Study Guide

for use with

Cost Management
A Strategic Emphasis

Third Edition

Edward J. Blocher
University of North Carolina – Chapel Hill

Kung H. Chen
University of Nebraska

Gary Cokins, CPIM
SAS / Worldwide Strategy

Thomas W. Lin
University of Southern California

Prepared by
Roger K. Doost
Clemson University

 **McGraw-Hill
Irwin**

Boston   Burr Ridge, IL   Dubuque, IA   Madison, WI   New York   San Francisco   St. Louis
Bangkok   Bogotá   Caracas   Kuala Lumpur   Lisbon   London   Madrid   Mexico City
Milan   Montreal   New Delhi   Santiago   Seoul   Singapore   Sydney   Taipei   Toronto

McGraw-Hill Irwin

Study Guide for use with
COST MANAGEMENT: A STRATEGIC EMPHASIS
Blocher, Chen, Cokins, Lin

Published by McGraw-Hill/Irwin, an imprint of The McGraw-Hill Companies, Inc., 1221 Avenue of the Americas, New York, NY 10020. Copyright © 2005, 2002, 1999 by The McGraw-Hill Companies, Inc. All rights reserved.

1 2 3 4 5 6 7 8 9 0 CUS/CUS 0 9 8 7 6 5 4

ISBN 0-07-283566-4

www.mhhe.com

Table of Contents

CHAPTER 1
COST MANAGEMENT AND STRATEGY: AN OVERVIEW

Highlights:

Cost management information includes all the information managers need to manage effectively. Cost management information includes both financial and non-financial information that is critical to the success of the firm. Management functions, to which cost management information is applied, include strategic management, planning and decision making, operational and management control and preparation of financial statements.

The new business environment have brought about an increase in global competition, advances in manufacturing and information technologies, a greater focus on the customer, new forms of management organization, and changes in social, political, and cultural environment of the business. Cost management can assist the firm in using the new management techniques such as, benchmarking, total quality management, continuous improvement, activity-based costing and management, reengineering, the theory of constraints, mass customization, target costing, life-cycle costing, and the balanced scorecard.

A variety of organizations support management accounting including the Institute of Management Accounting (IMA), the American Institute of Certified Public Accountants (AICPA), and the Financial Executives Institute (FEI), among others. Several relevant certification programs recognize competence and experience in management accounting; they include the Certified Management Accountant (CMA), and the Certified Financial Manager (CFM) programs of the IMA, and the Certified Public Accountant (CPA) program of the AICPA. There is a code of ethics for management accountants set forth by the IMA. The code includes competence, integrity, objectivity, and confidentiality.

Let us now review the individual objectives within this chapter and raise the relevant questions for your reflection.

Questions:

Learning Objective 1: Explain the use of cost management in each of the four functions of management and in different types of organizations with emphasis on the strategic management function.

1. What is cost management information?

2. What is the focus of financial versus non-financial information?

3. Who are the key players in the financial area?

4. What is the key distinction between financial accounting and management accounting?

5. What are the key functions of management and why are they needed?

6. What is strategic management?

7. What is a strategy?

8. What is operational control?

Learning Objective 2: Explain how the contemporary business environment has influenced cost management.

9. What changes in the business environment in recent years have caused significant modifications in cost management practices?

10. Contrast prior and contemporary business environments with regards to the following:
* Basis of competition:

 * Manufacturing process:

* Required labor skills:

* Emphasis on Quality:

* Products:

 * Markets:

* Type of information:

* Management organizational structure:

* Management focus:

11. What are the firm's **critical success factors (CSFs)**?

> **Learning Objective 3: Explain the contemporary management techniques and how they have influenced cost management.**

12. Identify the major contemporary management techniques.

13. Explain the major contemporary management techniques:

14. What is benchmarking?

15. What is total quality management?

16. What is continuous improvement?

17. What is activity-based costing (ABC)?

18. What is activity-based management (ABM)?

19. What is the theory of constraints (TOC)?

20. What is mass customization?

21. What is target costing?

22. What is life-cycle costing?

*Cost Management: A Strategic Emphasis, 3*e by Blocher/Chen/Cokins/Lin
© 2005 by The McGraw-Hill Companies, Inc.

23. What is balanced scorecard?

Learning Objective 4: Explain the different types of competitive strategy.

24. What is a strategy?

25. Give three examples of company mission statements:

26. What was the focus of cost management in the past?

27. What is the focus of cost management in today's business environment?

28. What are the financial measures of success?

29. What are the non-financial measures of success?

30. What are the consequences of lack of strategic information?

31. What is cost leadership?

32. What is differentiation?

33. What are the distinctive features of the differentiation strategy?

Learning Objective 5: Describe the professional environment of the management accountant, including professional organizations, professional certifications, and professional ethics.

---

34. What are the major professional organizations of interest to the accountant?

35. What are the major professional certifications offered?

Learning Objective 6: Understand the principles and rules of professional ethics and explain how to apply them.

---

36. What is the code of professional ethics? What are the steps one should take to resolve an ethical question within the firm?

Suggested responses to the above questions:
Now that you have attempted the above questions, you may want to compare your answers to the suggested answers below.

1. What is cost management information?

It is the information the manager needs to effectively manage the firm or not-for-profit organization. It includes both financial and non-financial information about productivity, quality, customer loyalty, and other key success factors for the firm.

Cost Management: A Strategic Emphasis, 3e by Blocher/Chen/Cokins/Lin
© 2005 by The McGraw-Hill Companies, Inc.

2. What is the focus of financial versus non-financial information?

The focus of financial information is short-term whereas non-financial information has a long-term focus.

3. Who are the key players in the financial area?

The chief financial officer (CFO) has the overall responsibility for the financial function, while the treasurer manages investor and creditor relationships, and the chief information officer (CIO) manages the firm's use of the information technology, including computer systems and communications. The controller who also reports to the CFO has the cost management responsibility as well as financial reporting, maintaining financial systems, and other reporting functions.

4. What is the key distinction between financial accounting and management accounting?

Financial accounting requires compliance with external reporting requirements, whereas cost management information is developed for use within the firm, to facilitate management. The main focus of management accounting, therefore, must be usefulness and timeliness, whereas the focus of financial reports must be accuracy in compliance with the reporting requirements.

5. What are the key functions of management and why are they needed?

The key functions of management are a) strategic management, b) planning and decision making, c) management and operational control, and d) preparation of financial statements. Strategic management is needed to make sound strategic decisions regarding choice of products, manufacturing methods, marketing techniques and channels, and other long-term issues. Planning and decision making information is needed to support recurring decisions regarding replacing equipment, managing cash flow, budgeting raw material purchases, scheduling production, and pricing. Management and operational control information is needed to provide a fair and effective basis for identifying inefficient operations, and to reward and support the most effective managers. Preparation of financial information is needed to provide accurate accounting for inventory and other assets, in compliance with reporting requirements, for the preparation of financial reports and for use in the three other management functions.

6. What is strategic management?

Strategic management is the development of a sustainable competitive position.

7. What is a strategy?

A strategy is a set of goals and specific action plans that, if achieved, provide the desired competitive advantage.

8. What is operational control?

Operational control exists when mid-level managers monitor the activities of operating-level managers and employees.

9. What changes in the business environment in recent years have caused significant modifications in cost management practices?

The primary changes are: a) increase in global competition, b) advances in manufacturing and information technologies, c) a greater focus on the customer, d) new forms of management organization, and e) changes in the social, political, and cultural environment of business.

10. Contrast prior and contemporary business environments with regards to the following:
* Basis of competition:
  - *Prior: economies of scale, standardization*
  - *Contemporary: quality, functionality, customer satisfaction*
* Manufacturing process:
  - *Prior: high volume, long production runs, significant level of in-process, and finished goods inventory.*
  - *Contemporary: low volume, short production runs, focus on reducing inventory levels, and other non-value-added activities and costs.*
* Manufacturing technology:
  - *Prior: assembly-line, automation, isolated technology applications*
  - *Contemporary: robotics, flexible manufacturing systems, integrated technology applications connected by networks.*
* Required labor skills:
  - *Prior: machine-paced, low-level skills*
  - *Contemporary: individual and team-paced, high-level skills*
* Emphasis on Quality:
  - *Prior: acceptance of a normal or usual amount of waste*
  - *Contemporary: goal for zero defects*
* Products:
  - *Prior: relatively few variations, long product life cycles*
  - *Contemporary: large number of variations, short product life cycles*
* Markets:
  - *Prior: largely domestic*
  - *Contemporary: global*
* Type of information:
  - *Prior: almost exclusively financial data*
  - *Contemporary: financial and operating data, the firm's strategic success factors*
* Management organizational structure:
  - *Prior: hierarchical, command and control*

Cost Management: A Strategic Emphasis, 3e by Blocher/Chen/Cokins/Lin

- Contemporary: network-based organization forms, teamwork focus, employee has more responsibility and control, coaching rather than command and control.
* Management focus:
- Prior: *Emphasis on short-term performance measures and compensation; concern for sustaining the current stock price, short tenure and high mobility of top managers.*
- Contemporary: *Emphasis on the long-term, focus on critical success factors, commitment to the long-term success of the firm, including adding shareholder value.*

11. What are the firm's **critical success factors (CSFs)**?

CSFs are measures of those aspects of the firm's performance that are essential to its competitive advantage, and therefore, to its success. Many of these critical success factors will be financial, but many will also be nonfinancial operating information such as, product quality and customer service.

12. Identify the major contemporary management techniques.

They include benchmarking, total quality management, continuous improvement (kaizen), activity-based costing, reengineering, the theory of constraints, mass customization, target costing, life-cycle costing, and the balanced scorecard.

13. Explain the major contemporary management techniques:

* *Benchmarking is a process by which a firm identifies its critical success factors, studies the best practices of other firms (or other units within a firm) for these critical success factors, and then, implements improvements in the firm's processes to match or beat the performance of those competitors.*

* *Total quality management (TQM) is a technique in which management develops policies and practices to ensure that the firm's products and services exceed customer's expectations.*

* *Continuous improvement (the Japanese word is kaizen) is a management technique in which managers and workers commit to a program of continuous improvement in quality and other critical success factors.*

* *Activity-based management (ABM) uses activity analysis to improve operational control and management control.*

* *Activity-based costing (ABC) is used to improve the accuracy of cost analysis by improving the tracing of costs to cost objects.*

* Reengineering is a process for creating competitive advantage in which a firm reorganizes its operating and management functions, often with the result that jobs are modified, combined, or eliminated.

* The theory of constraints (TOC) is a strategic technique to help firms effectively improve the rate at which raw materials are converted to finished goods. This is done through increasing throughput - the rate at which the firm generates cash through sales which is equal to sales less the materials required in products sold. The key issues here are dealing with bottlenecks and improving speed where needed.

* Mass customization is a management technique in which marketing and production processes are designed to handle the increased variety of delivering customized products and services to customers.

* Target costing determines the desired cost for a product upon the basis of a given competitive price, such that the product will earn a desired profit.

* Life cycle costing is a management technique used to identify, and monitor the costs of a product throughout its life cycle.

* The balanced scorecard is an accounting report that includes the firm's critical success factors in four areas: a) financial performance, b) customer satisfaction, c) internal business processes, and d) learning and innovation.

* The value chain is an analysis tool used to better understand the firm's strategy by identifying the specific steps to provide a competitive product or service to the customer.

14. What is benchmarking?

Benchmarking is a process by which a firm identifies its critical success factors, studies the best practices of other firms (or other units within a firm) for achieving these critical success factors, and then implements improvements in the firm's processes to match or beat the performance of those competitors.

15. What is total quality management (TQM)?

TQM is a technique by which management develops policies and practices to ensure that the firm's products and services exceed customers' expectations.

16. What is continuous improvement?

Continuous improvement (Kaizen) is a management technique by which managers and workers commit to a program of continuous improvement in quality and other critical success factors.

17. What is activity-based costing (ABC)?

ABC is used to improve the accuracy of cost analysis by improving the tracing of costs to products or to individual customers.

18. What is activity-based management (ABM)?

ABM uses activity analysis to improve operational control and management control.

19. What is the theory of constraints (TOC)?

TOC is a strategic technique to help firms effectively improve the rate at which raw materials are converted to finished product.

20. What is mass customization?

Mass customization is a management technique in which marketing and production processes are designed to handle the increased variety that results from delivering customized products and services to customers.

21. What is target costing?

Target costing determines the desired cost for a product on the basis of a given competitive price so that the product will earn a desired profit.

22. What is life-cycle costing?

Life-cycle costing is a management technique used to identify and monitor the costs of a product throughout its life cycle.

23. What is balanced scorecard?

The balanced scorecard is an accounting report that includes the firm's critical success factors in four areas: 1) financial performance, 2) customer satisfaction, 3) internal business processes, and 4) innovation and learning.

24. What is a strategy?

A strategy is a set of policies, procedures, and approaches to business that produce long-term success.

25. Give three examples of company mission statements:

*   * UPS: to move at the speed of business*
*   * Walt Disney: to make people happy*
*   * Merck: to preserve and improve human life*

26. What was the focus of cost management in the past?

The past focus was on financial reporting and cost analysis plus standardization and standard costs. The accountant was the financial scorekeeper.

27. What is the focus of cost management in today's business environment?

Today, cost management is used as a tool for the development and implementation of business strategy. The accountant is the business partner.

28. What are the financial measures of success?

Financial measures of success are sales growth, earnings growth, dividend growth, bond and credit ratings, cash flow, and increase in stock price.

29. What are the non-financial measures of success?

* Customer measures: market share and growth in market share, customer service, on-time delivery, customer satisfaction, brand recognition, positions in favorable markets.
* Internal business processes: high product quality, manufacturing innovation, high manufacturing productivity, cycle time, yield and reduction in waste.
* Learning and innovation: competence and integrity of managers, morale and firm-wide culture, education and training, innovation in new products and manufacturing methods.

30. What are the consequences of lack of strategic information?
* Decision making based on guesses and intuition only
* Lack of clarity about direction of goals
* Lack of a clear and favorable perception of the firm by customers and suppliers
* Incorrect investment decisions
* Inability to effectively benchmark competitors
* Failure to identify most profitable products, customers, and markets

31. What is cost leadership?

Cost leadership is a competitive strategy in which a firm succeeds by developing and maintaining a unique value for the product as perceived by consumers.

32. What is differentiation?

Differentiation is a competitive strategy in which a firm succeeds by developing a unique value for the product as perceived by consumers.

33. What are the distinctive features of the differentiation strategy?

With a differentiation strategy, the company focuses on a section of the market, produces or carries unique products or services, is very innovative in products and their specific features, and charges premium price.

34. What are the major professional organizations of interest to the accountant?

- *American Institute of CPAs (AICPA)*
- *Cost Accounting Standards Board (CASB)*
- *Federal Trade Commission (FTC)*
- *Financial Executives Institute (FEI)*
- *Institute of Internal Auditors (IIA)*
- *Institute of Management Accountants (IMA)*
- *Internal Revenue Service (IRS)*
- *Securities and Exchange Commission (SEC)*
- *Society of Management Accountants (SMA, Canada)*

35. What are the major professional certifications offered?

- *Certified Management Accountant (CMA) administered by the IMA. The exam covers the areas of a) economics, finance, and management, b) financial accounting and reporting, c) management analysis and reporting, d) decision analysis and information systems.*
- *Certified Financial Manager (CFM) also administered by the IMA. Topics include corporate financial management in addition to the topics covered on the CMA exam.*
- *Certified Public Accountant (CPA) exam is administered by the AICPA and is geared toward the practice of public accounting. It covers the areas of auditing, business law, accounting practice, and accounting theory.*

36. What is the code of professional ethics? What should you do for resolving an ethical conflict within an organization?

It is the commitment of the management accountant to provide a useful service for management. This commitment means that the management accountant has the competence, integrity, confidentiality, and objectivity to serve management effectively.

You should first approach your supervisor. If action is not taken, you should go to his superior. If the problem is not resolved satisfactorily, the management accountant can choose to resign. You would respond to government authorities only if you are summoned to do so. You should not take the initiative according to the Code.

Multiple choice questions:

Note: this review provides you with a broad overview of major themes in the chapter. You may need to refer to your text if you have difficulty answering some of the following questions.

1. Cost management information is the information that
   a) the manager needs to effectively manage the firm.
   b) the worker needs to do his job efficiently.
   c) the customer needs to assess the value of the product.
   d) the bank needs to accept or reject a loan application.
   e) none of the above.

2. The responsibility for cost management information typically falls within the role of the
   a) chief financial officer
   b) controller
   c) treasurer
   d) chief information officer
   e) none of the above

3. The main focus of management accounting information is,
   a) usefulness
   b) timeliness
   c) accuracy
   d) all of the above
   e) a and b only

4. The major functions of management are:
   a) strategic management, planning and decision making
   b) preparation of financial statements
   c) management and operational control
   d) all of the above
   e) a and c only

5. Life-cycle costing is a technique that monitors and identifies the cost of the product during
   a) research and development and product design
   b) manufacturing, quality inspection, and warehousing
   c) marketing, promotion, and distribution
   d) a and b only.
   e) all of the above

Cost Management: A Strategic Emphasis, 3e by Blocher/Chen/Cokins/Lin

6. A balanced scorecard is an accounting report that includes the firm's
   a) financial performance
   b) customer satisfaction factors
   c) internal business processes
   d) innovation and learning
   e) all of the above

7. In recent years,
   a) facilities' costs compared to labor and material costs have increased.
   b) facilities' costs compared to material costs have decreased.
   c) facilities' costs compared to labor costs have not changed.
   d) facilities' costs compared to labor and material costs has not changed.
   e) none of the above

8. Design decisions
   a) have impact on the costs incurred later in manufacturing and selling but not service aspects in the product life cycle.
   b) have impact on costs incurred in manufacturing but not selling and service aspects in a product life cycle.
   c) have impact on costs incurred in manufacturing, selling, and service aspects in a product life cycle.
   d) have no impact on costs incurred in manufacturing, selling, and service aspects in a product life cycle.
   e) none of the above

9. Managers' orientation has changed in recent years to
   a) low-cost production of large quantities
   b) quality, service, and timely delivery
   c) ability to respond to the customer's desire for specific features
   d) all of the above
   e) b and c only

10. In recent years, the focus of management has shifted
   a) from customer satisfaction and value to financial measures of performance.
   b) from customer satisfaction and value to profit-based measures of performance.
   c) from financial and profit-based measures to customer related and non-financial measures of performance.
   d) from customer related and non-financial measures to financial and profit-based measures of performance.
   e) none of the above

11. The organizational structures are being replaced with
   a) a command-and-control type of organization.
   b) flexible organizational forms.
   c) organizations that encourage teamwork and coordination among business functions.
   d) a and b
   e) b and c

12. Comparing prior business environment (BE) to its contemporary counterpart,
   a) prior BE focused on quality, functionality, and customer satisfaction.
   b) prior BE focused on low volume, short production runs, reduction of inventory levels.
   c) prior BE focused on value-added activities and costs.
   d) prior BE focused on robotics, flexible manufacturing systems, and integrated technology applications.
   e) none of the above

13. Comparing prior business environment (BE) to its contemporary counterpart (CC),
   a) CC focuses on machine-paced, low-level skills.
   b) CC focuses on the acceptance of a normal or usual amount of waste.
   c) CC focuses on relatively few variations and long production life cycle
   d) CC focuses on largely domestic products
   e) none of the above

14. Comparing prior business environment (BE) to its contemporary counterpart (CC),
   a) CC focuses on financial and operating data.
   b) CC focuses on network-based organization forms where employee has more responsibility and control
   c) CC focuses on team-paced, high-level skills
   d) all of the above
   e) b and c only

15. A firm's critical success factors include items such as
   a) quality and customer service
   b) labor relations and employee retraining
   c) data processing and product development
   d) all of the above
   e) a and b

Cost Management: A Strategic Emphasis, 3e by Blocher/Chen/Cokins/Lin

16. Which statement(s) is true?
    a) TQM promotes policies and practices to ensure that the firm's products and services exceed customer's expectations.
    b) TQM results in increased product functionality, reliability, durability, and serviceability.
    c) TQM is a very strictly narrow concept.
    d) all of the above
    e) a and b

17. Which statement is true?
    a) the Japanese word for critical success factors is kaizen.
    b) the Japanese word for TQM is kaizen.
    c) the Japanese word for continuous improvement is kaizen.
    d) the Japanese word for ABM is kaizen.
    e) none of the above

18. Activity-based costing (ABC)
    a) uses activity analysis to improve operational control.
    b) uses activity analysis to improve management control.
    c) is used to improve the accuracy of cost analysis by improving the tracing of costs to cost objects
    d) none of the above
    e) a and b

19. Reengineering is
    a) a process for creating competitive advantage in which a firm reorganizes its operating and management functions.
    b) a process which results in a strictly hierarchical organizational structure.
    c) a process that is applicable to manufacturing firms more so than services industries.
    d) all of the above
    e) a and c

20. The theory of constraints (TOC) is
    a) a strategic technique primarily used to reduce waste.
    b) a strategic technique used to help firms effectively improve the rate at which raw materials are converted to finished goods.
    c) a strategic technique used to help reduce labor costs
    d) all of the above
    e) b and c

21. Target costing
    a) determines the cost based on a predetermined standard cost.
    b) determines the cost such that the product will earn a desired profit.
    c) determines the cost based on budgeted raw material and labor rates.
    d) determines the cost based on anticipated market demand for the product.
    e) none of the above

22. Life-cycle costing
    a) is a technique used to monitor costs of a product throughout its life cycle.
    b) is a technique used to exclude costs related to marketing and promotion and service and include costs associated with design, testing, manufacturing, inspecting, packaging, and warehousing.
    c) is a technique used to exclude costs related to sales and service and include costs associated with manufacturing, inspecting, packaging, and warehousing.
    d) is a technique used to exclude costs related to marketing, promotion, service, and sales, and include costs associated with design, testing, manufacturing, inspecting, packaging, warehousing.
    e) none of the above

23. The balanced scorecard is
    a) an accounting report that includes financial performance and customer satisfaction indicators.
    b) an accounting report that includes internal business processes as well as learning and innovation indicators
    c) a management report which deals with the questions of employee morale and management satisfaction.
    d) all of the above
    e) a and b

24. The Certified Financial Manager (CFM) examination is administered by
    a) AICPA
    b) IMA
    c) IRS
    d) IIA
    e) SMAC

25. Standards of Ethical Conduct for Management Accountants as promulgated by the IMA include the elements of
    a) competence, confidentiality, integrity, and relevance
    b) competence, confidentiality, integrity, and objectivity
    c) competence, confidentiality, verifiability, and objectivity
    d) competence, openness, integrity, and objectivity
    e) conciseness, confidentiality, integrity, and objectivity

Cost Management: A Strategic Emphasis, 3e by Blocher/Chen/Cokins/Lin

Correct answers to multiple choice questions:

1-a; 2-b; 3-e; 4-d; 5-e; 6-e; 7-a; 8-c; 9-e; 10-c; 11-e; 12-e; 13-e; 14-d; 15-d; 16-e; 17-c; 18-c; 19-a; 20-b; 21-b; 22-a; 23-d; 24-b; 25-b

Important Exercise:

Do a computer search and see how many articles you can find on the recent ethical lapses dealing with Enron, Worldcom, Tyco, Arthur Andersen, major banks, major stock brokers, and New York Stock Exchange. If your instructor allows for an extra credit project or assigns you to an end of the semester paper, suggest to him that you want to do some research on any of the above. After all, if we learn all of the financial and cost-management concepts and do not totally comprehend how and why these multi-billion dollar frauds occurred and why the watch-dogs were sleeping when they occurred, they are bound to happen again! Whether the instructor requires it or not, write a page in your diary about this experience – particularly on how you would fight fraud and corruption when you enter the business world, and what criteria you would insist on with regards to your future employer. The future of our economic (and perhaps, political) success depends on it.

CHAPTER 2
IMPLEMENTING STRATEGY:
THE BALANCED SCORECARD AND THE VALUE CHAIN

Highlights:

The world has changed significantly in the past few decades. Today's accountant, particularly management accountant, is expected to do a lot more than merely maintaining the company's books and records. S/he is expected to be fully engaged and knowledgeable about the business operation. S/he must also take an active role in assisting management for taking actions to advance company goals and objectives. Firms succeed through having a *competitive strategy;* i.e., they must have a set of policies, procedures, and approaches to business to produce long-term success. In this vein, the firm must be aware of its *critical success factors* in the areas of cost, quality, and timely delivery and responsiveness. The firm must also periodically assess its strengths and weaknesses as well as external opportunities and threats to the business (SWOT analysis). *The balanced scorecard* reporting which provides a mix of financial and non-financial factors dealing with sales, production, employee development, and other matters is a helpful management tool. *Value-chain analysis* is another strategic analysis tool used to better understand the firm's competitive advantage, to identify where value to customers can be increased or costs reduced.

Questions:

> **Learning Objective 1: Explain how to implement a competitive strategy by using Strengths-Weaknesses-Opportunities-Threats (SWOT) Analysis.**

1. What are a firm's core competencies?

2. What is SWOT analysis? [Strength, Weaknesses, Opportunities, and Threats]

3. What are some of the firm's opportunities and threats?

4. Critical success factors deal with the question of quality, cost, and timely production and delivery. What is to be done next?

5. What is a competitive strategy?

6. What is the mission of the company and its relationship to the company strategy?

7. How have firms responded to the changes in business?

Learning Objective 3: Explain how to use competitive strategy using value chain analysis.
---

8. What is value chain analysis?

9. What is the objective of value chain analysis?

10. What are the six stages of the value chain in a manufacturing firm?

11. What are the three steps in value chain analysis? Identify and explain these steps.

12. How does value chain analysis support the firm's competitive advantage?

Learning Objective 4: Explain how to implement a competitive strategy using the balanced scorecard.

13. What is the balanced scorecard?

14. How can we make the balanced scorecard most effective?

15. What are the balanced scorecard leading and lagging indicators?

16. What are the major steps involved in value-chain analysis for a non-profit organization?

Learning Objective 5: Explain how to expand the balanced scorecard by integrating sustainability.

17. What is sustainability?

18. What is the expanded definition of sustainable growth?

19. What are the critical success factors as defined by World Resources Institute?

20. What are the implications of strategic analysis for cost management?

Suggested responses to the above questions:

1. What are a firm's core competencies?

A firm's core competencies are skills or competencies that the firm employs especially well. They include things such as innovation abilities, management's competence, effective marketing and promotional strategies, effective business strategies.

2. What is SWOT analysis? [Strength, Weaknesses, Opportunities, and Threats]

SWOT analysis is a systematic procedure for identifying a firm's critical success factors -- its internal strengths and weaknesses, and its external opportunities and threats.

3. What are some of the firm's opportunities and threats?

Opportunities and threats are identified by looking outside of the firm. Opportunities are important favorable situations in the firm's environment such as, demographic trends. In contrast, threats are major unfavorable situations in the firm's environment such as, unfavorable changes to the government regulations.

4. Critical success factors deal with the question of quality, cost, and timely production and delivery. What is to be done next?

After developing the critical success factors (CSFs), the firm must develop relevant and reliable measures for those CSFs in order to succeed.

5. What is a competitive strategy?

A strategy is a set of policies, procedures, and approaches to business to produce long-term success. A competitive strategy considers the business environment to gear itself toward a competitive advantage.

6. What is the mission of the company and its relationship to the company strategy?

A strategy begins with a mission of the company, and it is developed into specific performance objectives, which are then implemented by specific corporate strategies.

7. How have firms responded to the changes in business?

They have responded to the changes in business through reengineering operational processes, down-sizing the workforce, outsourcing service functions, and developing smaller, more efficient, and more socially responsible organizational objectives and strategies.

8. What is value chain analysis?

   Value chain analysis is a strategic analysis tool used to better understand the firm's competitive advantage, to identify where value to customers can be increased or costs reduced, and to better understand the firm's linkages with suppliers, customers, and other firms in the industry. The value chain identifies and links the various strategic activities of the firm.

9. What is the objective of value chain analysis?

   The objective of value chain analysis is to identify stages of the value chain where the firm can increase value to the customer or reduce cost. The reduction in cost or increased value makes the firm more competitive.

10. What are the six stages of the value chain in a manufacturing firm?

   They include a) design, b) raw material acquisition, c) manufacturing, testing, packaging, d) warehousing and distribution, e) retail sales, and f) customer service. Each selected firm may occupy a selected part or parts of this entire value chain.

11. What are the three steps in value chain analysis? Identify and explain these steps.

   The three steps are identified and explained as follows:
   - *First step: Identify the value chain activities. The firm identifies the specific value activities that firms in the industry must perform in the process of design, manufacturing, and customer service. Some firms may be involved in a single activity or a subset of the total activities.*
   - *Second step: Identify the cost driver(s) at each value activity. (Note: a cost driver is any factor that changes the level of total cost). The objective of the second step is to identify activities where the firm has a current or potential future cost advantage.*
   - *Third step: Develop a sustainable competitive advantage by reducing cost or adding value. In this stage, the firm determines the nature of its current and potential competitive advantage by studying the value activities and cost drivers identified.*

12. How does value chain analysis support the firm's competitive advantage?

   It supports the firm's strategic competitive advantage by facilitating the discovery of opportunities for adding value to the customers and/or by reducing the cost of providing the product or service.

13. What is a balanced scorecard?

The balanced scorecard is the accounting report developed from the strategic information system demonstrated in earlier questions. It is used for linking CSFs to strategy and for monitoring the firm's achievement toward its strategic goals. The balanced scorecard includes all the firm's CSFs including, a) financial performance, b) customer satisfaction, c) internal business processes, and d) learning and innovation.

14. How can we make the balanced scorecard (BSC) most effective?

This goal can be achieved by having BSC developed by employees at the most detail level so that employees can see how their actions contribute to the success of the firm. Moreover, employee compensation should be tied to achievement of company goals, to reinforce the importance that management places on achieving CSFs.

15. What are the BSCs leading and lagging indicators?

Leading indicators are those which point to future competitive success, such as patents earning in research and development. In contrast, lagging indicators are primarily output measures, such as unit costs and profits. Financial measures tend to be lagging indicators while non-financial indicators can be of either type.

16. What are the major steps involved in value-chain analysis for a non-profit organization?

The first step is to develop a statement of the organization's broad social mission, including the specific public needs served. The second step is to develop resources for the organization, including personnel and facilities. The third and fourth steps deal with operation of the organization and delivery of service to the public respectively.

17. What is sustainability?

Sustainability means the balancing of short and long term goals in all three dimensions of the company's performance.

18. What is the expanded definition of sustainable growth?

Sustainable growth seeks to make more of the world's people our customers – and to do so by developing markets that promote and sustain economic prosperity, social equity, and environmental integrity.

19. What are the critical success factors as defined by World Resources Institute?

They include operational indicators (potential stresses on the environment), management indicators (efforts to reduce environmental effects), and environmental condition indicators (measures of environmental quality).

Cost Management: A Strategic Emphasis, 3e by Blocher/Chen/Cokins/Lin
© 2005 by The McGraw-Hill Companies, Inc.

20. What are the implications of strategic analysis for cost management?

The introduction of new manufacturing and information technologies, the focus on the customer, the growth of worldwide markets, and other changes require that firms develop strategic information systems to effectively maintain their competitive advantage in the industry. This means that cost management must provide appropriate types of information that have not been provided under traditional cost accounting systems. Only by succeeding at the CSFs will the firm maintain its competitive advantage. The role of cost management must be to identify, measure, collect, and report information on the CSFs reliably and in a timely manner. This is the information (both financial and non-financial) that is reflected in the balanced scorecard. The efforts to sustain a competitive advantage require long-term plans. Success in the short term is no longer a measure of ultimate success, since long term success requires strategic, long-term planning and action. Finally, the strategic approach requires integrative thinking, that is, the ability to identify and solve problems from a cross-functional view.

Multiple choice questions:
You can further test your understanding of this chapter's contents by responding to the following questions. The correct answers appear on the last page, to this chapter, but promise not to look at them before you complete this exercise!

1. A balanced scorecard includes
   a) financial measures only
   b) non-financial measures only
   c) both financial and non-financial measures
   d) customer satisfaction and production quality issues only
   e) none of the above

2. Which statement is correct?
   a) cost leadership relies on outstanding quality or product features
   b) differentiation relies on lowest cost production and distribution
   c) focus strategy relies on differentiation but not cost leadership
   d) all of the above
   e) none of the above.

3. Critical success factors include items such as
   a) speed of customer service
   b) safety of workplace
   c) customer satisfaction
   d) all of the above
   e) b and c only.

4. SWOT analysis is a technique for
   a) identifying a firm's strengths but not weaknesses
   b) identifying a firm's weaknesses but not strengths
   c) identifying a firm's opportunities but not threats
   d) identifying a firm's threats but not opportunities
   e) none of the above.

5. Value chain analysis is a technique used for
   a) determining the strategic competitive advantage of the firm
   b) assisting the management accountant in identifying opportunities for reducing cost
   c) identifying opportunities for adding value to the firm's products and services
   d) all of the above
   e) b and c only.

6. The distinction between traditional accounting and cost management is
   a) the focus of the former on accounting matters and the latter on partnership with management in making the right decisions for staying on a competitive position
   b) the emphasis of former on record keeping and the latter on reporting
   c) the emphasis of former on cost accounting and the latter on managing
   d) the focus of the former on cost cutting and the latter on product differentiation
   e) the focus of the former on efficiency and the latter on quality.

7. Cost management information is the information
   a) the accountant needs to prepare the financial statements.
   b) the manager needs to be able to read the financial statements.
   c) the manager needs to effectively manage the firm.
   d) the manager needs to effectively manage not-for-profit organization.
   e) c and d.

8. The cost management function is usually under
   a) the chief information officer.
   b) treasurer.
   c) purchasing manager.
   d) controller.
   e) personnel manager.

9. The main focus of cost management information must be
   a) usefulness and accuracy.
   b) timeliness and accuracy.
   c) usefulness and timeliness.
   d) usefulness and good format.
   e) relevance and good format.

Cost Management: A Strategic Emphasis, 3e by Blocher/Chen/Cokins/Lin

10. The major functions of management are
    a) strategic management and long-range planning.
    b) planning and decision making.
    c) management and operational control.
    d) identifying threats and opportunities for the firm.
    e) all of the above.

11. With regard to the task of management's decision making, cost management information is needed to
    a) make sound strategic decisions regarding choice of products, methods, and techniques.
    b) support recurring decisions regarding replacement of equipment, managing cash flow, etc.
    c) provide a fair and effective basis for identifying inefficient operations.
    d) provide accurate accounting for inventory, receivables, and other assets.
    e) all of the above.

12. In the contemporary business environment, cost management focus is on
    a) financial reporting and cost analysis.
    b) common emphasis on standardization and standard costs.
    c) development and implementation of the business strategy. \
    d) a and c.
    e) b and c.

13. Financial measures of success as measures of critical success include
    a) customer service and growth in market share.
    b) on-time delivery and customer satisfaction.
    c) brand recognition and positioning in favorable markets.
    d) high product quality and increased productivity.
    e) none of the above.

14. The three major types of competitive strategy include
    a) cost leadership, differentiation, and productivity.
    b) cost leadership, focus, and productivity.
    c) differentiation, focus, and productivity.
    d) cost leadership, differentiation, and focus.
    e) none of the above.

15. Sustainability means the balancing of
    a) short term and long term goals in economic performance.
    b) short term and long term goals in social aspects.
    c) short term and long term goals in environmental aspects.
    d) all of the above.
    e) a and c.

Exercise 1:

ABC Company has prepared a SWOT analysis which is described below:
The company is close to the raw material source and saves $250,000 a year compared to the closest competitor in terms of proximity to raw material sources. Labor is cheap and plentiful in this area and provides a saving of $200 per worker per month as compared to the closest competitor for the 150 people employed in this plant. The region's political instability has scared the shareholders who now expect a return of 30% on their 2 million dollar investment as compared to the closest competitor whose return expectation is around 12%. Being away from the market for these goods is costing the firm approximately $145,000 a year more as compared to the closest competitors. The four top researchers who work for the competitor are paid an average of $75,000 a year whereas, that caliber of researcher demands an average pay of $115,000 in this region. As the firm could not afford to retain four researchers who monitored product quality, design, and engineering, it has retained only three of the four, paying them these top dollars. However, the company has fallen behind in product engineering and quality resulting in a ten percent reduction of the market share compared to last year. Last year's sales amounted to $21.6 million with a margin of 15%.

Based on your understanding of strategic cost management, provide a report to the manager suggesting what you think the appropriate course of action for the firm should be. Provide sufficient detail in your report.

Exercise 2:

Without regard to dollar amounts, construct a balanced scorecard composed of the four essential parts (financial and non-financial) and indicate why you think those items are important to be reported to management on a periodic basis. Indicate the leading and lagging indicators of success in your report.

Exercise 3:

Do an internet search for World Resources Institute (www.wri.org). Share your findings with your team.

Correct answers to multiple choice questions:

1-c; 2-e; 3-d; 4-e; 5-d; 6-a; 7-e; 8-d; 9-c; 10-e; 11-b; 12-c; 13-e; 14-d.; 15-d.

If your answer to any of these basic questions was incorrect, I strongly suggest that you go back and review the material. If you had no wrong answers, I congratulate you for your good work in mastering this important material.

Suggested answer to the exercise 1:

The above exercise is intended to help you think and get together with your fellow-students for discussion and analysis of some of these issues. A brief discussion is provided here to guide you in your work. You should compliment these numbers with further qualitative analysis.

Potential savings of this project:

Material	$250,000
Labor 150 * 200 * 12 =	360,000
Total annual savings	$610,000

Additional costs of this project:

Needed additional return:	2,000,000 * (.30 - .12) = $ 360,000
Additional marketing cost	145,000
Additional researchers' cost:	(115,000*3) – (75,000 * 4) = 45,000
Loss of market share:	21,600,000 * 10% * 15% = 324,000
Total additional cost	$874,000

Net annual disadvantage of this project: $ 264,000

Many questions need to be asked to determine how we may be able to deal with this situation:

- Is political instability easing or not? If not, is the shareholder's required return a good measure of the level of risk associated with this project? If we can produce and sell the same product where shareholders' expected return there is only 12%, this must be a serious consideration.
- Can we deal effectively with the shortage and cost of quality researchers? Is there a way for our three researchers to be able to accomplish as much as the competitor does with four? Can we train local personnel in this area to fill up the gap with lower salary expectations?
- Can the gap be filled to avoid the huge marketing cost differential?
- Can the loss of the market share be reversed and avoided in the future?
- Can we repair the deterioration in quality and customer service?

If satisfactory answers to these questions cannot be provided, a long-range plan of relocating the business to more favorable conditions may be worth pursuing. Threats and opportunities for long-term strategic advantage must be carefully measured and analyzed.

Exercise 2. If you have not mastered the elements of the balanced scorecard, refer to the text.

Exercise 3. Internet search.

CHAPTER 3
BASIC COST CONCEPTS

Highlights:

This chapter addresses many important concepts as related to the functions of management. In strategic management, the most important concepts relate to the four types of cost drivers: activity-based, volume-based, structural, and executional. Activity-based cost drivers are at a detail level of operations such as, equipment setup, materials handling, clerical or other tasks. In contrast, volume-based cost drivers are at an aggregate level, usually the number of units produced, direct labor hours, machine hours, etc. Variable costs, in the traditional sense, are volume-based and change with a variation in the level of cost driver. Direct costs are costs that can be traced directly to a cost object, in contrast to indirect costs, which cannot. Structural cost drivers involve decisions that have long-term effects while executional cost drivers are those with short-term decision frames.

The important concepts in product costing are product costs, which are the direct material, direct labor, and indirect manufacturing costs (called overhead). Non-product costs (also called period costs) are the selling, administrative, and other costs that are not involved with manufacturing. The inventory formula is used to determine the cost of materials used in production, the cost of materials manufactured (transferred from work in process to finished goods), and the cost of goods sold for a given period.

When considering options, the management accountant considers relevant costs, the costs which differ for each competing alternative and which will occur in the future. All past costs (also called sunk costs) are irrelevant because they will not change, and are already spent.

It is important to distinguish controllable costs from other costs, because managers should be evaluated only on the basis of controllable costs. It is also important to note that managers tend to be relatively risk-averse, which can cause managers to make decisions that are not consistent with the company's objectives.

Questions:

Learning Objective 1: Explain the cost driver concepts at the activity, volume, structural, and executional levels.

1. What is a cost driver?

2. What is a cost pool?

3. What is a cost object?

4. What is cost assignment?

5. What is a direct cost?

6. What is an indirect cost?

7. What is cost allocation?

8. What is a cost allocation base?

9. What does direct material account include?

10. What is indirect material?

11. What is direct labor?

*Cost Management: A Strategic Emphasis, 3*e by Blocher/Chen/Cokins/Lin

12. What is indirect labor?

13. What is factory overhead?

14. What are prime costs? What is conversion costs?

15. Explain the four kinds of cost drivers.

16. What is the relevant range?

17. What are fixed costs?

18. What are mixed costs?

19. What is a step-fixed cost?

20. What is unit cost?

21. What is marginal cost?

22. What are the executional cost drivers?

Learning Objective 2: Explain the cost concepts used in product and service costing.

23. What is cost of goods sold?

24. What is the difference between a product cost for a manufacturing firm versus a merchandising firm?

25. What are period costs?

Learning Objective 3: Demonstrate how costs flow through the accounts.

26. What is work in process inventory?

27. What are the steps involved in the manufacturing process?

Learning Objective 4: Prepare an income statement for both a manufacturing firm and a merchandising firm.

28. What are the steps involved in preparing an income statement for a manufacturing firm?

Learning Objective 5: Explain the cost concepts related to the use of cost information in planning and decision making.

29. What is a relevant cost?

30. What are differential costs?

31. What is opportunity cost?

32. What are sunk costs?

33. What is the system of internal accounting controls?

34. What is a controllable cost?

35. What are a manager's risk preferences?

Suggested responses to the above questions:

Now that you have attempted responding to these questions on your own, compare your responses to the suggested answers below and review the areas where you think you still do not have a mastery of the material.

1. What is a cost driver?

A cost driver is any factor that has the effect of changing the level of total cost.

2. What is a cost pool?

Costs are sometimes collected into meaningful groups, called cost pools. Cost pools may be by type of cost, by source, or by responsibility. They are often homogenous – in that, they are driven by a common cost driver.

3. What is a cost object?

A cost object is any product, service, or organizational unit to which costs are assigned for some management purpose.

4. What is cost assignment?

Cost assignment is the process of assigning costs to cost pools, or from cost pools to cost objects.

 Cost Management: A Strategic Emphasis, 3e by Blocher/Chen/Cokins/Lin

5. What is a direct cost?

A direct cost can be conveniently and economically traced directly to a cost pool or a cost object.

6. What is an indirect cost?

An indirect cost has no convenient or economical trace from the cost or cost pool to the cost pool or cost object.

7. What is cost allocation?

The assignment of indirect costs to cost pools and cost objects is called cost allocation.

8. What is a cost allocation base?

The cost drivers used to allocate costs are often called allocation bases.

9. What does direct material account include?

It includes the cost of materials in the product plus a reasonable allowance for scrap and defective units.

10. What is indirect material?

It includes materials used in manufacturing that are not physically part of the finished product, such as supplies, machine lubricants, etc.

11. What is direct labor?

It includes the labor used to manufacture the product or to provide the service plus nonproductive time that is normal and unavoidable.

12. What is indirect labor?

It includes discretionary and planned labor such as downtime, training, and set up time. It also includes supervision, quality control, inspection, purchasing and receiving, and other manufacturing support costs.

13. What is factory overhead?

Factory overhead includes all the indirect costs associated with a product. In other words, all manufacturing costs except for direct material and direct labor are considered as factory overhead.

14. What are prime costs? What are conversion costs?

Direct materials and direct labor are sometimes considered together and called prime costs. Direct labor and overhead are often combined into a single amount, which is called conversion costs. For firms with highly automated operations, the labor component of total manufacturing costs is relatively low, and these firms often choose to place their strategic focus on materials and facilities.

15. Explain the four kinds of cost drivers.

- *Activity-based cost drivers are developed at a detailed level of operations and are associated with a given manufacturing activity, such as machine setup, product inspection, material handling, or packaging.*
- *Volume-based cost drivers are developed at an aggregate level, such as the number of units produced.*
- *Structural and executional cost drivers involve strategic and operational decisions which affect the relationship between the cost drivers and total cost.*

16. What is the relevant range?

It is the range within which the association of costs and applicable cost drivers apply.

17. What are fixed costs?

Fixed costs are costs that do not change with a change in the quantity of the cost driver within the relevant range.

18. What are mixed costs?

Mixed costs are those costs that include the elements of fixed and variables in them, such as, maintenance costs.

19. What is a step-fixed cost?

A cost is said to be step-fixed when it varies with the cost driver, but in discrete steps.

20. What is unit cost?

Unit cost (or average cost) is the total of manufacturing costs (materials, labor, and overhead) divided by units of output.

21. What is marginal cost?

Marginal cost is the additional cost incurred as the cost driver increases by one unit.

22. What are the executional cost drivers?

Executional cost drivers are factors the firm can manage in short-term to reduce costs. These include workforce involvement, design of the production process, and better relationship with the suppliers.

23. What is cost of goods sold?

When inventory is sold, the cost of the product is transferred to the income statement as cost of goods sold. This is also the point where an asset (inventory) is converted into expense (cost of goods sold).

24. What is the difference between a product cost for a manufacturing firm versus a merchandising firm?

- Product costs for a manufacturing firm include only the costs necessary to complete the product; i.e., direct materials, direct labor, and factory overhead.

- Product costs for a merchandising firm include the purchase cost of the product plus the transportation costs paid by the retailer or wholesaler to get the product to the location from which it will be sold or distributed.

25. What are period costs?

Period costs are non-product expenditures for managing the firm and selling the product.

26. What is the work in process inventory?

Work in process inventory accounts for all costs put into manufacture of products that are started but not complete at the financial statement date.

27. What are the steps involved in the manufacturing process?

The first step of the manufacturing process is to purchase materials to be used in manufacturing. The second step involves adding the three cost elements to work in process; i.e. materials used, labor, and overhead. As the products are completed, these three factors of production are added to the work in process account. In the third step, as the production is completed, the production costs that have been accumulating in the work in process account are transferred to finished goods, and from there to cost of goods sold when the products are sold. The process in a merchandising firm is simpler because there are no raw materials involved to need conversion.

28. What are the steps involved in preparing an income statement for a manufacturing firm?

In case the firm maintains a periodic inventory system (adjusts inventory by taking a physical count periodically), the following steps are followed:

Step 1: Prepare a statement of cost of goods manufactured:
Material inventory beginning + Purchases - Material inventory ending = Material used.
Material used + Direct labor + Factory overhead = Costs to manufacture.
Costs to manufacture + Work in process inventory beginning - Work in process inventory ending = Costs of goods manufactured

Step 2: Prepare a statement of costs of goods sold:
Cost of goods manufactured + Finished goods inventory beginning - finished goods inventory ending = Costs of goods sold.

Step 3: Prepare income statement:
Sales - Costs of goods sold = Gross profit
Gross profit - selling and administrative expenses = Operating income
Operating income - interest expenses and extraordinary expenses = income before taxes
Income before taxes - taxes = Net income

Note: for a merchandising firm, there is no statement for cost of goods manufactured. Steps 2 and 3 are basically the same.

29. What is a relevant cost?

The concept of relevant cost arises in situations in which the decision maker must choose between two or more options. To determine which option is best, the decision maker will determine which option has the highest benefit, usually in dollars. A relevant cost is a cost that differs among competing alternatives and it is incurred in the future. It involves decisions such as, outsourcing, special order, dropping a segment, or replacing a machine.

30. What is differential costs?

Differential costs are costs that differ for each decision option and are therefore relevant.
Although most differential costs are variable. Some differential costs may be fixed. Fixed costs are more likely to be differential over long term.

31. What is opportunity cost?

Opportunity cost is the benefit lost when one chooses an option over a competing alternative. It is used to measure the impact of alternatives of a decision.

32. What are sunk costs?

Sunk costs are costs that have been incurred or committed in the past, and are therefore irrelevant.

33. What is the system of internal accounting controls?

The system of internal accounting controls is a set of policies and procedures that restrict and guide activities in the processing of financial data, with the objective of preventing or detecting errors and fraudulent acts. The controller is responsible for setting up such a system. External and internal auditors may assist in designing such a system. The auditors also periodically monitor and evaluate the system of internal control. Such a system is intended to provide timely, accurate, and useful information. Cost/benefit analysis is also relevant. Because a system's cost must not exceed the benefit that it can provide.

34. What is a controllable cost?

A cost is said to be controllable if the manager or employee has discretion in choosing to incur the cost or can significantly influence the amount of the cost within a given, usually short, period of time. Expenses such as rent and basic phone charges are not controllable in the shortrun.

35. What are a manager's risk preferences?

Risk preferences describe the way individuals differentially view decision options, because they place a weight on certain outcomes that differs from the weight others place on the same items.

Multiple choice questions:

1. A cost pool can be,
   a) a group of costs by type of costs such as moving costs.
   b) a group of costs by source such as departments.
   c) a group of costs by responsibility such as each manager's area of responsibility.
   d) all of the above
   e) a and b

2. A cost object is
   a) any product to which costs are assigned.
   b) any service to which costs are assigned.
   c) any organizational unit to which costs are assigned.
   d) all of the above
   e) a and c

3. Cost assignment is the process of
   a) assigning costs to cost pools.
   b) assigning costs from cost pools to cost objects.
   c) assigning costs from cost objects to cost pools.
   d) all of the above
   e) a and b

4. Direct costs are
   a) all variable costs that are identifiable with a cost object.
   b) all fixed costs that are identifiable with a cost object.
   c) all costs that are identifiable with a cost object.
   d) direct material and direct labor costs only.
   e) all step-fixed identifiable with a cost object.

5. Cost allocation is the process of
   a) assigning indirect costs to cost pools.
   b) assigning indirect costs to cost objects.
   c) assigning direct costs to cost pools.
   d) assigning direct costs to cost objects.
   e) a and b

6. Cost allocation bases are
   a) costs that must be allocated.
   b) costs that cannot be allocated.
   c) always in terms of units or weights.
   d) the cost drivers used to allocate costs.
   e) none of the above

Cost Management: A Strategic Emphasis, 3e by Blocher/Chen/Cokins/Lin

7. Direct labor and overhead when combined is called,
   a) prime cost
   b) conversion cost
   c) allocated cost
   d) assigned cost
   e) none of the above

8. Activities used in conjunction with cost drivers are items such as,
   a) patient scheduling
   b) insurance verification
   c) number of patients admitted
   d) all of the above
   e) a and b

9. Cost drivers can be items such as,
   a) number of checks
   b) number of moves
   c) number of billings
   d) all of the above
   e) a and c

10. Mixed costs are those that include,
    a) both fixed and variable costs.
    b) various forms of fixed costs.
    c) various forms of variable costs.
    d) step-fixed costs.
    e) none of the above

11. Number of purchase orders is an example of
    a) unit level costs
    b) batch level costs
    c) product level costs
    d) organizational level costs
    e) customer level costs.

12. Product design change is an example of
    a) unit level costs
    b) batch level costs
    c) product level costs
    d) organizational level costs
    e) customer level costs.

13. At 100 unit level, this company's costs were $210 per unit plus another $50 for the second group of costs. When production doubled, the first group of costs remained the same, and the latter was cut in half.
a) both of these costs are variable
b) both of these costs are fixed
c) the first group is variable and the second fixed
d) the first group is fixed and the second variable
e) none of the above.

Exercises:

E1. Statement of costs of goods manufactured

Omid Printing has asked you to prepare a statement of cost of goods manufactured for the month of November 2004 based on the following facts:

Raw material inventory as of 11/1/2004	$ 2,000
Purchases	17,800
Freight on above	700
Raw material inventory as of 11/30/2004	3,100
Direct labor	7,800
Total cost to manufacture	41,400
Work in process 11/1/2004	6,300
Work in process 11/30/2004	9,500

E2. Statement of costs of goods manufactured and sold

Saba Supply Company has asked you to prepare a statement of cost of goods manufactured and sold for the third quarter of 2004 based on the data given below: Raw material inventory beginning $3,100; Purchases $19,900; Raw material used $18,300; Direct labor $8,400; Factory overhead $24,900; Work in process beginning $8,700; Cost of goods manufactured $47,900; Finished goods inventory beginning $11,800; Finished goods inventory at the end of the quarter $20,600.

E3. Income statement

Arman Graphics has asked you to prepare an income statement for the year 2,000 based on the following facts. Cost of sales amounted to $39,100 with a gross profit of $22,400. Selling and administrative expenses amounted to $8,700 while extraordinary expenses amounted to $4,100. Taxes amount to 40% of income.

E4. Work in process inventory

Shahnaz Design Company has asked you to estimate the balance of its work in process inventory. Job 1 has used $12,000 of fabric and $8,000 of labor. This job is complete and is loaded on the truck for shipment to the customer. Job 2 is 60% complete with $3,900 of fabric and $5,700 of labor. Job 3 is about 40% complete with $8,700 worth of fabric and $12,800 of labor. Overhead amounts to 200% of labor cost.

Cost Management: A Strategic Emphasis, 3e by Blocher/Chen/Cokins/Lin
© 2005 by The McGraw-Hill Companies, Inc.

E5. Relevant costs and differential analysis

Iraj Super Store has two departments, Supplies and Pharmacy. The store rent amounts to $64,000 a year. The store has a total space of 3,200 square feet. The supplies area occupies 2,000 square feet with the balance used for the pharmacy area. Partial income statement for the year 2002 is as follows:

	Supplies	Pharmacy	Total
Sales	$240,000	$180,000	$420,000
Cost of sales	140,000	60,000	200,000
Direct expenses	60,000	60,000	120,000
Allocated expenses	50,000	40,000	90,000

Allocated expenses include rent, utilities, and common maintenance costs. If the supplies area is closed, it can be rented for $30,000 a year whereas currently it shows a loss of about $10,000. In addition, common expenses allocated will go down by $3,000. Also note that 50% of the copier depreciation which amounts to $1,800 in total is charged to the Supplies division. Considering the question of differential and relevant costs, prepare an analysis to evaluate the closing of supplies division and its impact on company profits.

E6. Do a search on General Electric Financial Statements. Review the amounts for sales, costs of sales, inventory, and net income for the next couple of years and share the results with your group.

Correct answers to multiple choice questions:
1-d; 2-d; 3-e; 4-c; 5-e; 6-d; 7-b; 8-e; 9-d; 10-a; 11-b, 12-c; 13-c.

Suggested answers to exercises:
E1. Cost of goods manufactured for November 2004

RM inventory as of 11/1/04	$ 2,000
Purchases plus freight	18,500
RM inventory as of 11/30/04	-3,100
Raw materials used	**17,400**
Direct labor	7,800
Overhead	**16,200**
Cost to manufacture	41,400
Work in process 11/1	6,300
Total available	47,700
Work in process 11/30	- 9,500
Cost of goods manufactured	**38,200**

E2. Cost of goods manufactured and sold

Raw materials inventory as of 7/1/04	$ 3,100	
Purchases	19,900	
Raw materials inventory as of 9/30/04	- **4,700**	
Raw materials used		18,300
Direct labor		8,400
Overhead	24,900	
Costs to manufacture		**51,600**
Work in process as of 7/1/04		8,700
Total available		60,300
Work in process as of 9/30/04	- **12,400**	
Costs of goods manufactured		47,900
Finished goods inventory as of 7/1/04	11,800	
Cost of goods available for sale	59,700	
Finished goods inventory as of 9/30/04	- 20,600	
Cost of goods sold	**39,100**	

E3. Income statement

Sales	$ **61,500**
Cost of sales	39,100
Gross profit	22,400
Selling and admin. exp.	8,700
Operating income	**13,700**
Extraordinary expenses	4,100
Income before taxes	**9,600**
Tax 40%	3,840
Net income	**5,760**

E4. Work in process inventory

Job 1 is complete and on its way and is not part of work in process.

	Job 2	Job 3
Fabric used	$ 3,900	$ 8,700
Labor	5,700	12,800
Overhead 200% of labor	11,400	25,600
Total	21,000	47,100

Total work in process inventory balance = $68,100

Cost Management: A Strategic Emphasis, 3e by Blocher/Chen/Cokins/Lin

© 2005 by The McGraw-Hill Companies, Inc.

E5. Relevant costs and differential analysis

Income if Supplies division is closed:

Expenses saved	200,000
Allocated costs saved	3,000
Rental income gained	30,000
Sales lost	-240,000
Additional loss	$ 7,000

Based on partial income statement provided in the problem, the income before closing the Supplies division amounts to $10,000. If we close Supplies division, the net income would be reduced to $3,000. Here is the proof of this:

Revenue from Pharmacy division	$180,000
Rental income	30,000
Direct costs	120,000
The balance of allocated costs	87,000
Income	3,000

CHAPTER 4
JOB ORDER COSTING

Highlights:

Product costing provides useful cost information for both manufacturing and non-manufacturing firms for the purposes of: 1) product and service cost determination and inventory valuation, 2) management planning, cost control, and performance evaluation, and 3) managerial decisions.

Cost systems can be classified by: 1) cost accumulation method -- job costing or process costing, 2) cost measurement method -- actual, normal, or standard costing systems; 3) overhead assignment method -- traditional or activity-based costing systems; and 4) treatment of fixed factory overhead costs -- variable or absorption costing systems.

Job costing systems accumulate costs by jobs as compared to process costing systems that accumulate costs by processes or departments. These systems provide information for managers to make strategic decisions regarding choice of products and customers, manufacturing methods, pricing decisions, overhead allocation methods, and other long-term issues.

Job costing uses several general ledger accounts to control the product cost flows. Direct material costs are charged to work in process (WIP) when materials are requested for use in production. Direct labor costs are charged to WIP when incurred. Actual factory overhead costs are charged to a control account when incurred. WIP is charged for overhead using predetermined overhead rates in normal costing and credited to the factory overhead applied account. When a job is complete, the cost of goods manufactured is transferred from the work in process control account to the finished goods control account.

The determination of a predetermined overhead rate has four steps: 1) determine the most appropriate cost driver(s) for charging the factory overhead costs; 2) budget the total amount or activity level of the chosen cost driver(s); 3) budget the factory overhead costs for an appropriate operating period, usually a year; 4) divide the budgeted factory overhead costs by the budgeted activity level of the chosen cost driver(s).

The difference between the actual factory overhead cost and the amount of the factory overhead applied is called the overhead variance which may be under or overapplied. It may be disposed in two ways: 1) adjust the cost of goods sold account, or 2) prorate the discrepancy among the amounts of the current period's applied overhead remaining in the ending balances of the WIP Control, the Finished Goods Control, and the Cost of Goods Sold accounts. The ideal criterion for choosing an allocation base is a cause-and-effect relationship. A plant-wide rate is appropriate when all products pass through the same processes, or all departments are similar. In some production processes, the relationship between factory overhead costs and various cost drivers differ substantially among production departments. Then, multiple overhead rates with multiple cost drivers, both volume-related and non-volume-related cost drivers based on consumption of activities should be used. Normal spoilage, abnormal spoilage, rework, and scrap must be accounted for when computing a job cost.

Questions:

1. What is product costing?

2. What is the purpose of product costing?

Learning Objective 1: Explain the types of costing systems.

3. What are the major types of product costing systems?

4. What factors should be considered in choosing a particular system?

5. Where is job costing or process costing method most appropriate?

6. Discuss actual, normal, and standard costing.

7. Why use activity-based costing (ABC) in overhead assignment?

8. Distinguish between variable and absorption costing?

Learning Objective 2: Describe the strategic role of job costing.

9. What is the strategic role of job costing?

10. Define job costing.

11. What type of firms use job costing? Process costing?

Learning Objective 3: Explain the flow of costs in a job order costing system.

12. What is a material requisition?

13. What is a time ticket?

14. What is an overhead application rate?

15. How are costs recorded on the job cost sheet?

16. Why use a predetermined factory overhead rate?

17. What are the primary cost drivers for allocation of factory overhead?

18. What is the process of overhead application?

19. What is an actual costing system?

20. What is a normal costing system?

Learning Objective 4: Explain the application of factory overhead costs in a job costing system.

21. How is a predetermined factory overhead rate calculated?

22. How is overhead applied to jobs?

*Cost Management: A Strategic Emphasis, 3*e by Blocher/Chen/Cokins/Lin

Learning Objective 6: Calculate underapplied and overapplied overhead and dispose of them properly at the end of the period.

23. What is the overapplied and underapplied overhead?

24. What should be done with the under or overapplied overhead?

25. When are departmental overhead rates more appropriate than a single plant-wide rate?

Learning Objective 6: Apply job costing to service industries.

26. What is different and similar in job costing for a service entity?

Learning Objective 7: Explain an operation costing system.

27. What is an operation costing system?

Appendix: Account for spoilage, rework, and scrap in job costing.

28. What is spoilage?

29. What is scrap?

30. What is rework?

31. What is normal spoilage?

32. What is abnormal spoilage?

33. What are the two types of normal spoilage?

34. How are the two types of normal spoilage accounted for?

35. How is rework charged to accounts?

Cost Management: A Strategic Emphasis, 3e by Blocher/Chen/Cokins/Lin

Suggested responses to the above questions:

1. What is product costing?

   Product costing is the process of accumulating, classifying, and assigning direct materials, direct labor, and factory overhead costs to products or services.

2. What is the purpose of product costing?

   Product costing systems provide useful information for managers to make strategic and operational decisions.

3. What are the major types of product costing systems?

   Product costing systems can be classified by: a) cost accumulation method -- job or process costing systems; b) cost measurement method -- actual, normal, or standard costing systems; c) overhead assignment method -- traditional or activity-based costing systems; and d) treatment of fixed factory overhead costs -- variable or absorption costing systems.

4. What factors should be considered in choosing a particular system?

   The choice of a particular system depends on a) the nature of the industry and the product or service, b) the firm's strategy and its management information needs, and c) the costs and benefits of acquiring, designing, modifying, and operating a particular system.

5. Where is job costing or process costing method most appropriate?

   Job costing system is appropriate in any environment where costs can be readily identified with specific products, batches, contracts, or projects. The process costing system, on the other hand, is usually used by firms having homogeneous products which are often mass-produced.

6. Discuss actual, normal, and standard costing.

   * An actual costing system uses actual amounts of costs incurred for all product costs including material, labor, and overhead. They are subject to wide fluctuation of costs and are rarely used.

   * A normal costing system uses actual costs for direct materials and direct labor, and normal costs for factory overhead using predetermined rates. The predetermined overhead rate is derived by dividing budgeted factory overhead costs by budgeted volume or activity levels.

   * A standard costing system uses standard rates (costs) and quantities for all three types of manufacturing costs -- direct materials, direct labor, and factory overhead.

Such a system is good for cost control, performance evaluation, and process improvement.

7. Why use activity-based costing (ABC) in overhead assignment?

Some factory overhead costs are not volume-based. For example, machine setup cost is batch-based and product design cost is product-based. Under ABC systems, factory overhead costs would be allocated to products using cause-and-effect criteria with multiple cost drivers.

8. Distinguish between variable and absorption costing?

In variable costing, all fixed manufacturing costs are treated as period costs and taken directly to income statement without being added to the finished goods value. The theory is that fixed costs do not vary with production and are costs of the "period". Absorption costing, on the other hand, makes no distinction between fixed and variable costs in determining a product's costs.

Generally accepted accounting principles and tax regulations require an absorption costing method for external reporting purposes. For internal managerial planning and control purposes, on the other hand, many firms prefer to use a variable costing method.

9. What is the strategic role of job costing?

Job costing systems provide information for managers to make strategic decisions regarding choice of products and customers, manufacturing methods, pricing decisions, and other long term issues. Traditional, volume-based costing may not be appropriate in many cases, and ABC method provides a much better information when there are more than one product that use different amounts of resources.

10. Define job costing.

Job costing is a product costing system that accumulates and assigns costs to a specific job. Both manufacturing and service organizations can use job costing systems.

11. What type of firms use job order costing? Process costing?

If the company produces specific products for individual customers, it must use a job order costing system. If it produces the same kind of products for all customers, it must use a process costing system.

12. What is a material requisition?

A material requisition form is a source document that the production department supervisor uses to request materials for production.

*Cost Management: A Strategic Emphasis, 3*e by Blocher/Chen/Cokins/Lin

13. What is a time ticket?

A time ticket shows the time an employee worked on each job, the pay rate, and the total cost chargeable to each job.

14. What is overhead application?

Overhead application is a process of assigning overhead costs to the appropriate jobs?

15. How are costs recorded on the job cost sheet?

A product costing system uses material requisition (MR) forms to document and control all materials issued. Based on the information on MR forms, costs of direct materials issued to production are recorded on the job cost sheet with a debit to WIP control and credit to Material control.

A time ticket shows, for each employee, the time worked on each job, the pay rate, and the total cost chargeable to each job. Analysis of time tickets provide information for assigning direct labor costs to individual jobs with a debit to WIP Control and a credit to the Accrued Payroll Control.

Overhead is charged to jobs with due consideration to appropriate cost drivers. For example, if the cost driver is direct labor costs, then, total overhead is divided by total direct labor to arrive at the rate of overhead to be charged per dollar of direct labor. Actual overhead costs are allocated to various jobs under an actual costing system. Factory overhead costs are costs incurred in an accounting period for indirect materials, indirect labor, and other indirect factory costs, including factory rent, insurance, property tax, depreciation, repairs and maintenance, power, light, heat, and employer payroll taxes for factory personnel.

Under normal costing, actual overhead costs are accumulated in a separate overhead account. A predetermined overhead rate, based on budget, is used to charge the applicable overhead to specific jobs with a debit to WIP Control and a credit to Factory Overhead Control. Jobs completed are transferred to inventory with a debit to Finished Goods Inventory and a credit to Work In Process Control.

16. Why use a predetermined factory overhead rate?

A predetermined factory overhead rate is used because it a) provides more accurate unit cost information which does not fluctuate with monthly changes in the level of output, and b) provides cost information on a timely basis.

17. What are the primary cost drivers for allocation of factory overhead?

Examples of cost drivers include direct labor hours, machine hours, number of set-ups, number of orders, manufacturing cycle time, and direct labor costs.

18. What is the process of overhead application?

Overhead application is a process of assigning overhead costs to the appropriate jobs.

19. What is an actual costing system?

An actual costing system uses actual costs incurred for direct materials and direct labor and assigns or applies actual factory overhead to various jobs.

20. What is a normal costing system?

Normal costing system uses actual costs for direct materials and direct labor and applies factory overhead to various jobs using a predetermined rate basis.

21. How is a predetermined factory overhead rate calculated?

Predetermined overhead rate =
Budgeted factory overhead for the year / expected level of activity

22. How is overhead applied to jobs?

Amount applied =
Predetermined overhead rate * actual level of the cost driver (s) selected.

23. What is the overapplied and underapplied overhead?

Overapplied overhead is the amount of factory overhead applied that exceeds the actual factory overhead cost. Underapplied overhead is the amount that the actual factory overhead exceeds the amount applied.

24. What should be done with the under or overapplied overhead?

The discrepancy between factory overhead applied and the actual amount of overhead can be disposed in two ways: a) Adjust the Cost of Goods Sold account, and b) Prorate the amount among Cost of Goods Sold, Finished Goods Inventory, and WIP accounts based on balances in these accounts. Generally, the under/overapplied amounts are written off directly to Cost of Goods Sold if such amounts are small or are a result of operation of the period. In either case, such adjustments are usually done at the end of the year.

The disposition of over/underapplied overhead will be further illustrated through the end of the chapter multiple choice questions and exercises.

25. When are departmental overhead rates more appropriate than a single plant-wide rate?

A plant-wide rate is appropriate when all products pass through the same processes, or all departments are similar. Departmental rates are appropriate when the converse is true.

26. What is different and similar in job costing for a service entity?

Job costing in service industries uses recording procedures and accounts similar to those of manufacturing, except that there are no direct materials involved (or the amount is insignificant). The primary focus is on direct labor performance. The overhead costs are usually applied to jobs based on direct labor hours or dollars.

27. What is an operation costing system?

Operation costing is a hybrid costing system that uses job costing to assign direct materials costs, and process costing to assign conversion costs to products or services. Such procedures may be found in clothing industry, for example.

28. What is spoilage?

Spoilage denotes unacceptable units that are discarded or sold for disposal value.

29. What is scrap?

Scrap is the part of the product that has little or no value.

30. What is rework?

Rework units are product units that are economically reworked into firsts and seconds and sold in regular channels.

31. What is normal spoilage?

Normal spoilage is what occurs under efficient operating conditions. It is uncontrollable in the short-term and is considered a part of product cost. That is, lost unit costs are absorbed by the good units produced.

32. What is abnormal spoilage?

Abnormal spoilage is that in excess of that expected under efficient operating conditions, and is charged as a loss to operations in the period detected.

33. What are the two types of normal spoilage?

a) normal spoilage for a particular job, and b) normal spoilage common to all jobs because it relates to the production process in general.

34. How are the two types of normal spoilage accounted for?

For the first type of spoilage, the particular job cost will be reduced by the estimated disposal price of the spoiled goods. For the second type of spoilage, the spoilage cost will be transferred out from the particular job cost into the factory overhead control account.

35. How is rework charged to accounts?

Rework is charged to one of three accounts depending on its nature. Normal rework due to a particular job is charged to the Work-in-process control of that specific job. Normal rework common to all jobs is charged to the Factory Overhead Control. Abnormal rework is charged to the Loss from Abnormal Rework account.

Multiple choice questions:
1. Product costing is the process of accumulating, classifying, and assigning
   a) direct materials costs to products or services.
   b) direct labor costs to products or services.
   c) factory overhead costs to products or services.
   d) direct materials, direct labor, and factory overhead costs to products or services.
   e) none of the above.

2. Product costing systems provide useful information for managers to make
   a) tactical decisions only.
   b) strategic decisions only.
   c) operational decisions only.
   d) strategic and operational decisions.
   e) none of the above.

3. Product costing systems can be classified by
   a) cost accumulation methods such as, actual, normal, or standard.
   b) cost measurement methods such as, job or process costing.
   c) treatment of fixed overhead costs such as, traditional or activity-based costing.
   d) overhead assignment methods such as, variable or absorption costing.
   e) none of the above.

4. Which statement is <u>false</u>?
   a) Job costing accumulates costs by jobs.
   b) Job costing is suitable for mass production of homogenous products.
   c) Unit cost is computed by dividing total job costs by units produced in job costing.
   d) Costs are accumulated by departments in process costing.
   e) none of the above.

5. A time ticket shows
   a) the time worked on each job for each employee.
   b) the pay rates of employees for a shift.
   c) the time worked on each job for all employees.
   d) the hours worked by each employee for a day.
   e) none of the above.

6. Cost allocation is the process of
   a) assigning overhead costs to the appropriate jobs.
   b) assigning costs to the appropriate products, services, or jobs.
   c) assigning costs to overhead cost pools.
   d) assigning revenues to the related departments.
   e) none of the above.

7. Actual factory overhead includes
   a) direct labor, indirect labor, and other factory costs.
   b) direct material, indirect material, and other factory costs.
   c) indirect material, indirect labor, and other factory overhead costs.
   d) indirect material, indirect labor, and budgeted other factory costs.
   e) none of the above.

8. The journal entry for charging overhead to jobs will be as follows:
   a) Factory Overhead Control   xxx
           Factory Overhead Applied   xxx
   b) Factory Overhead Applied   xxx
           Factory Overhead Control   xxx
   c) Work In Process Control   xxx
           Factory Overhead Applied   xxx
   d) Work In Process Control   xxx
           Indirect labor and material   xxx
   e) None of the above.

9. The predetermined overhead rate is calculated by taking
   a) budgeted factory overhead divided by the estimated activity level of the chosen cost driver.
   b) actual factory overhead divided by the estimated activity level of the chosen cost driver.
   c) actual factory overhead divided by the actual activity level of the chosen cost driver.
   d) budgeted factory overhead divided by the actual activity level of the chosen cost driver.
   e) none of the above.

10. Using a predetermined factory overhead results in
    a) more accurate unit cost information.
    b) providing cost information on a timely basis.
    c) less accurate unit cost information.
    d) b and c.
    e) a and b.

11. The factory overhead is charged to jobs based on
    a) predetermined overhead rate times budgeted level of cost driver activity.
    b) predetermined overhead rate times actual level of cost driver activity.
    c) actual overhead rate times budgeted level of cost driver activity.
    d) actual overhead rate times actual level of cost driver activity.
    e) b or d.

12. The amount of applied overhead can be greater than actual overhead because
    a) the actual level of the cost driver exceeded the estimate.
    b) the actual overhead was less than expected.
    c) the actual level of overhead was more than expected.
    d) a and b.
    e) a and c.

13. If the amount of overhead is underapplied and is insignificant in amount, the difference will be
    a) credited to Cost of Sales.
    b) debited to Cost of Sales.
    c) either debited or credited to Cost of Sales.
    d) always prorated between Cost of Sales, Finished Goods Inventory, and Work In Process accounts.
    e) none of the above.

Cost Management: A Strategic Emphasis, 3e by Blocher/Chen/Cokins/Lin

14. Normal cost of goods sold include
    a) actual direct materials, actual direct labor, and actual overhead.
    b) actual direct materials, actual direct labor, and applied overhead.
    c) actual direct materials, applied direct labor, and actual overhead.
    d) applied direct materials, actual direct labor, and actual overhead.
    e) none of the above.

15. In service industries, the overhead costs are usually applied to jobs based on
    a) direct material weight.
    b) direct labor hours or dollars.
    c) purchasing units or dollars.
    d) direct material cost.
    e) none of the above.

Exercise:

E1. Printing Impressions Inc. uses job costing for its printing operations. Budgeted overhead for 2003 amounts to $450,000 with an estimated machine time of 5,000 hours. Actual overhead amounted to $440,000 with total actual machine time of 4,400 hours. Material costs charged to Work in Process amount to $320,000 and direct labor amount to $132,000. Jobs J7, J8, and J9 are still open. Each one of them have associated material costs of $5,480 and direct labor costs of $1,750. The machine hours associated with these jobs are 25, 34, and 46 hours respectively. Sales for the year amounted to $974,500. Job # J6 which is complete is still in the warehouse and amounts to $17,650 - 40% of this sum is for applicable overhead. There was no inventory at the beginning of the year.

Required:
a) Determine the overhead rate per machine hour.
b) Determine the amount of overhead applied.
c) Determine the cost of Work in Process.
d) Determine the Cost of Goods Sold.
e) Determine the over/underapplied overhead amount.
f) Determine the disposition of the over/underapplied amount using the proration method.
g) Determine the amount of gross profit.
h) Prepare all the necessary journal entries.

E2. Search the internet for www.smithfabinc.com, www.gkurzind.com, and www.housingzone.com with regards to Smith Fabrication Inc., Kurz Industries, and Construction Remodeling Company. Find what you can about their product costing methods and discuss the concepts competitive pricing and other peculiarities in conjunction with the costing methods used by these firms.

Correct answers to multiple choice questions:
1-d; 2-d; 3-e; 4-b; 5-a; 6-b; 7-c; 8-c; 9-a; 10-e; 11-e; 12-d; 13-b; 14-b; 15-b.

Suggested answer to exercise:
a) Predetermined overhead rate: 450,000 / 5,000 = $90 per machine hour

b) The amount of overhead applied: 9,000 * 4,400 = $396,000

c) Jobs in work in process (see the answer on the following page)

d) Cost of goods sold: (320,000 + 132,000 + 396,000) - (31,140 + 17,650) = $799,210
   Note: this amount is before the application of the amount of underapplied overhead explained below.

e) Underapplied overhead: 440,000 - 396,000 = $44,000

c) Jobs in work in process:

Item	Job # J7	Job # J8	Job # J9	Total
Direct Materials	5,480	5,480	5,480	16,440
Direct Labor	1,750	1,750	1,750	5,250
Factory Overhead	2,250	3,060	4,140	9,450
Total WIP	9,480	10,290	11,370	31,140

f) Allocation of underapplied overhead:

Item	Amount	Percentage	Allocation
Finished Goods	7,060	1.78	783.20
Work in Process	9,450	2.39	1,051.60
Cost of Goods Sold	379,490	95.83	42,165.20
Total	396,000	100.00	44,000.00

g) Gross Profit: 974,500 - 799,210 - 42165.20 = $133,124.80

h)	Overhead Control	440,000	
	Various		440,000

	Work in Process	396,000	
	OH Applied		396,000

	Work in Process	320,000	
	Materials Inventory		320,000

	Work in Process	132,000	
	Wages Control		132,000

Finished Goods Inventory	816,860	
Work in Process		816,860

[320,000 + 132,000 + 396,000 – 31,140]

Finished goods inventory	783.20	
Work in process	1,051.60	
Cost of goods sold	42,165.20	
Overhead applied		44,000

To account for underapplied overhead

Overhead applied	440,000	
Overhead control		440,000

Cost of Goods Sold	799,210	
Finished Goods Inventory		799,210

Accounts Receivable	974,500	
Sales		974,500

CHAPTER 5
ACTIVITY-BASED COSTING AND MANAGEMENT

Highlights:

In recent years, companies have taken a number of innovative approaches such as 1) just-in-time inventory systems, 2) various automation techniques such as, robotics, computer-aided design, computer-aided manufacturing, 3) integration approaches such as, flexible manufacturing systems and computer-aided manufacturing to improve manufacturing productivity.

One major limitation of the traditional costing systems is the use of direct labor hours or other volume-based departmental overhead rates such as machine hours or direct material costs in firms with diverse processes and products. Many costs such as setup costs or material handling are activity-based and not volume-based, and the traditional treatment of such costs lead to major inaccuracies when firms produce a diverse mix of products with different volumes, sizes, and complexities.

Activity-based costing (ABC) assigns costs to product or services based on their consumption of activities wherever applicable. It is based on the premise that a firm's products or services are performed by activities and that the required activities incur costs. After resources are assigned to activities, activities are assigned to cost objects according to their use. ABC recognizes the causal relationship of cost drivers to activities. Activity-based Management (ABM) focuses on improving business efficiency and effectiveness, and increasing not only the value received by customers but also the firm. ABC and ABM have been successfully used in both manufacturing and non-manufacturing organizations.

Questions:

Learning objective 2: Explain why traditional costing systems tend to undercost or overcost products.

1. When are traditional, volume-based costing systems useful?

2. When are the traditional costing systems not suitable?

Learning Objective 2: Describe an activity-based costing system and its benefits, limitations, and two-stage allocation procedures.

3. What is an activity?

4. What is a resource?

5. What is a cost object?

6. What is a cost element?

7. What is a cost driver?

8. What is a resource driver? What is an activity driver?

9. What is an activity-based costing system?

10. What is a two-stage allocation procedure?

Cost Management: A Strategic Emphasis, 3e by Blocher/Chen/Cokins/Lin

11. What is unit-level activity?

12. What is batch-level activity?

13. What is product-sustaining activity?

14. What is facility-sustaining activity?

15. What are the two ways that resources can be assigned to activities?

16. Provide several examples of resource costs and related resource consumption drivers.

17. How are costs of activities assigned to cost objects?

18. What are some of the benefits of ABC?

19. How is ABC different compared to traditional costing systems with regards to cost allocation?

20. What are the steps in designing an activity-based costing system?

21. What are the limitations of ABC?

Learning Objective 3: Compute and contrast product costs under a traditional and an activity-based costing system.

The student must review the examples given in the textbook. Additional problems will be provided at the end of this chapter.

Learning Objective 4: Describe an activity-based management system and distinguish between value-added and non-value-added activities.

22. What is activity-based management?

23. What is cost driver analysis?

24. What is a cause-and-effect diagram?

25. What is a value-added activity?

26. What is a non-value-added activity?

> **Learning Objective 5: Describe how activity-based costing systems are used in the manufacturing industry.**

     The authors provide examples from Helwett Packard and Advanced Micro Devices on how ABC costing has been implemented in these companies.

> **Learning Objective 6: Describe how activity-based costing systems are used in marketing and administrative activities.**

     The authors provide several examples and tools used in such an analysis.

27. What is Pareto Analysis?

28. What is performance measurement?

> **Learning Objective 7: Demonstrate how activity-based costing systems are used in service and not-for-profit organizations.**

     The authors provide several examples of how ABC may be implemented in service industries.

> **Learning Objective 8: Relate activity-based costing to strategic cost management.**

29. How are activities related to strategic choices?

> **Learning Objective 9: Identify key factors for a successful ABC/ABM implementation.**

30. What are key factors for successful implementation of ABC/ABM?

31. What is meant by customer profitability analysis?

32. What factors affect the net amount received from a customer?

33. What cost activities and cost drivers relate to customers?

34. List several cost management strategy questions that can help the firm attain its strategic goals with the help of ABC and ABM.

Suggested responses to the above questions:

1. When are traditional, volume-based costing systems useful?

Traditional, volume-based costing systems are suitable when direct labor and materials are the predominant factors of production, when technology is stable, and when there is a limited range of products. These systems measure the resources consumed in proportion to the number of individual products produced.

2. When are the traditional costing systems not suitable?

Traditional costing systems are not suitable when activities such as setup and material handling are unrelated to the physical volume of units produced. Traditional cost allocation system, in such situations, causes serious distortions.

3. What is an activity?

An activity is work performed within an organization such as, actions, movements, or work sequences.

4. What is a resource?

A resource is an economic element that is applied or used in the performance of activities such as, salaries or materials.

5. What is a cost object?

A cost object is any end item for which the cost measurement is desired. Examples of cost objects include any customer, product, service, contract, project, or other work unit for which a separate cost measurement is desired.

6. What is a cost element?

A cost element is an amount paid for a resource consumed by an activity and included in a cost pool?

7. What is a cost driver?

*A cost driver is any factor that causes a change in the cost of an activity. It is also a measurable factor used to assign costs to activities and from activities to other activities, products, or services. The two kinds of activities are **resource drivers and activity drivers.***

8. What is a resource driver? What is an activity driver?

A resource driver is a measure of the quantity of resources consumed by an activity. An example of a resource driver is the percentage of square feet occupied by an activity.

An activity driver is a measure of frequency and intensity of demands placed on activities by cost objects. An example is the number of different parts in a finished product used to measure the consumption of material-handling activities by each product.

9. What is an activity-based costing system?

Activity-based costing (ABC) is a costing approach that assigns costs to products or services based on their consumption of the resources caused by activities.

10. What is a two-stage allocation procedure?

A two-stage allocation assigns a firm's resource costs, namely factory overhead costs, to cost pools and then to cost objects based on how cost objects use those resources. In traditional costing systems, factory overhead costs are assigned to plant or departmental cost pools or cost centers, and then to production outputs.

11. What is unit-level activity?

A unit level activity is performed for each unit of the cost object. Example: lubricating every item produced.

12. What is batch-level activity?

A batch-level activity is performed for each batch or group of cost objects; i.e., number of machine setups.

13. What is product-sustaining activity?

A product-sustaining activity supports the production of products in general; i.e., number of design changes.

14. What is facility-sustaining activity?

A facility-sustaining activity supports the production of products in general.

15. What are the two ways that resources can be assigned to activities?

The cost of resources can be assigned to activities by direct tracing or estimation.

16. Provide several examples of resource costs and related resource consumption drivers.

    * *Personnel / Number of workers*
    * *Storeroom / number of picks*
    * *Engineers / time worked*
    * *research and development / number of new items developed*

17. How are costs of activities assigned to cost objects?

The level of activity of the cost driver is used to allocate costs (based on the rates developed) to the cost object.

18. What are some of the benefits of ABC?

    * *Better profitability measures*
    * *Better decision and control*
    * *Readily available information*

Cost Management: A Strategic Emphasis, 3e by Blocher/Chen/Cokins/Lin

19. How is ABC different compared to traditional costing systems with regards to cost allocation?

ABC measures consumption of resources by activities, and then links the cost of these activities to cost objects such as products or services.

20. What are the steps in designing an activity-based costing system?

There are three steps in designing an activity-based costing system.
*The first step is to identify resource costs and conduct an activity analysis. Activities may take the form of unit-based, batch-level, product-sustaining, or facility-sustaining. A **unit level activity** is performed for each unit of production such as, material or labor. A **Batch-level activity** is performed for each batch of products rather than for each unit of production such as, machine setup, production scheduling, etc. A **product-sustaining activity** is performed to support the production of a different product such as product design, part administration, etc. A **facility-sustaining activity** is performed to support the production of products in general such as, maintenance, plant management, etc.*

The second step is assignment of resource costs to activities. Typical resource drivers include meters for utilities, number of employees for payroll related activities, etc.

The third step is assignment of costs to cost objects. Activity drivers are used to assign activity costs to the cost objects. Typical activity drivers are the number of purchase orders, number of parts stored, number of setups, etc.

21. What are the limitations of ABC?

Tthere will still be arbitrariness in allocation of certain costs such as those that are facility related. There is also the possibility of omission of some costs such as marketing and administrative costs. In addition, ABC is expensive and difficult to maintain. A general limitation of traditional costing is that it undercosts complex, low-volume products, and it overcosts high-volume products.
The student must review the examples given in the textbook. Additional problems will be provided at the end of this chapter.

22. What is activity-based management?

Activity-based management (ABM) is the management of activities to improve the value received by the customer and to increase the profit achieved by providing this value. AMB draws on ABC as its major source of information. ABM improves management's focus in reducing costs and focusing on value-added activities.

23. What is cost driver analysis?

Cost driver analysis is the examination, quantification, and explanation of the effects of cost drivers.

24. What is a cause-and-effect diagram?

It maps out a list of causes that affect an activity, process, stated problem, or a desired outcome.

25. What is a value-added activity?

It is an activity that contributes to customer value and satisfaction or satisfies an organization's needs.

26. What is a non-value-added activity?

A non-value-added activity does not contribute to customer value or to the organization's needs. Examples are waiting or moving time, reworking, repairing, storing, and inspection functions.
The authors provide examples from Helwett Packard and Advanced Micro Devices on how ABC costing has been implemented in these companies.

27. What is Pareto Analysis?

Pareto analysis is a management tool that shows 20 percent of a set of important cost drivers are responsible for 80 percent of the total costs incurred.

28. What is performance measurement?

Performance measurement identifies indicators of the work performed and the results achieved in an activity, process, or organizational unit. It could include financial and non-financial measures.

29. How are activities related to strategic choices?

Successful firms put their resources into those activities that lead to the greatest strategic benefit. ABC/ABM helps managers understand the relation between the firm's strategy and the activities and resources needed to put the strategy into place.

30. What are key factors for successful implementation of ABC/ABM?

For a successful implementation of ABC/ABM, management accountants need to cooperate with engineers, manufacturing, and operating managers to form a design team. Activities and cost drivers need to be identified; both financial and non-financial

Cost Management: A Strategic Emphasis, 3e by Blocher/Chen/Cokins/Lin

measures are required. Six factors are identified for a successful implementation strategy. These factors are:
1) *Involve management and employees in the creation of an ABC system.*
2) *Maintain a parallel system until people get used to it.*
3) *Use ABC/ABM on jobs that will succeed.*
4) *Keep the initial ABC/ABM design simple.*
5) *Create desired incentives.*
6) *Educate management*

31. What is meant by customer profitability analysis?

Customer profitability analysis traces and reports customer revenues and customer costs.

32. What factors affect the net amount received from a customer?

Customer revenue considers all activities that affect the net amount received from the customer including gross sales, sales discount, terms of payment, delivery, and sales return and allowances.

33. What cost activities and cost drivers relate to customers?

It includes customer unit-level costs such as sales commission. Customer batch-level costs such as, order processing and invoicing costs. Customer sustaining costs such as, collection costs for late payment. Distribution-channel costs such as, operating a regional warehouse, and sales-sustaining costs such as, general corporate headquarter costs.

34. List several cost management strategy questions that can help the firm attain its strategic goals with the help of ABC and ABM.

* How do a firm's cost structures and profits compare to those of its competition?
* How does switching from traditional costing to an ABC costing system impact pricing, product design, manufacturing technology, and product-line decisions?
* How will changes in activities and components affect the suppliers and customers in the value chain?
* How will changes in firm's processes impact the bottom line?

Multiple choice questions:

1. In an activity-based costing system
   a) some manufacturing costs may not be allocated to the cost object.
   b) some non-manufacturing costs may be allocated to the cost object.
   c) common costs are assigned to cost pools before being allocated to cost objects.
   d) facility-sustaining costs are often not allocated to cost objects.
   e) all of the above.

2. Product design changes is an example of ____ whereas plant utilities is an example of __
   a) batch level / product level.
   b) product level / batch level.
   c) product level / facility level.
   d) facility level / product level

3. Typically moving time is considered____ and storing is considered____
   a) value-added / non-value-added.
   b) non-value-added / value-added.
   c) non-value-added / non-value-added
   d) value-added / value-added
   e) none of the above.

4. Generally inspecting time is considered __ and delivering the product is considered __
   a) value-added / non-value-added.
   b) non-value-added / value-added.
   c) non-value-added / non-value-added.
   d) value-added / value-added.
   e) none of the above.

5. An appropriate cost driver for order filling, shipping, and warehousing may be
   a) weight of products.
   b) number of products.
   c) size of the products.
   d) any of the above.
   e) a and c only.

6. Monthly processing of customer statements is an example of
   a) customer unit-level costs.
   b) customer batch-level costs.
   c) customer-sustaining costs.
   d) distribution-channel costs.
   e) sales-sustaining costs.

7. Order processing costs or invoicing costs for customers are examples of
   a) customer unit-level costs.
   b) customer batch-level costs.
   c) customer-sustaining costs.
   d) distribution-channel costs.
   e) sales-sustaining costs.

Cost Management: A Strategic Emphasis, 3e by Blocher/Chen/Cokins/Lin
© 2005 by The McGraw-Hill Companies, Inc.

8. A resource is a (an)
   a) measure of frequency and intensity of demands placed on activities by cost objects
   b) measure of the quantity of resources consumed by an activity
   c) amount paid for a resource consumed by an activity and included in a cost pool
   d) economic element that is applied or used in the performance of activities
   e) none of the above

9. A cost element is a (an)
   a) measure of frequency and intensity of demands placed on activities by cost objects
   b) measure of the quantity of resources consumed by an activity
   c) amount paid for a resource consumed by an activity and included in a cost pool
   d) economic element that is applied or used in the performance of activities
   e) none of the above

10. A resource driver is a (an)
   a) measure of frequency and intensity of demands placed on activities by cost objects
   b) measure of the quantity of resources consumed by an activity
   c) amount paid for a resource consumed by an activity and included in a cost pool
   d) economic element that is applied or used in the performance of activities
   e) none of the above

11. An activity driver is a (an)
   a) measure of frequency and intensity of demands placed on activities by cost objects
   b) measure of the quantity of resources consumed by an activity
   c) amount paid for a resource consumed by an activity and included in a cost pool
   d) economic element that is applied or used in the performance of activities
   e) none of the above

12. A two-stage cost allocation is a (an)
   a) measure of frequency and intensity of demands placed on activities by cost objects
   b) measure of the quantity of resources consumed by an activity
   c) amount paid for a resource consumed by an activity and included in a cost pool
   d) economic element that is applied or used in the performance of activities
   e) none of the above

13. Unit-level activity is
   a) performed to support the production of products in general
   b) performed to support the production of a different product
   c) performed for each batch of products rather than for each unit of production
   d) performed for each unit of production
   e) none of the above

14. Batch-level activity is
    a) performed to support the production of products in general
    b) performed to support the production of a different product
    c) performed for each batch of products rather than for each unit of production
    d) performed for each unit of production
    e) none of the above

15. Product-sustaining activity is
    a) performed to support the production of products in general
    b) performed to support the production of a different product
    c) performed for each batch of products rather than for each unit of production
    d) performed for each unit of production
    e) none of the above

16. Facility-sustaining activity is
    a) performed to support the production of products in general
    b) performed to support the production of a different product
    c) performed for each batch of products rather than for each unit of production
    d) performed for each unit of production
    e) none of the above

17. Activity analysis is
    a) performed to support the production of products in general
    b) performed to support the production of a different product
    c) performed for each batch of products rather than for each unit of production
    d) performed for each unit of production
    e) none of the above

18. ABM
    a) and ABC are virtually the same
    b) is determining cost of products or services with proper association of activities to cost drivers
    c) is the management of activities to improve the value received by the customer and profit achieved by providing this value
    d) is the examination, quantification, and explanation of the effects of cost drivers
    e) maps out a list of causes that affect an activity, process, stated problem, or a desired outcome.

19. Cause-and-effect diagram
    a) and ABC are virtually the same
    b) is determining cost of products or services with proper association of activities to cost drivers
    c) is the management of activities to improve the value received by the customer and profit achieved by providing this value
    d) is the examination, quantification, and explanation of the effects of cost drivers
    e) maps out a list of causes that affect an activity, process, stated problem, or a desired outcome.

Cost Management: A Strategic Emphasis, 3e by Blocher/Chen/Cokins/Lin

20. Cost driver analysis
    a) and ABC are virtually the same
    b) is determining cost of products or services with proper association of activities to cost drivers
    c) is the management of activities to improve the value received by the customer and profit achieved by providing this value
    d) is the examination, quantification, and explanation of the effects of cost drivers
    e) maps out a list of causes that affect an activity, process, stated problem, or a desired outcome.

21. Pareto analysis is a management tool that shows
    a) 50 percent of important cost drivers are responsible for 50 percent of costs.
    b) 80 percent of important cost drivers are responsible for 20 percent of costs.
    c) 20 percent of important cost drivers are responsible for 80 percent of costs.
    d) 10 percent of important cost drivers are responsible for 90 percent of costs
    e) none of the above

22. Performance measurement
    a) identifies indicators of the work performed and the results achieved in an activity, process, or organizational unit
    b) is an activity that contributes to customer value and satisfaction or satisfies an organizational need
    c) does not contribute to customer value or to the organization's needs
    d) is used only in decentralized organizations
    e) none of the above.

23. A non-value-added activity
    a) identifies indicators of the work performed and the results achieved in an activity, process, or organizational unit
    b) is an activity that contributes to customer value and satisfaction or satisfies an organizational need
    c) does not contribute to customer value or to the organization's needs
    d) is used only in decentralized organizations
    e) none of the above.

Exercises:
E1.
Shahnaz Design Company had a total of $66,000 in overhead. A total of $33,000 is purchasing department overhead spent on 10 purchase orders, 4 of which were for customer A and the balance for customer B. A total of $11,000 of this overhead was related to warehousing cost. Ninety percent of the space occupied was for merchandise held for customer A and the balance for customer B. The balance of overhead was for general administration which was spent equally on the two jobs. Materials purchased for the two jobs amounted to $24,000, 2/3 of which was for customer A. Labor cost

amounted to $12,000 for a total of 600 hours, 1/3 for job A and 2/3 for job B. The company expects to have a margin of 20% on these two jobs.

Required: Determine a) the total cost of each job using the traditional costing system. Use direct labor cost as the basis for allocation of overhead; b) the total cost of each job using ABC technique for allocation of overhead; c) expected selling price under each method.

E2.

Identify a proper cost driver for the following resource costs:

Resource costs	Appropriate cost driver
• Utilities	
• Personnel costs	
• Cafeteria costs	
• Setup costs	
• Material moving costs	
• Machinery depreciation	
• Janitorial costs	
• Employee benefits	
• Vehicle costs	
• Printing costs	
• CPU costs	
• Computer storage costs	

E3.

Omid Printing Company has incurred the following overhead costs for the current fiscal year.

Material purchasing	$12,000
Direct labor support	60,000
Machine operation	48,000
Setup costs	20,000
Production order	30,000
Material handling	15,000
Parts administration	36,000
General administration	56,000

Appropriate cost drivers and their volumes are identified to be as follows:

Material costs	$200,000
Direct labor cost	150,000
Machine hours	4,000
Setup hours	2,000
Number of orders	1,000
Number of loads	300
Number of parts	18,000
Square footage occupied	112,000

Required: determine cost per unit of the cost drivers identified.

E4.
Refer to exercise 3 and also consider the following facts:

Two products resulted from the above operation, X and Y. Cost drivers associated with X are as follows:

Material costs	120,000
Direct labor costs	50,000
Machine hours	2,000
Setup hours	1,500
Number of orders	600
Number of loads	200
Number of parts	4,500
Square footage occupied	84,000

The operation resulted in 1,000 units of X and 2,000 units of Y.

Required: Determine cost per unit of X and Y.

E5.
Refer to exercise 3. Now assume that that a single overhead base was used for determination of overhead rate. Production of X remains at 1,000 units while 2,000 units of Y were produced.
Required: determine the overhead charged to X and Y assuming a) material cost as allocation base, b) direct labor cost as allocation base, and c) machine hours as allocation base.

E6.
Andrea Company was an E-retailing business. The activities were identified as servicing routine customers, electronic customer order processing, imaging and annotation, virtual storefront optimization, and customer acquisition and retention. **Identify a proper cost driver for each of these activities.**

Correct answers to multiple choice questions:
1-e; 2-c; 3-c; 4-b; 5-d; 6-c; 7-b; 8-d; 9-c; 10-b; 11-a; 12-e; 13-d; 14-c; 15-b; 16-a; 17-e; 18-c; 19-e; 20-d; 21-c; 22-a; 23-c

Suggested answers to exercises:

E1.

Title	Cust. A	Cust. B	Total
a) Job cost under the traditional method:			
Material	16,000	8,000	24,000
Labor	4,000	8,000	12,000
Overhead	22,000	44,000	66,000
Total	42,000	60,000	102,000
b) Job cost under Activity-based costing:			
Material	16,000	8,000	24,000
Labor	4,000	8,000	12,000
Purchasing	13,200	19,800	33,000
Warehousing	9,900	1,100	11,000
Administration	11,000	11,000	22,000
Total	54,100	47,900	102,000
c1) Sales value under traditional costing			
20% margin5250	52,500	75,000	127,500
c2) Sales value under ABC method			
20% margin	67,625	59,875	127,500

E2.

Resource costs	Appropriate cost driver
• Utilities	Meters for utilities
• Personnel costs	Number of employees
• Cafeteria costs	Number of meals served
• Setup costs	Number of setups
• Material moving costs	Number of moves
• Machinery depreciation	Machine hours
• Janitorial costs	Square feet occupied
• Employee benefits	Gross payroll amount
• Vehicle costs	Number of miles driven
• Printing costs	Number of lines printed
• CPU costs	CPU minutes
• Computer storage costs	Storage units

Cost Management: A Strategic Emphasis, 3e by Blocher/Chen/Cokins/Lin

E3.

Material purchasing	$12,000/200,000	=	.06 per dollar of material costs
Direct labor support	60,000/150,000	=	.40 per dollar of direct labor
Machine operation	48,000/4000	=	$12 per machine hour
Setup costs	20,000/2,000	=	$10 per setup hour
Production order	30,000/1,000	=	$30 per order
Material handling	15,000/300	=	$50 per load
Parts administration	36,000/18,000	=	$2 per part
General administration	56,000/112,000	=	.50 per square foot

E4.

Cost of X

Material purchasing	.06 * 120,000	=	$7,200
Direct labor support	.40 * 50,000	=	20,000
Machine operation	12 * 2,000	=	24,000
Setup costs	10 * 1,500	=	15,000
Production order	30 * 600	=	18,000
Material handling	50 * 200	=	10,000
Parts administration	2 * 4.500	=	9,000
General administration	50 * 84,000	=	42,000
Total overhead			$145,200
Material cost			120,000
Direct labor			50,000
Total cost			315,200
Number of units			1,000
Cost per unit of X			315.2

Cost of Y

Material purchasing	.06 * 80,000	=	$ 4,800
Direct labor support	.40 * 100,000	=	40,000
Machine operation	12 * 2,000	=	24,000
Setup costs	10 * 500	=	5,000
Production order	30 * 400	=	12,000
Material handling	50 * 100	=	5,000
Parts administration	2 * 13,500	=	27,000
General administration	50 * 28,000	=	14,000
Total overhead			131,800
Material cost			80,000
Labor cost			100,000
Total cost of Y			311,800
Number of units			2,000
Cost per unit of Y			155.90

E5.

a) Overhead rate based on direct material costs $277,000/200,000 = $1.385

     Overhead charged to X   120,000 * 1.385 = 166,200

     Overhead charged to Y   80,000 * 1.385 = 110,800

b) Overhead rate based on direct labor costs   277,000/150,000 = $1.8466

     Overhead charged to X   50,000 * 1.8466 = 92,330

     Overhead charged to Y   100,000 * 1.8466 = 184,670

c) Overhead rate based on machine hours   277,000/4,000 = 69.25

     Overhead charged to X   2,000 * 69.25 = $138,500

     Overhead charged to Y   2,000 * 69.25 = 138,500

E6.

Activity	Cost drivers
Service routine customers	E-mail and phone inquiries
Electronic customer order processing	Time (hardware/software depreciation
Imaging and annotation	Number of changes to inventory data base
Virtual storefront optimization	Time (hours dedicated to Web page development
Customer acquisition and retention	number of targeted customers

CHAPTER 6
COST ESTIMATION

Highlights:
It is important for managers to have accurate and timely estimates of product and service costs. Five estimation methods are presented. The account classification, visual fit and high-low methods are relatively simple, but they are not very accurate. The account classification method uses the accountant's classification of ledger cost accounts, as either variable or fixed costs, to develop the estimation equation as fixed cost plus average per unit variable cost. The visual fit method requires the accountant to graph the data and to visually draw the estimation equation. The high-low method develops an estimation equation using algebra and the representative low and high points in the data. The chapter skips the accountant classification and the scatter diagram and pays attention to the other methods.

Two statistical methods are also presented -- work measurement and regression analysis. Work measurement is a study of work activity that measures the time or input required per unit of output. Regression analysis is a statistical method that obtains the best-fitting line for the data. The three key measures of the precision and reliability of the regression; R-squared, the t-value, and the standard error of the estimate are explained.

Questions:
1. What is cost estimation?

Learning Objective 1: Understand the strategic role of cost estimation.

---

2. Why does strategic management require accurate cost estimates?

3. For what cost drivers can cost estimation be used?

4. How are cost drivers identified?

Learning Objective 2: Apply the six steps of cost estimation.

5. What are the six steps in cost estimation?

6. What are the trade-offs in cost estimation?

Learning Objective 3: Use of each of the cost estimation methods: high-low method, work measurement, and regression analysis.

7. What is the mean absolute percentage error (MAPE)?

8. What is the visual fit method and what are its limitations?

9. What is the high-low method and what are its limitations?

Cost Management: A Strategic Emphasis, 3e by Blocher/Chen/Cokins/Lin
© 2005 by The McGraw-Hill Companies, Inc.

10. What is work measurement?

11. What is regression analysis?

12. What are outliers?

13. What is a dummy variable?

Note: Regression analysis produces several statistical measures: a) R-squared, also called the coefficient of determination, b) the t-statistic, or t-value, and SE, the standard error of the estimate.

14. What is R-squared?

15. What is t-value?

16. What is multicollinearity?

17. What is correlation?

18. What is standard error of the estimate (SE)?

Learning Objective 4: Explain the data requirements and implementation problems of the cost estimation methods.

---

19. What are the three aspects of data collection that significantly affect precision and reliability of the regression line?

20. What are some of the non-linearity problems?

Appendix:

Learning Objective 5: Use learning curves in cost estimation when learning is present.

---

21. What is learning curve analysis?

22. What is the learning rate?

23. What decisions are affected by learning rate?

24. What are the limitations of learning curve analysis?

Learning Objective 6: Use statistical measures to evaluate a regression analysis.

25. What is simple linear regression in contrast to multiple regression?

26. What is variance?

27. What are the degrees of freedom?

28. What is mean squared variance?

29. What does the analysis of variance table provide?

30. What are the six key statistical measures in regression?

31. What is precision of the regression?

32. What is a confidence interval?

33. What is Goodness of Fit (R-squared)?

34. What is the F-statistic?

35. What is the t-value?

36. What is non-constant variance?

37. What is rank-order correlation?

38. What are non-independent (Durbin-Watson) errors?

Cost Management: A Strategic Emphasis, 3e by Blocher/Chen/Cokins/Lin

Suggested responses to the above questions:

1. What is cost estimation

Cost estimation is the development of a well-defined relationship between a cost object and its cost drivers, for the purpose of predicting the cost.

2. Why does strategic management require accurate cost estimates?

- *To facilitate strategic positioning analysis.*
- *To facilitate value chain analysis.*
- *To facilitate target costing and life cycle costing.*

3. For what cost drivers can cost estimation be used?

Cost estimation can be used for any of the four cost drivers: activity-based, volume-based, structural, or executional.

4. How are cost drivers identified?

Cost drivers are identified by using the judgment of product designers, engineers, and manufacturing personnel. Cost estimation itself can also sometimes play a discovery role in the process.

5. What are the six steps in cost estimation?

- *Define the cost object to be estimated. Example: auto expense.*
- *Determine the cost drivers. Example: number of miles to be driven.*
- *Collect consistent and accurate data.*
- *Graph the data.*
- *Select and employ the estimation method; i.e., visual fit, regression, etc.*
- *Assess the accuracy of the cost estimate.*

6. What are the trade-offs in cost estimation?

The more accurate the method (regression), the more costly.
The less accurate the method (account classification) the less costly.

7. What is the mean absolute percentage error (MAPE)?

MAPE is an estimation method to compare the estimates to the actual results over time which is calculated by taking the absolute value of each error, and then averaging these errors and converting the result to a percentage of the actual values of overhead.

8. What is the visual fit method and what are its limitations?

The visual fit method calls for viewing the data in either tabular or graphical form. It is also simple and allows for a quick estimation of costs. Its limitations are that a) the scale of a graph may affect the viewer's ability to estimate costs accurately, and b) users of both tabular and graphical reports make significant perception errors. Note: the method is not explicitly discussed in the chapter but its understanding helps in realizing what the other methods attempt to accomplish.

9. What is the high-low method and what are its limitations?

It uses algebra to determine a unique estimation line between representative low and high points in the data. It is represented by the equation, $Y = a + bX$, where Y is the value of the estimated cost, X is the cost driver, a represents the fixed cost, and b is the slope of the line which is often interpreted as the unit variable cost. The graph is objectively prepared. However, it can only represent the best possible line for the two selected points, and the selection of the two points requires judgment.

10. What is work measurement?

*Work measurement is a cost estimation method that makes a detailed study of some production or service activity with the objective of measuring the time or input required per unit of output. The most common method of work measurement is **work sampling.** This is a statistical method that makes a series of measurements about the activity under study.*

11. What is regression analysis?

It is a statistical method for obtaining the unique equation that best fits a set of data points. Least squares regression is widely viewed as one of the most effective methods for estimating costs. The dependent variable is the cost to be estimated (Y). The independent variable is the cost driver that is used to estimate the value of the dependent variable (X). The regression method has both an intercept (a), and a slope (b). In addition, the estimation error (e) is considered explicitly in the regression estimate.

12. What are outliers?

Outliers are unusual data points that strongly influence a regression analysis. Each outlier must be reviewed to determine whether it is due to a data-recording error, normal operating conditions, or a unique and non- recurring event.

13. What is a dummy variable?

A dummy variable is used to represent the presence or absence of a condition; i.e., we must consider a high or low volume for a particular month due to seasonality if not already present in the data provided.

Note: Regression analysis produces several statistical measures: a) R-squared, also called the coefficient of determination, b) the t-statistic, or t-value, and SE, the standard error of the estimate.

14. What is R-squared?

R-squared is a number between zero and 1, and it is often described as a measure of the explanatory power of the regression, that is, the degree to which changes in the dependent variable can be predicted by changes in the independent variable(s).

15. What is the t-value?

The t-value is a measure of the reliability of each of the independent variables, that is, the degree to which an independent variable has a valid, stable, long-term relationship with the dependent variable.

16. What is multicollinearity?

Multicollinearity means that two or more independent variables are highly correlated with each other. However, independent variables are supposed to be independent of each other, and not correlated.

17. What is correlation?

Correlation means that a given variable tends to change predictably in the same (or opposite) direction for a given change in the other correlated variable.

18. What is standard error of the estimate (SE)?

It is a measure of the accuracy of the regression's estimates. A regression estimate of $2,000 with the SE of $300 means that there is reasonable confidence that the unknown actual value lies in the range of $2,000 +/- $300. SE must be interpreted in terms of its relationship to the average size of the dependent variable resulting in good precision or relatively poor precision.

19. What are the three aspects of data collection that significantly affect precision and reliability of the regression line?

They are data accuracy, the choice of the time period, and non-linearity.

20. What are some of the non-linearity problems?

- *Trend and/or seasonality: this occurs due to changing prices or seasonal nature of some transactions. Adjustments can be made through the use of a price change index, use of a decomposition technique that extracts the seasonality of the data series, addition of a trend variable, replacement of the original values of each of the variables with the **first differences** for each variable, that is, the difference between each value and the succeeding value in the time series.*
- *Outliers: outliers can significantly decrease the precision and reliability of the estimate, and they should be corrected or adjusted (using, for example, a dummy variable) if it is clear that they are unusual or non-recurring.*
- *Data Shift: if the unusual business condition is long lasting, such a shift should be included in the estimate.*

Appendix:
21. What is learning curve analysis?

It is a systematic method for estimating costs when learning is present.

22. What is the learning rate?

It is the percentage by which average time (or total time) falls from previous levels, as output doubles.

23. What decisions are affected by learning rate?

- *The make or buy decision*
- *Preparation of bids for production contracts; life-cycle costing*
- *Cost-volume-profit analysis*
- *Development of standard product costs*
- *Capital budgeting*
- *Budgeting production levels and labor needs*
- *Operational and management control*

24. What are the limitations of learning curve analysis?

- *It is most appropriate for labor-intensive, repetitive tasks; not suitable in flexible manufacturing environment.*
- *The learning rate is assumed to be constant while in actual applications, the decline in labor time may not be constant.*
- *It may be unreliable because the observed change in productivity could be due to other factors.*

Cost Management: A Strategic Emphasis, 3e by Blocher/Chen/Cokins/Lin

25. What is simple linear regression in contrast to multiple regression?

Simple linear regression is based on a single independent variable whereas, multiple regression includes two or more independent variables. The lack of independence among the independent variables (multicollinearity) is a concern in multiple regression analysis.

26. What is variance?

*Variance is a measure of the degree to which the values of the dependent variable vary about its mean. Total variance is composed of "error" and "explained" components. Part of the change which is **not** due to change in the dependent variable is the residual or error variance.*

27. What are the degrees of freedom?

The degrees of freedom for each component of variance represents the number of independent choices that can be made for that component.

28. What is mean squared variance?

Mean squared variance is the ratio of the amount of variance of a component to the number of degrees of freedom for that component.

29. What does the analysis of variance table provide?

The analysis of variance table is used to separate the total variance of the dependent variable into both "error" and "explained" variance components. It can also provide statistics on the degrees of freedom and the mean squared variance.

30. What are the six key statistical measures in regression?

<u>Precision</u>
1. Precision of the regression (measured by the standard error of the estimate).

<u>Reliability</u>
2. Goodness of fit (R-squared)
3. Statistical reliability (F statistic)
4. Statistical reliability for each independent variable (t value)
5. Reliability of precision (Rank order correlation)
6. Non-independence of errors (Durbin-Watson statistic)

31. What is precision of the regression?

It is measured by standard error (SE). SE is interpreted as a range of values around the regression estimate such that we can be approximately 67% confident that the actual value will lie in this range. Doubling the range will give us 95% confidence. Thus, there is an inverse relationship between precision and confidence level. It can be computed by taking the square root of the mean square error.

32. What is a confidence interval?

It is a range around the regression line within which one can be confident the actual value of the predicted cost will fall.

33. What is Goodness of Fit (R-squared)?

R-squared (also called the coefficient of determination) is a measure of the percentage of variance in the dependent variable that can be explained by the independent variable; i.e., Sum of squares (explained) / Sum of squared (total).

34. What is the F-statistic?

It is a useful measure of the statistical reliability of the regression; i.e., F = Mean square (explained) / mean square (errors).

35. What is the t-value?

t value is a measure of the reliability of each independent variable; i.e., t value = ratio of the coefficient of the independent variable / standard error of the coefficient.

36. What is non-constant variance?

It is the condition when the variance of the errors is not constant over the range of the independent variable.

37. What is rank-order correlation?

It is a statistic that measures the degree to which two sets of numbers tend to have the same order, rank. A relatively high rank-order correlation would be evidence of non-constant variance.

38. What are non-independent (Durbin-Watson) errors?

If the data is non-linear because of seasonality or when learning is present, then, regression will be unreliable and subject to greater than expected estimation errors. It is a measure of the extent of non-linearity in the regression.

Multiple choice questions:

1. Fill in the blank: Cost estimation is the development of _____ for the purpose of predicting costs:
   a) a well-defined relationship between a cost object and a cost element.
   b) a well-defined relationship between a cost object and a cost center.
   c) a well-defined relationship between a cost object and a cost driver.
   d) a well-defined relationship between a cost object and a cost account.
   e) a well-defined relationship between a cost object and a cost entity.

2. Accurate cost estimates
   a) are needed to facilitate strategic positioning analysis.
   b) are not needed in facilitating value chain analysis.
   c) are needed to facilitate target costing and life cycle costing.
   d) all of the above.
   e) a and c.

3. Cost estimation can be used for
   a) activity-based cost drivers.
   b) volume-based cost drivers.
   c) structural cost drivers.
   d) executional cost drivers.
   e) all of the above.

4. The heating expense for the building and temperature to be maintained in the building is an example of relationship between,
   a) cost driver, and cost to be estimated.
   b) cost to be estimated, and cost driver.
   c) cost to be estimated, and cost element.
   d) cost to be estimated, and cost objective.
   e) none of the above.

5. If the club expense includes a rent of $2,000 plus a charge of $40 per member and the club has 80 members,
   a) fixed costs amount to $2,000 and variable cost amounts to $3,200.
   b) fixed costs amount to $3,200 and variable cost amounts to $2,000.
   c) all costs are fixed.
   d) all costs are variable.
   e) cannot be determined.

6. Which cost estimation method requires classification of each cost account in the financial records as either a fixed or variable cost?
   a) regression
   b) high-low method
   c) visual fit
   d) account classification
   e) work measurement

7. To estimate costs, we include only two points from a series of observations in this method:
   a) regression
   b) high-low method
   c) visual fit
   d) account classification
   e) work measurement

8. In the high-low method of cost estimation,
   a) Y represents independent variable.
   b) X represents dependent variable.
   c) a represents the slope of the line.
   d) b represents the fixed cost or quantity.
   e) none of the above.

9. Concerning regression,
   a) the independent variable is the cost to be estimated.
   b) the dependent variable is the cost to be estimated.
   c) the intercept is the cost to be estimated.
   d) the slope of the line is the cost to be estimated.
   e) none of the above.

10. Coefficient of determination
   a) is same as R-squared.
   b) is a number between zero and 1.
   c) is a measure of the explanatory power of the regression.
   d) is the degree to which changes in the dependent variable can be predicted by changes in the independent variable.
   e) all of the above.

Cost Management: A Strategic Emphasis, 3e by Blocher/Chen/Cokins/Lin

11. Multicollinearity
    a) is a measure of the accuracy of the regression's estimate.
    b) means that a given variable tends to change predictably in the same (or opposite direction for the given change in the other variable.
    c) is the degree to which an independent variable has a valid, stable, long-term relationship with the dependent variable.
    d) means that two or more independent variables are highly correlated with each other.
    e) none of the above.

12. Correlation
    a) is a measure of the accuracy of the regression's estimate.
    b) means that a given variable tends to change predictably in the same [or opposite] direction for the given change in the other variable.
    c) is the degree to which an independent variable has a valid, stable, long-term relationship with the dependent variable.
    d) means that two or more independent variables are highly correlated with each other.
    e) none of the above.

13. The t-value
    a) is a measure of the accuracy of the regression's estimate.
    b) means that a given variable tends to change predictably in the same (or opposite direction for the given change in the other variable.
    c) is the degree to which an independent variable has a valid, stable, long-term relationship with the dependent variable.
    d) means that two or more independent variables are highly correlated with each other.
    e) none of the above.

14. The standard error of the estimate (SE)
    a) is a measure of the accuracy of the regression's estimate.
    b) means that a given variable tends to change predictably in the same or opposite direction for the given change in the other variable.
    c) is the degree to which an independent variable has a valid, stable, long-term relationship with the dependent variable.
    d) means that two or more independent variables are highly correlated with each other.
    e) none of the above.

15. The learning rate
    a) is a systematic method for estimating costs when learning is present.
    b) is the percentage by which average time (or total time) rises from previous levels, as output doubles.
    c) is the percentage by which average time (or total time) falls from previous levels, as output doubles.
    d) is the percentage by which average time (or total time) falls from previous levels, as output triples.
    e) none of the above.

16. Total variance of Y is computed by taking the difference between
    a) dependent variable Y and mean of Y.
    b) dependent variable Y and regression prediction for Y.
    c) mean of Y and regression prediction for Y.
    d) explained variance and error variance.
    e) none of the above.

17. Error variance is computed by taking the difference between
    a) dependent variable Y and mean of Y.
    b) dependent variable Y and regression prediction for Y.
    c) mean of Y and regression prediction for Y.
    d) explained variance and error variance.
    e) none of the above.

18. Explained variance is computed by taking the difference between
    a) dependent variable Y and mean of Y.
    b) dependent variable Y and regression prediction for Y.
    c) mean of Y and regression prediction for Y.
    d) explained variance and error variance.
    e) none of the above.

19. Mean squared variance is computed by taking the difference between
    a) dependent variable Y and mean of Y.
    b) dependent variable Y and regression prediction for Y.
    c) mean of Y and regression prediction for Y.
    d) explained variance and error variance.
    e) none of the above.

20. Durbin-Watson statistic
    a) is a measure of the extent of linearity in the regression.
    b) is a measure of the extent of non-linearity in the regression.
    c) is calculated from the amount and change of the errors over the range of the independent variable.
    d) a and c.
    e) b and c.

Exercises:

E1.

Consider the following observations of maintenance costs in the past six months:

Month	Machine hours	Amount $
January	200	$2,800
February	350	3,000
March	450	4,000
April	500	5,000
May	600	5,200
June	580	5,800

Required: Using the high-low method, determine the cost estimation equation. What would be the maintenance cost estimate if the anticipated machine hours for July is 580 hours?

E2.

Assume a regression estimate of $5,800 and the SE of $400.

Required: Compute the confidence interval with a) one standard deviation b) two standard deviations. In each case explain your level (percentage) of confidence.

E3.

Mailboxes Unlimited has hired a graphic artist. It is estimated that this artist's learning rate is at 70% and his first quarter's output has amounted to 300 fairly equal job outputs which took him a total of 50 hours to complete. Output is expected to double in every succeeding quarter.

Required: Compute the total output, and total time requirement for the 5th quarter.

E4.

Consider four observations for Y with amounts of 300, 350, 400, and 450, and a regression prediction for these values of Y to be 310, 325, 375, and 475.

Required: given these facts, compute mean of Y, total variance of Y, Explained variance of Y and error variance of Y. Also explain these numbers.

E5.

Assume that sum of squares of explained errors amounts to 900, and the sum of total standard error amounts to 1,300, and mean square error amounts to 400.

Required: Compute SE, R-squared, and F-statistic.

E6.

Search the site (www.lubys.com/financials/2001 ar.pdf) in conjunction with Luby's Inc. chain of Texas-based restaurants that uses regression analysis to predict cash flows at its different locations as part of the overall financial planning at the corporate level. To see why or how this company uses regression analysis in conjunction with its restaurants' operations. Share the results with your group.

1-c; 2-e; 3-e; 4-b; 5-a; 6-d; 7-b; 8-e; 9-b; 10-e; 11-d; 12-b; 13-c; 14-a; 15-c; 16-a; 17-b; 18-c; 19-e; 20-e.

Suggested answers to exercises:

E1.

Change in $ / Change in volume

$b = (5,200 - 2,800) / (600 - 200) = 6$

$a = Y - bX$

$a = 5,200 - (6 * 600) = \$1,600$

OR

$a = 2,800 - (6 * 200) = \$1,600$

$Y = a + bX$

$Y = 1,600 + (6 * 580)$

$Y = \$5,080$

Note that in conjunction with high-low (or regression) method, you start with the independent variables (X) to see what costs were at each volume level. Sometimes, at the highest volume, the cost may not be the highest, and at the lowest volume, the cost may not be the lowest. But those would be the numbers that we choose for such analysis.

E2.

a) with one standard deviation: $\$5,800 +/- \$400 = 5,400$ to $6,200$; We can be 67% sure that the actual costs would fall between $5,400 and $6,200.

b) with two standard deviations: $\$5,800 +/- (2 * 400) = 5,000$ to $6,600$; We can be 95% sure that the actual costs would fall between $5,000 and $6,600.

E3.

Cumulative output	Average time	Total time
300 units	50 hours	50 hours
600 units	50 * .70 = 35 hours	35 * 2 = 70 hours
1,200 units	35 * .70 = 24.5 hours	24.5 * 4 = 98 hours
2,400 units	24.5 hours * .70 = 17.15 hours	17.15 * 8 = 137.2 hours
4,800 units	17.15 hours * .70 = 12.005 hours	12.005 * 16 = 192.08 hrs

E4.

Variable Y	Mean of Y	Predicted Y	Total Var.	Regression V	Error V
300	375	310	-75	-65	-10
350	375	325	-25	-50	25
400	375	375	25	0	25
450	375	475	75	100	-25

Cost Management: A Strategic Emphasis, 3e by Blocher/Chen/Cokins/Lin

<u>E5.</u>

SE = Square root of 400 = 20

SE signifies the range of values around the regression estimate such that we can be approximately 67% sure that the actual value lies in a range of computed amount +/- 20.

R-squared = 900/1,300 = .692

R-squared signifies the percentage of variance in the dependent variable that is explained by the independent variable.

F-statistic = 900/400 = 2.25; when this number is low, it is indicative of the fact that the regression line may not be totally trusted due to significant error factor.

CHAPTER 7
COST-VOLUME-PROFIT ANALYSIS

Highlights:

Cost-volume-profit (CVP) analysis provides a linear model of the relationship between costs, revenues and output levels. Such analysis is used for break-even computations, revenue planning, and cost planning. Break-even is the point at which profits are zero. It is used in planning and budgeting to assess the desirability of current and potential products and services. It is also used in revenue planning to determine the sales needed to achieve a desired profit level, by adding desired profit to the break-even equation.

Activity-based costing breaks fixed costs and variable costs into batch and unit related costs, so CVP analyses can be done at either (or both) the batch or unit level. Sensitivity analysis is useful because profits of firms with relatively high fixed costs are more sensitive to changes in the level of sales. The sensitivity is measured by the margin of safety (expected sales less break-even sales) and operating leverage (the ratio of total contribution margin to profit).

When there are two or more products, the use of CVP analysis requires the assumption of a constant sales mix between the products, and the weighted average contribution margin is used to calculate the break-even point. Taxes are relevant beyond break-even. They must also be considered in such analysis.

Questions:

Learning Objective 1: Explain cost-volume-profit (CVP) analysis, the CVP model, and the strategic role of CVP analysis.

1. What is CVP analysis?

2. What is unit contribution margin?

3. What is contribution margin ratio?

4. What is the contribution income statement?

5. What is the strategic role of CVP analysis?

Learning Objective 2: Apply CVP analysis for break-even planning.

6. What is the formula for break-even (BE) and what is the logic for it?

7. What is the BE formula in dollars?

Learning Objective 3: Apply CVP analysis for revenue planning and cost planning.

8. How do we determine a sales level which produces a desired amount of profit?

9. Show a typical application of BE in target costing?

*Cost Management: A Strategic Emphasis, 3*e by Blocher/Chen/Cokins/Lin

10. How can we incorporate income taxes into CVP analysis?

Learning Objective 4: Apply CVP analysis for activity-based costing.

11. How can we incorporate ABC into the CVP model?

12. What is the advantage of CVP analysis?

Learning Objective 5: Employ sensitivity analysis to more effectively use CVP analysis when actual sales are uncertain.

13. What is margin of safety?

14. What is margin of safety ratio?

15. What is operating leverage?

Learning Objective 6: Adapt CVP analysis for multiple products.

16. How can CVP formula be adapted to multiple product situations?

<hr>

Learning Objective 7: Apply CVP analysis in service firms and not-for-profit organizations.

<hr>

17. What is a unique characteristic of CVP for non-for-profit organizations?

<hr>

Learning Objective 8: Identify the assumptions and limitations of CVP analysis and their affect the proper interpretation of the results.

<hr>

18. What are the major limitations and assumptions of CVP analysis?

Suggested responses to the above questions:

1. What is CVP analysis?

CVP analysis is a method for analyzing how various operating decisions and the marketing decisions will affect net income. It is based on an understanding of the relationship between variable costs, fixed costs, unit selling prices, and the output level.

2. What is unit contribution margin?

The unit contribution margin is the difference between unit sales price and unit variable cost, and it is a measure of the increase in profit for a unit increase in sales.

3. What is contribution margin ratio?

It is the ratio of the unit contribution margin to unit sales price, (p-v)/p. It may also be determined by taking the ratio of total contribution to total sales. More profitable products have a higher contribution margin ratio.

4. What is the contribution income statement?

It focuses on variable costs and fixed costs, in contrast to the conventional income statement that focuses on product costs and non-product costs. It is more useful in CVP analysis.

5. What is the strategic role of CVP analysis?

- *In life cycle costing, CVP analysis is used in the early stages of the product's cost life cycle to determine whether the product is likely to achieve the desired profitability.*
- *CVP analysis is also used in later stages of the product's life cycle to determine the most cost-effective manufacturing process, and to determine the best marketing and distribution systems.*
- *CVP analysis is used in target costing by showing the effect on profit of alternative product designs, at expected sales levels.*

6. What is the formula for break-even (BE) and what is the logic for it?

BE Sales = Fixed costs / Unit contribution margin
   $$Q = f / (p-v)$$
Break-even sales in units is where there is enough contribution to cover fixed costs.

7. What is the BE formula in dollars?

BE $ = Fixed costs / Contribution margin ratio
Where contribution margin ratio = $(p-v)/p$
p = selling price; v = variable cost per unit

8. How do we determine a sales level which produces a desired amount of profit?

Simply add the desired profit level (N) to fixed costs in the BE formula and continue; i.e., $Q = (f+N)/(p-v)$. In dollars, we replace contribution margin with contribution margin ratio (cm%); i.e.,
$ = (f+N)/cm%$

9. Show a typical application of BE in target costing?

Example: Unavoidable fixed costs have risen by $3,000 from its current level of $28,000. How much should variable costs change from its current level of $40 a unit to maintain the current level of profit ($8,000). p = 160.

Sales volume before the change:
(28,000 + 8,000) / (160 - 40) = 300 units
New variable cost required:
(28,000 + 3,000 + 8,000) / (160 - v) = 300 units; v = 30. This means that the target variable cost should be reduced by $10 a unit from its current level of $40 a unit in order to maintain the current level of profit.

10. How can we incorporate income taxes into CVP analysis?

Taxes should be considered similar to an addition to fixed costs. In order to determine the amount of tax (t), the net income(ni) should be converted to before tax income(bti); i.e.,
bti = ni / (1 -t%).

11. How can we incorporate ABC into the CVP model?

This can be done by breaking down the fixed costs into volume based fixed costs and batch level based fixed costs. Then, we estimate the number of units in each batch and recompute the BE. Batch level fixed costs are now treated as a variable cost and subtracted from the price. Q = f / (p - v1 - v2).

12. What is the advantage of CVP analysis?

A CVP analysis based on activity-based costing can provide a more precise analysis of the relationship between volume, costs, and profits, by treating batch-level costs as variable costs.

13. What is margin of safety?

Margin of safety measures the potential effect of the risk that sales will fall short of planned levels. Margin of safety may be determined in units or in dollars.
Margin of safety = Planned Sales - Break-even Sales

14. What is margin of safety ratio?

Margin of safety ratio = margin of safety / planned sales
It is a useful measure for comparing the risk of two alternative products, or for assessing the riskiness in any given product.

15. What is operating leverage?

*Operating leverage is the ratio of the contribution margin to profit. Firms with high fixed costs will have much wider swings in profits due to volume change and are riskier. Firms with high variable costs will have smaller swings in profit with changes in volume. Percentage increase in sales * degree of operating leverage = % increase in profits.*

Cost Management: A Strategic Emphasis, 3e by Blocher/Chen/Cokins/Lin

16. How can CVP formula be adapted to multiple product situations?

The only additional requirement is that we have to know the sales mix. Sales mix percentages are used to compute a weighted average contribution margin (wc); Q = f / wc. In order to calculate BE in dollars, we must compute weighted average contribution margin ration (wc%).

17. What is a unique characteristic of CVP for non-for-profit organizations?

In most non-for-profits, fixed costs are high, and a minor change in contract amounts can have a significant impact on the level of service to be provided.

18. What are the major limitations and assumptions of CVP analysis?
- *Selling price, fixed costs, and variable costs per unit do not change.*
- *Sales equals production.*
- *Sales mix remains constant.*
- *Cost/volume relationship is linear.*
- *Prices and costs are known.*
- *The relevant range can be approximated.*
- *Step-fixed costs do not exist*
- *Costs are clearly classifiable into fixed and variable.*

Multiple choice questions:

1. The purpose of CVP analysis is to
    a) analyze how fixed costs change while variable costs do not.
    b) analyze how variable costs change while fixed costs do not.
    c) analyze how selling prices change while costs do not.
    d) analyze how various operating and marketing decisions will affect income.
    e) none of the above

2. Revenue for CVP analysis is composed of
    a) fixed costs + variable costs + profit after tax.
    b) fixed costs + variable costs + profit before tax
    c) fixed costs + variable costs + taxes.
    d) fixed costs + variable costs + mixed costs.
    e) fixed costs + variable costs + step-fixed costs.

3. Contribution margin can be defined as
    a) total sales less variable cost per unit.
    b) selling price per unit less total variable costs.
    c) selling price per unit less variable cost per unit.
    d) selling price less variable cost per unit divided by selling price.
    e) selling price less variable cost per unit divided by variable cost per unit.

4. Contribution margin ratio can be defined as
   a) total sales less variable cost per unit.
   b) selling price per unit less total variable costs.
   c) selling price per unit less variable cost per unit.
   d) selling price less variable cost per unit divided by selling price.
   e) selling price less variable cost per unit divided by variable cost per unit.

5. Break-even formula in dollars can be shown as
   a) f / (s - v) ; where f = fixed costs, s = selling price, v = unit variable cost.
   b) f / [(s - v)/s]
   c) f/ [(s - v)/v]
   d) f/ [(s - v)/c]; where c is contribution margin.
   e) f/ [(s - v)/c%]; where c% is contribution margin ratio.

6. When we incorporate ABC into CVP analysis, we consider batch level costs as
   a) fixed costs.
   b) variable costs.
   c) mixed costs.
   d) step-fixed costs.
   e) none of the above.

7. Margin of safety measures
   a) sales less variable costs
   b) sales less fixed costs.
   c) sales less break-even sales.
   d) sales less fixed and variable costs.
   e) none of the above.

8. Margin of safety ratio is
   a) margin of safety/planned sales.
   b) planned sales/margin of safety.
   c) margin of safety/planned costs.
   d) planned sales/planned costs.
   e) none of the above.

9. Operating leverage is
   a) the ratio of contribution margin to profit.
   b) the ratio of profit to contribution margin.
   c) the ratio of contribution margin to variable costs.
   d) the ratio of contribution margin to fixed costs.
   e) the ration of contribution margin to total costs.

*Cost Management: A Strategic Emphasis, 3*e by Blocher/Chen/Cokins/Lin

10. Operating leverage * % increase in sales =
   a) profit.
   b) % increase in profit
   c) sales
   d) sales increase in dollars
   e) none of the above

Exercises:

E1.

Jennifer's flower shop has been selling flower vases for $45 each. The costs include $6 for each vase and $19 for flowers. Rent and salary of the shop attendant amount to $2,400 a month. Jennifer expects a net profit of $960 a month where taxes are at the rate of 20%.
Required: Determine the needed level of sales in dollars.

E2.

Nassim's Bake Shop makes two pastries. Pastry A costs $12 and sells for $24 each. Pastry B costs $7 and sells for $10 each. The above costs are only the variable costs. The shop's fixed costs per period amount to $4,014. Current sales volume amounts to 300 units of A and 700 units of B. The same mix will hold in the future.
Required: Determine the dollar sales of A and B at break-even point.

E3.

ABC Manufacturing Company has just determined that its fixed costs have increased by $5,000 per period from its current level of $38,000 due to mandated salary increases. However, it is determined to maintain its current profit before taxes of $12,000 even though sales are not anticipated to increase from its current level. Selling price is $80 per unit. Variable cost amounts to $60 per unit.
Required: How much should variable costs decrease to achieve the above?

E4.

Gissu's Frame Shop has a total fixed cost of $6,000 with a unit contribution margin of 30% (selling price is $20). However, it has determined that $2,000 of this fixed cost is related to number of orders placed. An average of 50 orders are placed per period. Each order is enough for 20 jobs.
Required: Compute break-even under traditional and ABC method.

E5.

Parisian Blanket Factory has a total sales of $95,000 and break-even sales amount to $70,000 where the fixed costs amount to $42,000.
Required: Compute margin of safety and operating margin. If sales increase by 20% by how much would profit increase?

E6.

Saba Electronics has a total fixed costs of $40,000 with a profit of $8,000 whereas, Omid Printing has the same profit with a contribution margin amounting to $96,000. Saba's variable costs are at 80% of sales. Omid's variable costs are at 40% of sales.

Required: Compute sales and operating leverage for both companies. If sales for both firms increase by 20% by how much would their profits increase? (Use the OL concept in your calculations).

E7.

As explained in the chapter, using the data from the U. S. Social Security Administration (www.ssa.gov) it is possible to develop a breakeven model to determine when a retired person should apply for benefits. Use the web site www.social-security-table.com to search for appropriate answers assuming a retirement age of 62, 63, 64, and 65 with an assumed level of income. Share the results with your group.

Correct answers to multiple choice questions:
1-d; 2-b; 3-c; 4-d; 5-b; 6-b; 7-c; 8-a; 9-a; 10-b.

Suggested answers to exercises:

E1.

Profit before tax = 960 / .80 = 1,200
Contribution margin ratio = 20/45 = .4444
Required sales = (2,400 + 1,200) / .4444 = $8,100

E2.

Item	Product A	Product B
Selling price	24	10
Variable costs	12	7
Contribution margin	12	3
Current sales volume	300	700
Sales $	7,200	7,000
Contribution margin $	3,600	2,100
Sales % $	50.7%	49.3%

Contribution margin ratio = (3,600 + 2,100) / (7,200 + 7,000)
= 40.14%

Break-even sales = 4014 / 40.14% = $10,000
Sales of A at BE = 10,000 * 50.7% = $ 5,070
Sales of B at BE = 10,000 * 49.3% = $4,930

E3.

Current contribution margin ratio: (80 - 60) / 80 =25%
Current sales: (38,000 + 12,000) / 25% = $200,000
Expected contribution margin ratio: (50,000 + 5,000) / x = 200,000; x = 27.5%
Targeted variable cost per unit: (80 - x)/80 = 27.5%; x = $58
Therefore, variable cost should decrease by $2 per unit; 60 - 58

Cost Management: A Strategic Emphasis, 3e by Blocher/Chen/Cokins/Lin

E4.

Current break-even point:	$6,000 / .30 = $20,000
Current variable cost:	20 * (1 - .30) = $14
Cost per order:	$2,000 / 50 = 40
Cost per job:	$40 / 20 = 2
ABC contribution margin:	20 - 14 - 2 = 4
ABC contribution margin ration:	4 / 20 = 20%
ABC break-even point:	(6,000 - 2,000) / 20% = $20,000

E5.

Margin of safety = 95,000 – 70,000 = $25,000	
Variable costs at BE:	70,000 – 42,000 = $28,000
Variable cost ratio:	28,000/70,000 = 40%
Current profit:	95,000 – (.40 * 95,000) – 42,000 = $15,000
Current contribution margin:	95,000 – (.40 * 95,000) = $57,000
Operating leverage:	57,000 / 15,000 = 3.8
Effect of 20% increase on sales on profit: 3.8 * 20% = 76%	
Profit at this level:	15,000 * 1.76 = $26,400

E6.

Item	Saba Electronic	%	Omid Printing	%
Sales	240,000	100	160,000	100
Variable costs	192,000	80	64,000	40
Contribution margin	48,000	20	96,000	60
Fixed costs	40,000		88,000	
Profit	8,000		8,000	
Operating leverage	6 times		12 times	
Increase in profit if sales increases by 20%	120%		240%	
Amount of increase in profit	$9,600		$19,200	

CHAPTER 8
STRATEGY AND THE MASTER BUDGET

Highlights:

A budget is a quantitative plan that identifies the resources and commitments required to fulfill the organization's goals for the budget period. It is also a good way to communicate within the organization and let employees participate in this process. A good budgeting system can help a company know its needs in advance and plan for them properly. It can also help the company in managing its cash flows.

A firm carries out its strategy through long-range plans and master budgets. A successful budget becomes personalized and has the support of top management. The budgeting process includes formation of a budget committee; determination of the budget period; specification of budget guidelines; preparation of the initial budget proposal; budget negotiation, review, and approval; and budget revision. The master budget includes sales, production, direct materials, direct labor, factory overhead, selling, administration expense budgets, the budgeted cash statement, income statement, and balance sheet.

Budgets which are updated monthly or quarterly for the subsequent 12 months or four quarters are known as continuous budgets. Activity-based budgeting is prepared in line with activity-based costing. Zero-base budgets start every year fresh from point zero whereas, incremental budgets start the beginning point from the last year's budgeted numbers. Budgets are prepared for manufacturing, merchandising, and service organizations. The difference is that a service organization does not have the production or merchandise inventory factor to consider.

Ethics should be on the forefront of all business actions, particularly in today's environment with rampant business frauds and misdeeds. Ethical issues include preventing concealment of information, avoidance of accepting a higher budget goal, inclusion of budget slack, and spending the budget to avoid having it cutback. There are benefits and drawbacks to participative versus imposed budgets. The controller serves as the coordinator in the organization in the budgeting process.

Questions:

Learning Objective 1: Describe the role of a budget in planning, communicating, motivating, controlling, and evaluating performance.

1. What is a budget?

2. What is budgeting?

Learning Objective 2: Discuss the importance of strategy and its role in budgeting; identify factors common to successful budgets.

3. Why is good strategy very important?

4. How is a strategy formulated?

5. How is a strategy implemented?

6. What is capital budgeting?

7. What is a master budget?

8. What are operating budgets?

9. What are financial budgets?

Cost Management: A Strategic Emphasis, 3e by Blocher/Chen/Cokins/Lin

Learning Objective 3: Outline the budgeting process.

10. What is the budgeting process?

11. What is a continuous budget?

Learning Objective 4: Prepare a master budget and explain the relationships among its supporting schedules.

12. What are the master budget components?

Learning Objective 5: Identify unique budgeting characteristics of service and not-for-profit organizations operating in international settings.

13. What are some of the unique characteristics of the organizations listed in objective 5?

14. What is zero-base budgeting?

15. What is activity-based budgeting (ABB)?

16. What is Kaizen budgeting?

Be aware of issues such as budgetary slack, padding the budget, "spending" the budget, etc. Top management involvement helps for taking budget seriously and for motivating lower-level employees. The controller and his staff should take an active role in the process, be good communicators, and assist in making the budget an effective and useful document.

17. What is goal congruence?

18. Why is an easily attainable budget not necessarily a good budget?

19. Distinguish between authoritative budget and participative budget?

Suggested responses to the above questions:

1. What is a budget?

A budget is the operation plan for an organization that identifies the resources and commitments required to fulfill the organization's goals for the budgeted period. It includes both the financial and non-financial aspects.

2. What is budgeting?

Budgeting is the process of preparing a budget.

3. Why is good strategy very important?

Without a good strategy, an organization may not be able to take full advantage of its opportunities and its strengths. Missed opportunities may cause an organization to stagnate.

4. How is a strategy formulated?

- *Analyze external factors (competition, economic, political, and social climate, etc.).*
- *Identify opportunities, limitations, and threats,*
- *Assess internal factors (financial, managerial, etc.).*
- *Recognize strengths, weaknesses, and competitive advantages.*
- *Match opportunities with strengths and competitive advantages of the firm.*

5. How is a strategy implemented?

A strategy is implemented through long-range planning, the capital budget, and the master budget. Strategy provides the framework for the long-range plan which is typically for a 5 to 10-year period. Long-range planning often entails capital budgeting.

6. What is capital budgeting?

It is a process for evaluating an organization's proposed long-range major projects.

7. What is a master budget?

*It is a plan of operations for a business unit for a current budget period. The plan of operations is formulated based on the goals of the strategic and long-range plans, expected future events, and the recent actual operating results of the organization. The master budget comprises **operating budgets and financial budgets.***

8. What are operating budgets?

   Operating budgets deal with uses of resources in operating activities and with the acquisition of these resources. They include production budgets, purchase budgets, personnel budget, and sales promotion budgets.

9. What are financial budgets?

   Financial budgets identify sources and uses of funds for the budgeted operations and the expected operating results for the period.

10. What is the budgeting process?

   - *Formation of a budget committee*
   - *Determination of the budget period; often same as fiscal year, also continuous budget, and continuously updated budget*
   - *Specification of the budget guidelines*
   - *Preparation of the initial budget proposal*
   - *Budget negotiation; negotiation occurs at all levels of the organization.*
   - *Review*
   - *Approval*
   - *Budget revision*

11. What is a continuous budget?

   A continuous (rolling) budget maintains at all times a budget for a set number of months, quarters, or years at all times.

12. What are the master budget components?
   - *Budgeting for sales: start with the sales forecast. Show the expected sales in units and in dollars.*
   - *Production budget: use the sales budget and consider the inventory level anticipated at the beginning and end of the period.*
   - *Direct materials usage budget: explode the production into basic ingredients through the use of bill of materials; then, consider the expected inventory levels beginning and end of the period to arrive at usage quantities. Obtain anticipated prices from purchasing department.*
   - *Direct labor budget: use industrial engineering guidelines and production needs to estimate labor requirements. Personnel should provide the labor rates for the skill levels required.*
   - *Factory overhead: considering internal and external factors, cost drivers, and fixed and variable costs, the overhead amount is estimated.*
   - *Cost of goods manufactured and sold: considering cost of goods produced and finished goods inventory levels, cost of goods sold can now be determined.*

Cost Management: A Strategic Emphasis, 3e by Blocher/Chen/Cokins/Lin

- *Merchandise purchases budget: this budget can be prepared considering the usage for the period and the anticipated raw material inventory levels as well as anticipated prices.*
- *Selling and general administrative budget: the variable and fixed cost components need to be identified and the amounts verified considering contractual obligations as well as other committed and discretionary costs.*
- *Cash budget: this item generally includes cash available, cash disbursements, and financing needs. Considering terms of sales cash receipts are anticipated. Considering terms of purchases, cash disbursements are forecasted. And considering cash balances any financing or investing needs will now be finalized.*
- *Budgeted income statement: having all the elements of income statements from sales to production and cost of sales and other expenses, the forecasted income statement is now prepared.*
- *Budgeted balance sheet: this starts with last period balances, and incorporating activities mentioned above, final balances in terms of cash, receivables, inventories, fixed assets, accounts payables, other liabilities, and equities are anticipated.*

13. What are some of the unique characteristics of the organizations listed in objective 5?

Many firms in service industries have people as their principal assets.
Non-profit organizations do not have a bottom-line account. The objective is often provision of a service efficiently and effectively. Budget revision is rare in such organizations.
In international settings, fluctuating monetary exchange rates, and discrepancies in inflation rates of different countries cause unique budgeting issues for multinational companies.

14. What is zero-base budgeting?

In this system, managers are required to start the budget from ground zero and justify each dollar of expenditure.

15. What is activity-based budgeting (ABB)?

ABB is a budgeting process that focuses on costs of activities and cost drivers necessary for production and sales. ABB facilitates continuous improvement.

16. What is Kaizen budgeting?
It is a budgeting approach that explicitly demands continuous improvement and incorporates all the expected improvements in the resultant budget.
Be aware of issues such as budgetary slack, padding the budget, "spending" the budget, etc.

Top management involvement helps for taking budget seriously and for motivating lower-level employees. The controller and his staff should take an active role in the process, be good communicators, and assist in making the budget an effective and useful document.

17. What is goal congruence?

Goal congruence is consistency between the goals of the firm and the goals of its employees. A budget that does not consider the goals of the employees is bound to fail.

18. Why is an easily attainable budget not necessarily a good budget?

An easily attainable budget target may fail to bring out the employees' best efforts. A budget target that is very difficult to achieve, on the other hand, can discourage managers to even trying to attain it. So budget targets should be challenging, yet attainable.

18. Distinguish between authoritative budget and participative budget?

An authoritative budget does not communicate; it posts orders and often fails to elicit employee's commitment.
A participative budget is a good communication device and is more likely to gain the commitment of the employees to fulfill the budgetary goals.

Multiple choice questions:

1. Budgeting is
   a) a quantitative plan of operations for an organization that identifies the resources and commitments required to fulfill the organization's goals for the budgeted period.
   b) the process of preparing a budget.
   c) a guideline for operations and gauge for controlling operations.
   d) a basis for performance evaluation.
   e) none of the above.

2. The budget is a
   a) profit or operating plan.
   b) basis for resource allocation.
   c) communication and authorization device.
   d) all of the above.
   e) a and c.

Cost Management: A Strategic Emphasis, 3e by Blocher/Chen/Cokins/Lin

3. The budget is a
   a) motivating device
   b) guideline for operations and gauge for controlling operations.
   c) basis for performance evaluation.
   d) all of the above.
   e) b and c.

4. In formulating a strategy, we must
   a) analyze external factors
   b) assess internal factors
   c) match opportunities with strengths and competitive advantage of the firm.
   d) all of the above.
   e) b and c.

5. In formulating a strategy, we must
   a) Identify opportunities, limitations, and threats.
   b) Recognize strengths, weaknesses, and competitive advantages.
   c) Match opportunities with strengths and competitive advantages of the firm.
   d) all of the above.
   e) a and c.

6. In formulating a strategy, we must analyze
   a) competition.
   b) economic and political factors.
   c) technological and regulatory factors.
   d) social and environmental factors.
   e) all of the above.

7. In formulating a strategy, we must analyze
   a) financial factors.
   b) managerial factors.
   c) functional issues.
   d) cultural issues.
   e) all of the above.

8. A master budget
   a) is an organization's proposed long-range plan for major projects.
   b) is a plan of operations for a business unit during a budgeted period.
   c) deals with uses of resources in operating activities and with the acquisition of these resources.
   d) identifies sources and uses of funds for the budgeted operations and the expected results for the period.
   e) none of the above.

9. A financial budget
   a) is an organization's proposed long-range plan for major projects.
   b) is a plan of operations for a business unit during a budgeted period.
   c) deals with uses of resources in operating activities and with the acquisition of these resources.
   d) identifies sources and uses of funds for the budgeted operations and the expected financial position of the firm.
   e) none of the above.

10. An operating budget
   a) is an organization's proposed long-range plan for major projects.
   b) is a plan of operations for a business unit during a budgeted period.
   c) deals with uses of resources in operating activities and with the acquisition of these resources.
   d) identifies sources and uses of funds for the budgeted operations and the expected results for the period.
   e) none of the above.

11. A continuous budget
   a) is prepared for 3 to 5 years at one time.
   b) is prepared for 5 to 10 years at one time.
   c) has a budget for a set number of months, quarters, or years at all time.
   d) incorporates new information as the year unfolds.
   e) none of the above.

12. A continuously updated budget
   a) is prepared for 3 to 5 years at one time.
   b) is prepared for 5 to 10 years at one time.
   c) has a budget for a set number of months, quarters, or years at all time.
   d) incorporates new information as the year unfolds.
   e) none of the above.

13. In activity-based budgets compared to traditional budgets
   a) fixed costs are usually less and variable costs are usually more.
   b) fixed costs are usually more and variable costs are usually less.
   c) fixed and variable costs are usually more.
   d) fixed and variable costs are usually less.
   e) none of the above.

14. Zero-based budgeting requires
   a) managers to prepare budgets from ground zero.
   b) focuses on costs of activities.
   c) focuses on cost drivers.
   d) explicitly demands continuous improvement.
   e) consistency between the goals of the firm and the goals of its employees.

Cost Management: A Strategic Emphasis, 3e by Blocher/Chen/Cokins/Lin

Exercises:

E1. Production budget:

Namazi Fabrics has two products M and N with an inventory beginning of 195 yards of M and 345 yards of N. Sales for the coming period is anticipated to amount to 2,900 yards for M and 3,760 yards for N. The company policy is to keep at least 15% of the period's sales in inventory.

Required: Determine how much the company needs to produce?

E2. Raw material budget:

Namazi Fabrics has decided to produce 3,200 yards of product M and 3,900 yards of product N. Product M uses 70% nylon and 30% rayon. Product N is 100% wool. Each yard of M weighs 1.5 lb. and each yard of N weighs 2 lb.. The price of nylon is at $2.50 a lb., rayon $1.75 a lb., and wool $3.90 a lb. Inventory beginning amounts to 225 lb. of nylon, 135 lb. of rayon, and 185 lb. of wool. Inventory ending is required to be 20% of the period's usage.

Required: Determine material usage in lb. as well as needed amount to be purchased in lb. and dollars for this period. Also compute material cost per yard of product M and N.

E3. Accounts receivable and cash receipts budget:

Namazi Fabrics is anticipating to sell 2,900 yards of product M and 3,760 yards of product N at $9.50 and $24.50 per yard respectively in the month of March. Terms of sales are 30% cash, 50% in 30 days and 20% in 60 days. However, 25% of the latter amount is expected to be uncollectible. The uncollectible balance is written off to bad debts fifteen days after the last installment is paid.

Required: Prepare a cash received and receivable schedule for March sales as of 3/31, 4/30, 5/31, and 6/30. Assume no other transactions but March sales.

E4. Income statement budget:

Namazi Fabrics is anticipating production of 3,200 yards of M and 3,900 yards of N at a cost of $6.70 for M and $16.50 per yard for N. Sales amounted to 2,900 yards of M and 3,760 yards of N. Selling price for M is $9.50 and for N is $24.50. Ending inventory amounts to 20% of the period's production. Selling expense amounts to 10% of sales, and administration expense amounts to $4,950. Taxes are at 20% of income.

Required: Prepare a budgeted income statement.

E.5. Sensitivity analysis using an Excel worksheet

Use any of the above problems and enter the data into an Excel worksheet – using formulas wherever needed. Change your assumptions with regard to sales, ending inventory, prices, etc., and see the impact of those changes in your worksheet.

Correct answers to multiple choice questions:
1-b; 2-d; 3-d; 4-d; 5-d; 6-e; 7-e; 8-b; 9-d; 10-c; 11-c; 12-d; 13-a; 14-a.

Suggested answers to exercises:

E1. Production budget:

Description	Product M	Product N
Sales Forecast	2,900 yards	3,750 yards
Desired ending inventory	435 "	563 "
Total available	3,335 "	4,313 "
Beginning inventory	195 "	345 "
Budgeted production	3,140 "	3,968 "

E2. Material budget:
Material usage:

Nylon usage: 3,200 yards of M * 1.5 = 4,800 lb.; 4,800 * .70 = 3,360 lb.

Rayon usage: 3,200 yards of M * 1.5 = 4,800 lb.; 4,800 * .30 = 1,440 lb.

Wool usage: 3,900 yards of N * 2 = 7,800 lb.

Material purchases:

Description	Nylon	Rayon	Wool
Usage per above	3,360 lb.	1,440 lb.	7,800 lb.
Desired ending inventory	672 "	288 "	1,560 "
Total available	4,032 "	1,728 "	9,360 "
Less: beginning inventory	225 "	135 "	185 "
Total purchases	3,807 "	1,593 "	9,175 "
* Price per lb.	$2.50	$1.75	$3.90
Total purchases = $48,087.75	9,517.50	2,787.75	35,782.50

Material costs per yard of fabric:

Product M: (1.5 lb. * .70 nylon * 2.50) + (1.5 lb. * .30 rayon * 1.75) = $3.4125

Product N: 2 lb. * 3.90 = $7.80

E3. Accounts receivable and cash receipts budget:
Sales:

M: 2,900 * 9.50 = $27,550; N: 3,760 * 24.50 = $92,120; Total sales = $119,670

Cash receipts:

March:	119,670 * .30 =	$35,901
April:	119,670 * .50 =	59,835
May:	119,670 * .15 =	17,950.50

Accounts receivable:

As of 3/31/xx	119,670 * .70 = $83,769
As of 4/30/xx	119,670 * .20 = 23,934
As of 5/31/xx	119,670 * .05 = 5,983.50
As of 6/30/xx	The 5% uncollectible amount is written off to bad debts

Cost Management: A Strategic Emphasis, 3e by Blocher/Chen/Cokins/Lin

E4. Budgeted income statement:

	Product M	Product N	Total
Sales	2,900 * 9.5	3,760 * 24.5	
Sales $	$ 27,550	$ 92,120	$ 119,670
Cost of sales @ 6.7,16.5	19,430	62,040	81,470
Gross profit	8,120	30,080	38,200
Selling expense	2,755	9,212	11,967
Separable income	5,365	20,868	26,233
Administrative costs			4,950
Income before taxes			21,283
Taxes			4,256.60
Net income			$ 17,026.40

CHAPTER 9
DECISION MAKING WITH RELEVANT COSTS
AND A STRATEGIC EMPHASIS

Highlights:

Relevant costs are those future costs that differ among the decision maker's options. Relevant cost decision-making applies to manufacturing, service, and not-for-profit organizations. Examples are: special order decision; make, lease, or buy decision; sell before or after further processing; keep or drop a product or service; and evaluating programs and projects. With two or more products, the concern is for the correct product mix. With production constraint, the answer is to produce and sell as much as possible of the product that has the highest contribution margin per unit of time on the constrained activity. Too much attention to relevant costs can cause the manager to overlook important opportunity costs and strategic considerations. It can also lead to a short-term orientation, thus, ignoring or discounting fixed costs in decisions.

Questions:

1. What are relevant costs?

Learning Objective 1: Define the decision making process and identify the types of cost information relevant for decision making.

---

2. What is relevant cost analysis?

3. What is strategic relevant cost analysis?

4. What is the decision-making process?

Learning Objective 2: Use relevant and strategic cost analysis to make special order decisions.

5. How do we make special order decisions?

Learning Objective 3: Use relevant and strategic cost analysis in the make, lease or buy decision.

6. How do we make lease or buy decisions?

Learning Objective 4: Use relevant and strategic cost analysis in the decision to sell before or after additional processing.

7. How do we make the decision of selling before or after further processing?

Learning Objective 5: Use relevant or strategic cost analysis in the decision to keep or drop products or services.

8. How do we make the decision of keeping or dropping a product or service?

Learning Objective 6: Use relevant or strategic cost analysis to evaluate programs.

Expand the thought process regarding relevant costs to enhance and strengthen decision-making in the firm, but be always aware of short-term versus long-term aspects of the issue.

Cost Management: A Strategic Emphasis, 3e by Blocher/Chen/Cokins/Lin

Learning Objective 7: Analyze decisions involving multiple products and limited resources.

9. What should be done when there is only one production constraint and excess demand?

10. What should be done when there are two or more constraints and excess demand?

Learning Objective 8: Discuss the behavioral, implementation, and legal issues in decision making.

11. What are the primary behavioral and implementation issues of relevant cost analysis?

12. Discuss the issue of improper management incentives under relevant cost analysis.

13. What is the wrongly placed incentive of replacing variable costs with fixed costs?

14. What is the tendency of focusing on irrelevant information?

Suggested responses to the above questions:

1. What are relevant costs?

   Relevant costs are costs to be incurred at some future time and that differ for each option available to the decision maker.

2. What is relevant cost analysis?

   - *Short-term focus*
   - *Not linked to strategy*
   - *Product cost focus*
   - *Precise and quantitative*
   - *Focused on individual product or decision situation*

3. What is strategic relevant cost analysis?

   - *Long-term focus*
   - *Linked to the firm's strategy*
   - *Customer focus*
   - *Broad and subjective*
   - *Integrative: considers all customer-related factors*

4. What is the decision-making process?

   - *First: Determine the strategic issues*
   - *Second: specify the criteria and identify the alternative actions*
   - *Third: analyze relevant costs: identify and collect relevant information, predict future values of relevant costs and revenues*
   - *Fourth: select and implement the best course of action*
   - *Fifth: evaluate performance*

5. How do we make special order decisions?

   Special order decisions are made by considering the costs that would be incremental if such an order is accepted as compared to the revenue that it would bring. It is assumed that such a special order will not affect the current market. It is also assumed that the firm is not working at full capacity. Otherwise, we need to consider the opportunity cost involved. In such situations, generally unit level and batch level costs are relevant in decisions of this type. Product level and facility level costs would not change and will be irrelevant.

6. How do we make lease or buy decisions?

   The two options are compared to see which one is advantageous. If we lease a machine and pay by meter versus purchase of same, we can put up an equation to determine the indifference point. However, it must be remembered that with purchase,

Cost Management: A Strategic Emphasis, 3e by Blocher/Chen/Cokins/Lin

there is long-term commitment, and there is the cost of financing the project. On the other hand, with the lease option, there is more flexibility. In make or buy (outsourcing) decisions, generally unit level, batch level, and product level costs are relevant whereas, facility level costs which would not change remain irrelevant.

7. How do we make the decision of selling before or after further processing?

The decision is made by considering the incremental revenue that additional processing will bring versus the incremental cost associated with further processing.

8. How do we make the decision of keeping or dropping a product or service?

The decision is made by considering the revenues and costs eliminated if a product or service is discontinued versus if it is not. Many costs which may be allocated to a certain product-line or service may continue regardless of the decision. The critical scrutiny of such items is important. Consider strategic factors, such as the potential that the loss of one product line will affect the sales of another. Also consider opportunity costs. What will you do with the released capacity?

Expand the thought process regarding relevant costs to enhance and strengthen decision-making process in the firm, but be always aware of short-term versus long-term aspects of the issue. When a section or a factory is closed, generally all costs that can be saved including unit-level, batch-level, product-level, and facility-level costs will be relevant in such decisions. Only past costs (sunk) will remain irrelevant.

9. What should be done when there is only one production constraint and excess demand?

With one production constraint such as limited quantity of material or labor hours or machine hours, it is generally best to focus production and sales on the product with the highest contribution per unit of constraining factor (scarce resource).

10. What should be done when there are two or more constraints and excess demand?

With two or more constraints, algebraic or graphic solution should be used to derive a mix that provides the highest contribution per unit of constraining factors.

11. What are the primary behavioral and implementation issues of relevant cost analysis?

- *Management incentives under relevant cost analysis that distort effective decision making.*
- *The incentive to replace variable costs with fixed costs, and*
- *the tendency to focus on irrelevant information.*

12. Discuss the issue of improper management incentives under relevant cost analysis.

Management could improperly use relevant cost analysis to achieve a short-term benefit and potentially suffer a significant long-term loss. This happens particularly when managers' incentives are tied to current rather than long-term profits.

13. What is the wrongly placed incentive of replacing variable costs with fixed costs?

Contribution margin analysis has the potential danger of the manager replacing, say, a machine with manual labor, even though the overall cost of this change may be higher.

14. What is the tendency of focusing on irrelevant information?

It is easy for untrained managers to mistakenly include sunk costs or allocated costs in such evaluations. Effective use of relevant cost analysis requires careful identification of relevant costs, those future costs that differ among competing alternatives as well as any opportunity costs that need be considered.

Multiple choice questions:

1. Relevant costs are costs
   a) which may have been incurred in the past for competing alternatives.
   b) to be incurred at some future time for competing alternatives.
   c) to be incurred at some future time and differ among competing alternatives.
   d) of already purchased machinery and equipment.
   e) c and d.

2. In decision making,
   a) fixed costs are always irrelevant.
   b) variable costs are always irrelevant.
   c) fixed and variable costs are always relevant.
   d) fixed and variable costs may be relevant.
   e) only mixed costs are relevant.

3. Relevant costs generally have
   a) short-term focus and are not linked to strategy.
   b) product cost focus and are precise and quantitative.
   c) have long-term focus and customer focus, and are broad and subjective.
   d) b and c.
   e) a and b.

Cost Management: A Strategic Emphasis, 3e by Blocher/Chen/Cokins/Lin

4. Opportunity costs are particularly relevant when the firm is working
    a) below capacity.
    b) more than one shift.
    c) more than two shifts.
    d) at full capacity
    e) none of the above.

5. The decision of selling before or after further processing can be answered by determining
    a) incremental costs of further processing.
    b) incremental revenues of further processing.
    c) total costs of further processing.
    d) total revenues of further processing.
    e) incremental costs and revenues of further processing.

6. In deciding which products to eliminate,
    a) net income for such products must be reviewed.
    b) unit contribution margin for such products must be reviewed.
    c) total contribution margin for such products must be reviewed.
    d) total contribution less relevant fixed costs must be reviewed.
    e) none of the above.

7. The decision of which product to produce when we have limited manpower available is solved by producing the product(s) which have
    a) the highest selling prices
    b) the highest contribution margin.
    c) the lowest cost.
    d) the highest contribution per unit of the constraining factor.
    e) none of the above.

8. The decision of which product to produce when we have limited machine hours available and there is a constraint on how much we can sell can be solved by producing the product(s) which have
    a) the highest selling prices considering the sales constraint.
    b) the highest contribution margin considering the sales constraint.
    c) the lowest cost considering the sales constraint.
    d) the highest contribution per unit of the constraining factor and also considering the sales constraint.
    e) none of the above.

9. When we have two products with two production constraints (material and labor availability), the optimal solution on a graph is often
   a) the highest point on the vertical axis.
   b) the highest point on the horizontal axis.
   c) the intersecting point of the two lines on the graph.
   d) a or b.
   e) none of the above.

10. There is a tendency for managers to focus on
    a) long-term goals because their compensation is tied to net income.
    b) short-term goals because their compensation is tied to net income.
    c) short-term goals because their compensation is tied to increase in value of stock.
    d) short-term goals because their compensation is tied to net income and increase in stock value.
    e) none of the above.

Exercises:
E1. Keeping or replacing an old machine:
Walter Ceramics Company wants to acquire a new machine to replace one of its old machines. The new machine would cost $95,000 and has estimated useful life of five years with a salvage value of $5,000. Variable operating costs would be $92,000 a year. The old machine has a book value of $60,000 and a remaining life of five years. Its disposal value in five years would be $9,000. Variable operating costs would be $120,000 a year.
Required: Considering the five years in total, but ignoring the time value of money and income taxes, what would be the difference in operating income by acquiring the new machine as opposed to retaining the old one?

E2. Make or buy decision:
Walter Ceramics produces and sells 20 units of product H at a cost of $1,130 a piece as follows:

Direct materials	$ 650
Direct labor	120
Overhead 300%	360 (40% of overhead is variable)
Total cost per unit of H	1,130

Siena Ceramics has suggested to sell 20 units of H to Walter Ceramics for $950 each. As an additional incentive Siena will pay a rent of $2,000 a month for the space saved for not producing product H in the factory. Fixed costs will remain whether this product is produced or not except for $20 a piece which is directly applicable to this order.
Required: Determine whether Walter should accept Siena's offer.

E3. Keeping or eliminating a product line:

Shahnaz Interiors has two product lines furniture and accessories. The manager is concerned about the recent loss situation of accessories and has threatened to close that product line, terminate its manager, and rent the space to a vendor who is willing to pay $1,500 a month for the released space. The manager says that although the $5,000 allocated cost of his salary and rent will remain but it would be partly offset by the subleasing arrangement. The Average monthly income numbers for the company follow:

	Furniture	Accessories	Total sales
Sales	$18,000	$10,600	$28,600
Cost of goods sold	9,000	6,360	15,360
Sales commission	1,800	1,060	2,860
Fixed costs	1,500	1,400	2,900*
Allocated costs	2,500	2,500	5,000

* Includes dept. manager salary and benefits only.
Required: Prepare a complete income statement and determine if the manager should carry out his threat.

E4. Maximizing contribution per unit of limiting factor:

Siena Company produces and sells two products A and B for $29 and $19 a piece respectively. Variable costs amount to $14 for A and $12 for B. It takes 1.5 hours to make one unit of A and 1/2 hour to make one unit of B. Total manpower available per month is 1300 hours and maximum demand for A is 1,800 units of A and 1,700 units of B.
Required: Determine the optimal product mix to maximize profit.

E5.

Search for an internet site for Dell Company and its various products. Prepare a brief statement on why sales forecast, availability of materials, and flexibility in pricing are particularly important for Dell to remain competitive in the market place.

Correct answers to multiple choice questions:
1-c; 2-d; 3-e; 4-d; 5-e; 6-d; 7-d; 8-d; 9-c; 10-b.

Suggested answers to exercises:
E1. Keeping or replacing an old machine:

	Old $	New $	Difference
New machine's cost		95,000	(95,000)
Salvage value	(9,000)	(5,000)	(4,000)
Variable costs	600,000	460,000	140,000
Total	591,000	550,000	41,000

Purchase of the new machines would increase profit by $41,000 in five years. Note that the cost of the old machine is a sunk cost and is irrelevant in decision making.

E2. Make or buy decision:

Variable overhead cost of producing H: 360 * 40% = $144

Relevant cost of product H: (650 + 120 + 144 + 20) = $934 per unit;

Total relevant cost of product H: 934 * 20 = $18,680

Cost of buying from Siena: 950 * 20 = 19,000; 19,000 - 2,000 (rent) = $17,000

Advantage of buying from Siena: 18,680 - 17,000 = $1,680

E3. Keeping or eliminating a product line:

	Furniture	Accessories	Total $
Sales	$ 18,000	$ 10,600	$ 28,600
Cost of sales	9,000	6,360	15,360
Sales commission	1,800	1,060	2,860
Direct fixed costs	1,500	1,400	2,900
Section margin	5,700	1,780	7,480
Allocated costs	2,500	2,500	5,000
Income before tax	3,200	(720)	2,480

If Accessories department is closed:

Section margin lost	$1,780
Rental to be received	1,500
Disadvantage of closing per month	280

E4. Maximizing contribution per unit of the constraining factor:

	Product A	Product B
Selling price	29	19
Variable cost	14	12
Contribution margin	15	7
Labor hours per unit	1.5	.5
CM per hour	10	14
Demand	1,800	1,700

To maximize profit, we must first satisfy the demand for B and then use the remaining time to produce A within the constraint of the 1300 labor hours.

Time needed to produce 1700 units of B: 1700 * .5 = 850 hours
Balance of time to produce A: 1300 - 850 = 450 hours; 450/1.5 = 300 units

Total CM: (1700 * 7) + (300 * 15) = 11,900 + 4,500 = 16,400
OR
Total CM: (850 hours * 14) + (450 hours * 10) = $16,400

Cost Management: A Strategic Emphasis, 3e by Blocher/Chen/Cokins/Lin

CHAPTER 10
COST PLANNING FOR THE PRODUCT LIFE CYCLE: TARGET COSTING, THEORY OF CONSTRAINTS, AND LONG-TERM PRICING

Highlights:

There are three cost management methods used to analyze the product or service's cost life cycle: target costing, the theory of constraints and life-cycle costing. Target costing is a tool for analyzing the cost structure to help management identify the proper design features and manufacturing methods to allow the firm to meet a competitive price. The five steps in target costing are 1) determine the market price, 2) determine the desired profit, 3) calculate the target cost (market price less desired profit), 4) use value engineering to identify ways to reduce product cost, and 5) use costing and operational control to further reduce costs. Target costing focuses on the design phase to make the right product at a sellable price.

The theory of constraints (TOC) is a tool that assists managers in identifying bottlenecks and scheduling production to maximize throughput and profits. There are five steps to TOC analysis: 1) identify the binding and non-binding constraints, 2) determine the most efficient utilization for each binding constraint, 3) manage the flows through the binding constraint, 4) add capacity to the binding constraint, and 5) redesign the manufacturing process for flexibility and fast throughput. TOC is a short term measure until bottlenecks can be dealt with more effectively in the long-term.

Life cycle costing assists managers in minimizing total cost over the product or service's entire life cycle. Life-cycle costing brings a focus to the upstream activities (research and development, engineering) and downstream activities (marketing, distribution, service), as well as the manufacturing and operating costs that cost systems focus on.

The second part of the chapter considers strategic pricing and cost management issues as the product or service moves through the different phases of its sales life cycle. In the production introduction phase, value chain analysis and the master budget are important. In the growth phase, managers are more likely to need advanced costing methods such as activity-based costing and capital budgeting to deal with the increased complexity and growth of the manufacturing process. In the final two phases of the sales life cycle, maturity and decline, cost management focuses on operational and management control, the flexible budget and activity-based management.

Questions:
1. What is the cost life cycle?

2. What is the sales life cycle?

3. What is target costing?

4. What are the five steps in implementing a target costing approach?

5. What is value engineering and how is it used?

6. What is functional analysis?

7. What is design analysis as used in value engineering?

8. What are cost tables?

9. What is group technology?

10. What is the theory of constraints (TOC)?

11. What is throughput margin?

12. What are the five steps in TOC analysis?

13. What is a network diagram?

14. What is task analysis?

15. What is the drum-buffer-rope system?

16. What are the main characteristics of the TOC?

17. What are the main characteristics of ABC?

Learning Objective 3: Describe how life-cycle costing facilitates strategic management.

18. What is basic engineering?

19. What is prototyping?

20. What is templating?

21. What is concurrent engineering?

Learning Objective 4: Outline the objectives and techniques of strategic pricing.

22. What is the contrast of sales life cycle to the cost life cycle?

*Cost Management: A Strategic Emphasis, 3*e by Blocher/Chen/Cokins/Lin

23. What are the four phases of sales life cycle?

Suggested responses to the above questions:

1. What is the cost life cycle?

The cost life cycle is the sequence of activities within the firm that begins with research and development, followed by design, manufacturing, distribution, and customer service.

2. What is the sales life cycle?

The sales life cycle is the sequence of phases in the product or service's life in the market from the introduction of the product or service to growth in sales and finally maturity, decline, and withdrawal from the market.

3. What is target costing?

Target costing is a method by which the firm determines the target cost for the product, given a competitive market price, such that the firm can earn a desired profit.
Target cost = Competitive price - Desired profit

4. What are the five steps in implementing a target costing approach?

1) determine the market price, 2) determine the desired profit, 3) calculate the target cost at market price less desired profit, 3) use value engineering to identify ways to reduce product cost, 5) use costing and operational control to further reduce costs.

5. What is value engineering and how is it used?

Value engineering is used in target costing to reduce product cost by analyzing the trade-offs between 1) different types and levels of product functionality and 2) total product cost.

6. What is functional analysis?

Functional analysis is a common type of value engineering in which each major function or feature of the product is examined.

7. What is design analysis as used in value engineering?

In design analysis, the design team prepares several possible designs of the product, each having similar features that have different levels of performance, and different costs.

8. What are cost tables?

Cost tables are computer-based databases that include comprehensive information about the firm's cost drivers. They may be used in conjunction with cost reduction efforts.

9. What is group technology?

Group technology is a method of identifying similarities in the parts of products a firm manufactures, so the same part can be used in two or more products, thereby reducing costs.

10. What is the theory of constraints (TOC)?

TOC focuses on the overall profitability of the firm by maximizing the overall rate of manufacturing output, the throughput of the firm.

11. What is throughput margin?

Throughput is defined as sales less direct material costs, including purchased components and materials handling costs.

12. What are the five steps in TOC analysis?

a) Identify the binding constraint(s).
b) Determine the most efficient utilization for each binding constraint.
c) Manage the flow through the binding constraint
d) Add capacity to the binding constraints
e) Redesign the manufacturing process for flexibility and fast throughput

13. What is a network diagram?

A network diagram is a flowchart of the work done that shows the sequence of processes and the amount of time required for each.

14. What is task analysis?

Task analysis describes the activity of each process in detail. It could also be used to identify binding constraints.

Cost Management: A Strategic Emphasis, 3e by Blocher/Chen/Cokins/Lin

15. What is the drum-buffer-rope system?

The drum-buffer-rope system is a system for balancing the flow of production through a binding constraint, thereby reducing the amount of inventory at the constraint and improving overall productivity.

16. What are the main characteristics of the TOC?

TOC has a short-term focus and deals with maximization of throughput based on available resources and limitations. It does not directly use the cost driver concept. It attempts to optimize production flow and short-term product mix.

17. What are the main characteristics of ABC?

ABC has a long-term focus and analyzes all product costs. It is not directly concerned with constraints. It focuses on cost driver analysis. Its major use is in strategic pricing and profit planning.

18. What is basic engineering?

Basic engineering is the method in which product designers work independently from marketing and manufacturing to develop a design from specific plans and specifications. It is a quick way to design. The design cost is relatively low. Downstream costs (marketing and production) are relatively high, because they are not integral in the design process.

19. What is prototyping?

Prototyping is a method in which functional models of the product are developed and tested by engineers and trial customers. It is a slow process in designing. Design cost is significant and includes material, labor, and time. It provides a potentially significant reduction in downstream costs.

20. What is templating?

Templating is a design method in which an existing product is scaled up or down to fit the specifications of the desired new product. It is a fast way to design. The design costs are relatively modest. The effect on downstream costs is often unknown as the results are not known until introduced into the market.

21. What is concurrent engineering?

Concurrent engineering, or simultaneous engineering, is an important new approach in which product design is integrated with manufacturing and marketing throughout the product's life cycle. The design speed is continuous. The design cost is significant. It is the best method for reducing downstream costs.

22. What is the contrast of sales life cycle to the cost life cycle?

The sales life cycle refers to the phase of the product or services' sales in the market from introduction of the product or service to decline and withdrawal from the market. The cost life cycle composes the activities of research and development, design, manufacturing, marketing, distribution, and customer service.

23. What are the four phases of sales life cycle?

a) *Product introduction where there is little competition...*
b) *Growth where there is the benefit of differentiation. Competition begins to soften. Adequate capacity, financing, and good distribution channels are vital.*
c) *Maturity where sales continue to increase but at a decreasing rate. There are fewer competitors at this phase.*
d) *Decline where sales begin to decline as well as the number of competitors. Prices stabilize. Emphasis on differentiation returns. Survivors are able to control costs and deliver quality and excellent service. Prices are now set by a mature, competitive market.*

Multiple choice questions:

1. The cost life cycle is
   a) a method that attempts to determine the product cost given a competitive market price and a desired level of profit.
   b) the sequence of phases in the product or service's life in the market from the introduction of the product or service to growth in sales and finally maturity, decline, and withdrawal from the market.
   c) the sequence of activities within the firm that begins with research and development, followed by design, manufacturing, marketing, distribution, and customer service.
   d) the sequence of activities from purchase of raw materials to production and transfer to the finished goods warehouse.
   e) none of the above.

2. The sales life cycle is
   a) a method that attempts to determine the product cost given a competitive market price and a desired level of profit.
   b) the sequence of phases in the product or service's life in the market from the introduction of the product or service to growth in sales and finally maturity, decline, and withdrawal from the market.
   c) the sequence of activities within the firm that begins with research and development, followed by design, manufacturing, marketing, distribution, and customer service.
   d) the sequence of activities from purchase of raw materials to production and transfer to the finished goods warehouse.
   e) none of the above.

Cost Management: A Strategic Emphasis, 3e by Blocher/Chen/Cokins/Lin

3. Target costing is
   a) a method that attempts to determine the product cost given a competitive market price and a desired level of profit.
   b) the sequence of phases in the product or service's life in the market from the introduction of the product or service to growth in sales and finally maturity, decline, and withdrawal from the market.
   c) the sequence of activities within the firm that begins with research and development, followed by design, manufacturing, marketing, distribution, and customer service.
   d) the sequence of activities from purchase of raw materials to production and transfer to the finished goods warehouse.
   e) none of the above.

4. Research has shown that about
   a) 80% or more of total product life-cycle costs are committed at the service stage
   b) 80% or more of total product life-cycle costs are committed at the distribution stage
   c) 80% or more of total product life-cycle costs are committed at the manufacturing stage
   d) 80% or more of total product life-cycle costs are committed at the design stage
   e) none of the above

5. Target costing with its positioning
   a) in the early, downstream phases of the cost life cycle, can clearly help a firm reduce total costs.
   b) in the early, upstream phases of the cost life cycle, can clearly help a firm reduce total costs.
   c) in the late, downstream phases of the cost life cycle, can clearly help a firm reduce total costs.
   d) in the late, upstream phases of the cost life cycle, can clearly help a firm reduce total costs.
   e) none of the above

6. Value engineering
   a) is used in target costing to reduce product cost by analyzing the trade off between different types and levels of product functionality and total product cost.
   b) is the process by which each major function or feature of the product is examined.
   c) is the process by which several possible designs of the product are examined.
   d) is the process by which the management accountant determines the sales value of the product.
   e) none of the above.

7. Design analysis
   a) is used in target costing to reduce product cost by analyzing the trade off between different types and levels of product functionality and total product cost.
   b) is the process by which each major function or feature of the product is examined.
   c) is the process by which several possible designs of the product are examined.
   d) is the process by which the management accountant determines the sales value of the product.
   e) none of the above.

8. Functional analysis
   a) is used in target costing to reduce product cost by analyzing the trade off between different types and levels of product functionality and total product cost.
   b) is the process by which each major function or feature of the product is examined.
   c) is the process by which several possible designs of the product are examined.
   d) is the process by which the management accountant determines the sales value of the product.
   e) none of the above.

9. Kaizen costing
   a) is used in target costing to reduce product cost by analyzing the trade off between different types and levels of product functionality and total product cost.
   b) is the process by which each major function or feature of the product is examined.
   c) is the process by which several possible designs of the product are examined.
   d) is the process by which the management accountant determines the sales value of the product.
   e) none of the above.

10. Group technology is a method
    a) that includes comprehensive information about the firm's cost drivers.
    b) of identifying similarities in the parts of products so the same part can be used in two or more products.
    c) of identifying similarities in the parts of products so the same part may not be used in two or more products.
    d) that focuses on the overall profitability of the firm by maximizing the overall company throughput.
    e) none of the above

11. The theory of constraints is a method
    a) that includes comprehensive information about the firm's cost drivers.
    b) of identifying similarities in the parts of products so the same part can be used in two or more products.
    c) of identifying similarities in the parts of products so the same part may not be used in two or more products.
    d) that focuses on the overall profitability of the firm by maximizing the overall company throughput.
    e) none of the above

Cost Management: A Strategic Emphasis, 3e by Blocher/Chen/Cokins/Lin

12. Task analysis
    a) is a flowchart of the work done that shows the sequence of processes and the amount of time required for each.
    b) describes the activity of each process in detail, to help identify binding constraints.
    c) is a system for balancing the flow of production through a binding constraint, thereby reducing the amount of inventory at the constraint and improving overall productivity.
    d) a and b
    e) none of the above

13. A network diagram
    a) is a flowchart of the work done that shows the sequence of processes and the amount of time required for each.
    b) describes the activity of each process in detail, to help identify binding constraints.
    c) is a system for balancing the flow of production through a binding constraint, thereby reducing the amount of inventory at the constraint and improving overall productivity.
    d) a and b
    e) none of the above

14. The drum-buffer-rope system
    a) is a flowchart of the work done that shows the sequence of processes and the amount of time required for each.
    b) describes the activity of each process in detail, to help identify binding constraints.
    c) is a system for balancing the flow of production through a binding constraint, thereby reducing the amount of inventory at the constraint and improving overall productivity.
    d) a and b
    e) none of the above

15. TOC
    a) has a short-term focus, develops an understanding of cost drivers, and is used in strategic profit planning.
    b) has a short-term focus, has no direct utilization of cost drivers, and is used for strategic pricing.
    c) has a short-term focus, has no direct utilization of cost drivers, and is used for optimization of production flow.
    d) has a long-term focus, develops an understanding of cost drivers, and is used in strategic profit planning.
    e) has a long-term focus, develops an understanding of cost drivers, and is used for optimization of production flow.

16. ABC
    a) has a short-term focus, develops an understanding of cost drivers, and is used in strategic profit planning.
    b) has a short-term focus, has no direct utilization of cost drivers, and is used for strategic pricing.
    c) has a short-term focus, has no direct utilization of cost drivers, and is used for optimization of production flow.
    d) has a long-term focus, develops an understanding of cost drivers, and is used in strategic profit planning.
    e) has a long-term focus, develops an understanding of cost drivers, and is used for optimization of production flow.

17. Upstream costs include
    a) marketing, distribution, and service.
    b) purchasing and manufacturing
    c) research, development, and design
    d) design, purchasing, and service
    e) research, design, and manufacturing

18. Downstream costs include
    a) marketing, distribution, and service.
    b) purchasing and manufacturing
    c) research, development, and design
    d) design, purchasing, and service
    e) research, design, and manufacturing

19. Manufacturing costs include
    a) marketing, distribution, and service.
    b) purchasing and manufacturing
    c) research, development, and design
    d) design, purchasing, and service
    e) research, design, and manufacturing

20. Basic engineering
    a) is a design approach in which the engineering design process takes place throughout the cost life cycle using cross-functional teams.
    b) is a method in which functional models of the product are developed and tested by engineers and trial customers.
    c) is the method in which product designers work independently from marketing and manufacturing to develop a design from specific plans and specifications.
    d) is a design method in which an existing product is scaled up or down to fit the specifications of the desired new product.
    e) none of the above

Cost Management: A Strategic Emphasis, 3e by Blocher/Chen/Cokins/Lin

21. Prototyping
    a) is a design approach in which the engineering design process takes place throughout the cost life cycle using cross-functional teams.
    b) is a method in which functional models of the product are developed and tested by engineers and trial customers.
    c) is the method in which product designers work independently from marketing and manufacturing to develop a design from specific plans and specifications.
    d) is a design method in which an existing product is scaled up or down to fit the specifications of the desired new product.
    e) none of the above

22. Concurrent engineering
    a) is a design approach in which the engineering design process takes place throughout the cost life cycle using cross-functional teams.
    b) is a method in which functional models of the product are developed and tested by engineers and trial customers.
    c) is the method in which product designers work independently from marketing and manufacturing to develop a design from specific plans and specifications.
    d) is a design method in which an existing product is scaled up or down to fit the specifications of the desired new product.
    e) none of the above

23. Templating
    a) is a design approach in which the engineering design process takes place throughout the cost life cycle using cross-functional teams.
    b) is a method in which functional models of the product are developed and tested by engineers and trial customers.
    c) is the method in which product designers work independently from marketing and manufacturing to develop a design from specific plans and specifications.
    d) is a design method in which an existing product is scaled up or down to fit the specifications of the desired new product.
    e) none of the above.

24. Basic engineering incorporates
    a) fast design speed, significant design cost, and low downstream costs.
    b) continuous design speed, significant design cost, and low downstream costs.
    c) fast design speed, modest design costs, and unknown downstream costs.
    d) slow design speed, significant design costs, and low downstream costs.
    e) fast design speed, relatively low design cost, and high downstream costs.

25. Prototyping incorporates
    a) fast design speed, significant design cost, and low downstream costs.
    b) continuous design speed, significant design cost, and low downstream costs.
    c) fast design speed, modest design costs, and unknown downstream costs.
    d) slow design speed, significant design costs, and low downstream costs.
    e) fast design speed, relatively low design cost, and high downstream costs.

26. Templating incorporates
    a) fast design speed, significant design cost, and low downstream costs.
    b) continuous design speed, significant design cost, and low downstream costs.
    c) fast design speed, modest design costs, and unknown downstream costs.
    d) slow design speed, significant design costs, and low downstream costs.
    e) fast design speed, relatively low design cost, and high downstream costs.

27. Concurrent engineering incorporates
    a) fast design speed, significant design cost, and low downstream costs.
    b) continuous design speed, significant design cost, and low downstream costs.
    c) fast design speed, modest design costs, and unknown downstream costs.
    d) slow design speed, significant design costs, and low downstream costs.
    e) fast design speed, relatively low design cost, and high downstream costs.

Exercises:

E1.

Nahid Sign Company is introducing a new metal-based, neon sign which has an estimated market value of $2,900. The anticipated sales volume is 100 of these signs. The investment in the project amounts to $80,000, and expected return on this investment is 25% per year. The current selling and administrative costs amount to $25,000. Management is determined to bring this cost down by 36% for the coming period.
Required: determine the target cost under this scenario.

E2.

Nahid Automotive Company manufactures mufflers. The selling price per muffler is $79 each at the current production of 1,000 units per month. Major cost per period includes material cost of $40,000, $2,000 scrap, $4,000 material handling, $16,000 in labor costs, plus $13,000 in direct and indirect overhead. The company works 8 hours per day and 25 days per month.
Required: compute total throughput, throughput per unit, and throughput per hour.

E3.

Assume the same facts in problem 2. Further assume that the scrap currently at the rate of 5% is reduced by 80%. Material handling costs are reduced by 50%. The resulting efficiency has contributed to increased sales for the units saved from being scrapped.
Required: compute total throughput with the new assumption.

E4.

Arman Software Company produces two software, software A and software B. Total revenue amounts to $420,000, 60% of which is for software A. Cost of sales amounts to $280,000, 45% of which is for software A. Research and development cost amounted to $60,000, 80 percent of which is for software A. Selling expense amounts to 8% of total sales. Service costs amounts to $25,000, 70% of which is for product A.
Required: Prepare a life-cycle costing income statement.

 Cost Management: A Strategic Emphasis, 3e by Blocher/Chen/Cokins/Lin

E5.

Houshang Medical Technology has two produces product X. Capacity limit is at 2500 units per year. The current sales amount to 2000 units at $390 per unit. Fixed costs amount to $300,000 and variable costs amount to $190 per unit. Reduction of selling price by 10% will result in 20% increase in sales.

Required: Determine if sales price should be reduced.

E6.

Starbucks, McDonalds, and the U. S. Postal Office are accepting the swipeable credit cards from their customers. Refer to the chapter material and use your imagination to see how this innovation can help in reducing customer paying time, increase their sales, reduce their cash handling costs, and provide a happier customer base.

Correct answers to multiple choice questions:

1-c; 2-b; 3-a; 4-d; 5-b; 6-a; 7-c; 8-b; 9-e; 10-b; 11-d; 12-b; 13-a; 14-c; 15-c; 16-d; 17-c; 18-a; 19-b; 20-c; 21-b; 22-a; 23-d; 24-e; 25-d; 26-c; 27-b

Suggested answers to exercises:

E1.

Desired return on investment (profit):	25% * 80,000 = $20,000
Desired profit per sign:	20,000 / 100 = $200
Anticipated selling and administration cost per unit:	16,000 / 100 = $160
Target cost:	2,900 - (200 + 160) = $2,540

E2.

Total sales	$79,000
Material	$40,000
Scrap	2,000
Handling	4,000
Total costs	46,000
Total throughput	$33,000
Throughput per hour:	33,000/200 = 165
Throughput per unit:	33,000/1000 = 33

E3.

Reduction of scrap by 80%:	2,000 * (1 - .80) = $400
Equivalent units of saved scrap	1000 * 5% * (1 - .20) = 40 units
Total sales 1040 * 79	$82,160
Material	1040 * 40 = 41,600
Scrap	400
Material handling	2,000
Total throughput	38,160

E4.

Item	Software A	Software B	Total
Sales	$ 252,000	$ 168,000	$ 420,000
Cost of sales	126,000	154,000	280,000
Gross Margin	126,000	14,000	140,000
Research & Dev.	48,000	12,000	60,000
Selling expense	20,160	13,440	33,600
Service cost	17,500	7,500	25,000
Profit or Loss	40,340	(18,940)	21,400

E5.

Sales $\qquad$ 2,000 * 390 = $780,000

Cost of sales:

Fixed costs		$300,000
Variable costs 2000 * 190 =		380,000
		680,000
Profit		100,000

Sales (if prices are reduced by 10%) 2,000 * 1.20 * 390 * .90 = $842,400

Cost of sales:

Fixed costs	300,000	
Variable costs 2000 * 1.20 * 190 =	456,000	756,000
Profit		86,400

Therefore, sales price should not be reduced.

Cost Management: A Strategic Emphasis, 3e by Blocher/Chen/Cokins/Lin

CHAPTER 11
PROCESS COSTING

Highlights:

Process costing is a product costing method wherein costs are accumulated in processing departments and then allocated to all units processed during the period, including both completed and partially completed units. It is used by firms producing homogeneous products on a continuous basis, to assign manufacturing costs to units in production during the period. Firms that use process costing include paint, chemical, oil refining, and food processing companies. Process costing systems provide information for managers to make strategic decisions regarding choice of products and customers, manufacturing methods, pricing decisions, overhead allocation methods, and other long term issues.

The preparation of a production cost report, the key document in a typical process costing system, includes five steps: 1) analysis of physical units, 2) calculation of equivalent, numbers of units, 3) determination of total costs to account for, 4) computation of unit costs, and 5) assignment of total costs. Equivalent units are the number of like or similar completed units that could have been produced given the amount of work actually performed on both complete and partially completed units.

There are two methods of preparing the departmental production cost report in process costing practices; 1) weighted average method, and 2) first-in, first-out method (FIFO). The weighted average method includes all costs, both those incurred during the current period and those incurred in the prior period that are shown as the beginning work in process inventory of this period, in calculating the unit cost. The FIFO method includes only costs incurred during the current period in calculating equivalent unit cost. It considers the beginning inventory as a batch of goods separated from the goods started and completed within the current period. FIFO assumes that all the beginning work in process were completed first before other work is done during the current period.

Most manufacturing firms have several departments or use processes that require several steps. As the product passes from one department to another, the cost has to follow. The costs that come from the prior department are called transferred-in costs or prior department costs. Process costing with multiple departments should include the transferred-in cost as the fourth cost element in addition to direct material, direct labor, and factory overhead costs. Journal entries in process costing are basically same as job order costing, except that the former does not have identification by jobs.

The Appendix covers the concept of spoilage in process costing. Normal spoilage is considered as part of the product cost. Abnormal spoilage is charged as a loss to operations in the period detected.

Questions:

1. What is process costing?

1. What type of firms use process costing?

2. What are the equivalent units?

3. What are "units to account for"?

4. What are "units accounted for"?

5. What are conversion costs?

6. What is a production cost report?

7. What are the five steps in determining process costs?

*Cost Management: A Strategic Emphasis, 3*e by Blocher/Chen/Cokins/Lin
© 2005 by The McGraw-Hill Companies, Inc.

Learning Objective 4: Demonstrate the weighted average method of process costing.

8. What are the two methods of process costing? What are the primary features of the weighted average method?

Learning Objective 5: Demonstrate the FIFO method of process costing.

9. How is FIFO method different from the weighted average method?

Learning Objective 6: Analyze process costing with multiple departments.

10. Describe process costing with multiple departments.

Learning Objective 7: Prepare journal entries to record the flow of costs in a process costing system.

11. Provide representative journal entries in a process costing system.

Note that related departments within WIP would be debited or credited for the appropriate charges.

Learning Objective 8: Explain how process costing systems are implemented and enhanced in practice.

12. Discuss the major impact of the new manufacturing technologies on process costing:

Appendix:
Learning Objective 10: Account for spoilage in process costing.

13. What are Spoilage, Scrap, and Rework?

14. Define Normal versus Abnormal Spoilage?

Suggested responses to the above questions:

1. What type of firms use process costing?

Process costing systems are used in many industries such as chemicals, oil refining, textiles, paints, flour, canneries, rubber, steel, glass, food processing, mining, paper, lumber, leather goods, metal products, sporting goods, cement and watches. Process costing can also be used by service organizations with homogeneous services and repetitive processes such as check processing in a bank or mail sorting in a courier.

2. What are the equivalent units?

The equivalent units are the number of like or similar completed units that could have been produced given the amount of work actually performed on both completed and partially-completed units.

3. What are "units to account for"?

Units to account for are the sum of beginning inventory units and number of units started during the period.

Cost Management: A Strategic Emphasis, 3e by Blocher/Chen/Cokins/Lin

4. What are "units accounted for"?

Units accounted for are the sum of units transferred out and units in ending inventory (and spoilage where applicable).

5. What are conversion costs?

Conversion costs are the sum of direct labor and factory overhead costs. In firms using non-labor based cost drivers for their factory overhead costs, it is more appropriate to calculate separate equivalent units of production for factory overhead and direct labor costs.

6. What is a production cost report?

A production cost report is a report which summarizes the physical units and equivalent units of a department, the costs incurred during the period, and costs assigned to both units completed and transferred out and ending work in process inventories.

7. What are the five steps in determining process costs?

The five steps in determining process costs are as follows:
- *Analyzing physical flow of production units.*
- *Calculating equivalent units of production for all manufacturing cost elements.*
- *Determining total cost for each manufacturing cost element.*
- *Computing cost per equivalent unit for each manufacturing cost element.*
- *Assigning the total manufacturing cost to units completed and transferred out and units of work in process at the end of the period.*

8. What are the two methods of process costing?

The two methods of process costing are weighted average method and FIFO method. Weighted average method includes all costs, both those incurred during the current period and those incurred in the prior period that are shown as the beginning work in process inventory of this period, in calculating the unit cost. FIFO method includes only costs incurred and work effort during the current period in calculating the unit cost.

9. How is FIFO method different from the weighted average method?

The FIFO method does not combine beginning inventory costs with current cost when computing equivalent unit costs. It considers the beginning inventory as a batch of goods separate from the goods started and completed within the same time period and completed within the same period. The costs from each period are treated separately. The same five steps as in the weighted average method are followed in determining product costs. For firms with a cost leadership strategy, the FIFO method is preferred because of calculating costs per unit for each period independent of other periods. FIFO method is also more closely related to the continuous improvement concept.

10. Describe process costing with multiple departments.

As the product passes from one department to another, so does the cost pass from department to department. The costs that come from the prior department are called transferred-in costs or prior department costs. Transferred-in costs can be computed in the same manner as direct materials that are added at the beginning of a process. Both weighted average price or FIFO methods may be used.

11. Provide representative journal entries in a process costing system.

- *Issuance of raw materials: Dr. WIP, Cr. Material inventory*
- *Charges direct labor: Dr. WIP, Cr. Accrued payroll*
- *Applying factor overhead: Dr. WIP, Cr. Factory Overhead Control*
- *Transferred in Costs: Dr. WIP dept. Y, Cr. WIP dept. X*
- *Product units completed: Dr. Finished Goods Inv., Cr. WIP*

Note that related departments within WIP would be debited or credited for the appropriate charges.

12. Discuss the major impact of the new manufacturing technologies on process costing:

JIT methodology has three major impacts on process costing procedures: a) the difference in unit cost between the FIFO and weighted average methods is reduced by the reduction of inventory units, b) under JIT, there is much less difference between units completed and WIP ending inventory, c) new cost drivers or activity bases (other than direct labor) are needed to assign factory overhead to processes and products.
More manufacturing firms are moving toward flexible manufacturing systems (FMS) and cellular manufacturing systems (CMS). A FMS is an automated production system that produces one or more items in a family of parts in a flexible manner. A CMS is to form a cell for machinery and equipment needed to manufacture parts that have similar processing requirements. Under the CMS, the traditional process costing is less useful than the activity-based costing with cell-level cost pools.

13. What are Spoilage, Scrap, and Rework?

- *Spoilage denotes unacceptable units that are discarded or sold for disposal value.*
- *Scrap is the part of the product that has little or no value.*
- *Rework units are product units that are economically reworked into firsts and seconds and sold in regular channels.*

Cost Management: A Strategic Emphasis, 3e by Blocher/Chen/Cokins/Lin
© 2005 by The McGraw-Hill Companies, Inc.

14. Define Normal versus Abnormal Spoilage?

- *Normal spoilage is what occurs under efficient operating conditions. Such lost unit costs are absorbed by the good units produced.*
- *Abnormal spoilage is the excess spoilage and is charged as a loss to operations in the period detected.*

Exercises:
E1.

Iraj Manufacturing Company uses process costing in the production of plastic sheets. Work in process beginning includes 30 units which were 80% complete with regard to material and 60% complete with regard to processing. The cost of WIP beginning was $3,000 – 60% of which was for materials. Two hundred units were added during the period at a cost of $28,000, 70% of which is for materials. WIP ending amounted to 60 units which was 90% complete with regards to materials and 40% complete with regards to conversion.

Required:
a) **Prepare a cost of production report using weighted average price method.**
b) **Prepare a cost of production report using the FIFO method.**
c) **Prepare all of the necessary journal entries under each method.**

E2.

Refer to the above problem to answer to this exercise. As the controller of Iraj Manufacturing, you have received the cost of production report prepared under the above two methods and analyzed the costs in terms of material and conversion costs for the prior period and current period and concluded that there must be significant errors in prior period cost computations. You are satisfied that the cost data is accurate and concluded that the error is primarily due to the fact that the equivalent number of units for the beginning inventory was in fact 65% complete with regards to materials and 85% with regards to conversion costs.

Required:
a) **Prepare a Table showing unit cost for prior period and current period before any adjustments. Also list and compare unit cost under weighted average price.**
b) **Redo the cost of production report with the new information under the FIFO method.**
c) **Discuss whether the unit cost under the weighted average price method would be any different with the newly discovered information. Why or why not?**
d) **Prepare a new Table showing unit cost for prior period and current period after the above adjustments.**

E3.

Siena Melamine Factory uses process costing. It has two departments: mixing (M) and finishing (F). The finishing department receives the mixed components from the mixing department and finishes them. F's WIP beginning amounts to 8,000 units which are 100% complete with regard to transferred in, 60% complete as to materials, and 40% complete as to conversion costs. WIP ending amounted to 15000 units – complete on transferred in, 90% complete on materials, and 60% complete on conversion costs. WIP beginning in F was composed of $96,000 in transferred in, $19,200 in materials, and $9,600 in conversion costs. Added costs during the period included $500,000 in transferred in, $175,140 in material, and $131,920 in conversion costs.

Required:

a) **Prepare a cost of production report for F under weighted average price method.**
b) **Prepare a cost of production report for F using FIFO method.**
c) **Compute prior period's cost per unit.**

E4.

Payam Textile Company has a work in process inventory of 250 yards, 100% complete with regard to material, and 80% complete with regard to conversion. Normal spoilage amounted to 5% of completed units. Abnormal spoilage amounted to 490 yards, caused primarily due to malfunctioning machinery. WIP end of the period was 80% complete with regard to materials and 60% complete with regard to conversion costs. The cost of WIP beginning was $3,500, $2500 of which was for materials. From the total of $132,280 of added costs, $94,870 was for material costs.

Required:

a) **Prepare a cost of production report using FIFO method detailing cost per equivalent unit, cost per unit of units completed, and prior period's cost per unit.**
b) **Prepare the journal entries required for goods completed and normal as well as abnormal spoilage.**

Cost Management: A Strategic Emphasis, 3e by Blocher/Chen/Cokins/Lin
© 2005 by The McGraw-Hill Companies, Inc.

Suggested answers to exercises:
E1.
a) Weighted average method:

1. Unit reconciliation:

WIP beginning	30
Units added	200
Total to account for	230

Units completed	170
WIP ending	60
Total accounted for	230

2. Equivalent no. of units:

	Total	Material	Conversion
Units completed	170	170	170
WIP ending: 90%, 40%	60	54	24
Total equivalent number of units	230	224	194

3. Costs to account for:

	$	$	$
WIP beginning: 60%, 40%	3,000.00	1,800.00	1,200.00
Added costs: 70%, 30%	28,000.00	19,600.00	8,400.00
Total costs to account for	31,000.00	21,400.00	9,600.00

4. Unit cost: $ /

	145.0203	95.5357	49.4845

5. Costs accounted for:

Cost of goods completed	24,653.44	16,241.07	8,412.37
Cost of WIP ending	6,346.56	5,158.93	1,187.63
Total costs accounted for	31,000.00	21,400.00	9,600.00

b) FIFO method:

1. Unit reconciliation:
(Same as part a above)

2. Equivalent number of units:

	Total	Material	Conversion
Units completed	170.00	170.00	170.00
WIP ending 90%, 40%	60.00	54.00	24.00
Less: WIP beginning	-30.00	-24.00	-18.00
FIFO Equivalent no. of units	200.00	200.00	176.00

3. Cost to account for
(Same as part a above)

4. Cost per unit

	145.73	98.00	47.73

5. Costs accounted for:

Costs of goods completed	24,562.55	16,108.00	8,454.55
Cost of WIP ending	6,437.45	5,292.00	1,145.45
Total costs accounted for:	31,000.00	21,400.00	9,600.00

c) Journal entries:

Under weighted average price method :

Work in process – Materials	19,600	
Work in process – Conversion	8,400	
Raw materials inventory		19,600
Various accounts		8,400

Finished goods inventory	24,653.44	
Work in process – Materials		16,241.07
Work in process – Conversion		8,412.37

Under FIFO method:

First entry is identical

Finished goods inventory	24,652.55	
Work in process – Materials		16,108.00
Work in process – Conversion		8,454.55

E2.

a) Unit costs for prior period and current period before any adjustment:

Note: prior period unit costs are computed based on WIP beginning dollars and equivalent number of units.

Prior period unit cost:	$75.00 + 66.67 = 141.67$
Current period unit cost (weighted)	$95.54 + 49.48 = 145.02$
Current period unit cost (FIFO)	$98.00 + 47.73 = 145.73$
Unit cost of completed goods (FIFO)	$94.75 + 49.73 = 144.48$

Cost Management: A Strategic Emphasis, 3e by Blocher/Chen/Cokins/Lin

b) Cost of production report using FIFO:

1. Unit reconciliation
(same as previous problem)

2. Equivalent number of units:	Total	Material	Conversion
Unit completed	170.00	170.00	170.00
Work in process ending: 90%, 40%	60.00	54.00	24.00
Less: WIP beginning: 65%, 85%	-30.00	-19.50	-25.50
Total Equivalent number of units	260.00	204.50	168.50
3. Costs to account for (no change)	31,000.00	21,400.00	9,600.00
4. Unit cost	145.70	95.84	49.85
5. Costs accounted for:			
Costs of goods completed	24,628.01	16,224.45	8,403.56
Cost of WIP ending	6,371.99	5,175.55	1,196.44
Total costs accounted for	31,000.00	21,400.00	9,600.00

c) In computation of costs under weighted average, total units must be considered. The total units have not changed. Unit cost would be different where prior period cost per unit is different from current period cost per unit for material and/or conversion costs.

d) Prior period unit cost after adjustments:
    $92.3077 + 47.0588 = 139.3665$
  Adjusted unit cost under FIFO:
    $95.8435 + 49.8516 = 145.6951$

E3.
a) Cost of production report using weighted average method:

Work in process beginning	8,000.00			
Units added	40,000.00			
Total units to account for	48,000.00			

Units in work in process ending	15,000.00			
Units completed	33,000.00			
Total units accounted for	48,000.00			

	Total units	Transferred	Materials	Conversion
Equivalent number of units				
WIP ending: 100%, 90%, 60%	15,000.00	15,000.00	13,500.00	9,000.00
Units completed	33,000.00	33,000.00	33,000.00	33,000.00
Total equivalent number of units		48,000.00	46,500.00	42,000.00

Costs to account for:				
Work in process beginning	124,800.00	96,000.00	19,200.00	9,600.00
Costs added	807,060.00	500,000.00	175,140.00	131,920.00
Total costs to account for	931,860.00	596,000.00	194,340.00	141,520.00

Unit cost	19.97	12.42	4.18	3.37

Costs accounted for:				
Cost of WIP ending	272,997.00	186,250.00	56,421.29	30,325.71
Cost of goods completed	658,863.00	409,750.00	137,918.71	111,194.29
Total costs accounted for	931,860.00	596,000.00	194,340.00	141,520.00

Cost Management: A Strategic Emphasis, 3e by Blocher/Chen/Cokins/Lin

b) Cost of production report using FIFO method:

1. Units to account for (same as part a)

2. Equivalent number of units:	Total	Transferred i	Materials	Conversion
WIP ending 100%, 90%, 60%	15,000.00	15,000.00	13,500.00	9,000.00
Units completed	33,000.00	33,000.00	33,000.00	33,000.00
Less: WIP beginning: 100%, 60%,	8,000.00	-8,000.00	-4,800.00	-3,200.00
Total equivalent number of units		40,000.00	41,700.00	38,800.00

3. Costs to account for:				
Cost of WIP beginning	124,800.00	96,000.00	19,200.00	9,600.00
Costs added	807,060.00	500,000.00	175,140.00	131,920.00
Total costs to account for	931,860.00	596,000.00	194,340.00	141,520.00

4. Unit cost	20.10	12.50	4.20	3.40

5. Costs accounted for:				
Cost of WIP ending	274,800.00	187,500.00	56,700.00	30,600.00
Cost of goods completed	657,060.00	408,500.00	137,640.00	110,920.00
Total costs accounted for	931,860.00	596,000.00	194,340.00	141,520.00

c) Prior period's unit cost: $12 + 4 + 3 = 19.00$

<u>E4.</u>
a) Cost of production report using FIFO:

1. Unit reconciliation:

Work in process beginning	250.00
Units added	9,250.00
Total units to account for	9,500.00

Units completed	7,200.00
Normal spoilage 5%	360.00
Abnormal spoilage	490.00
Work in process ending	1,450.00
Total units accounted for	9,500.00

2. Equivalent number of units:

	Total	Material	Conversion
Units completed	7,200.00	7,200.00	7,200.00
Normal spoilage	360.00	360.00	360.00
Abnormal spoilage	490.00	490.00	490.00
WIP ending: 80%, 60%	1,500.00	1,200.00	900.00
Less: WIP beginning: 100%, 80%	-250.00	-250.00	-200.00
Total equivalent number of units		9,000.00	8,750.00

3. Costs to account for:

Cost of WIP beginning	3,500.00	2,500.00	1,000.00
Costs added	132,280.00	94,870.00	37,410.00
Total costs to account for	135,780.00	97,370.00	38,410.00

4. Unit costs

4. Unit costs	14.82	10.54	4.28

5. Costs accounted for:

	Units			
WIP beginning		3,500.00	2,500.00	1,000.00
Costs to finish WIP 50 units		213.77		213.77
Total cost of completed WIP beginning		3,713.77	2,500.00	1,213.77
Normal spoilage	360.00	5,333.95	3,794.80	1,539.15
Started and completed this period	6,950.00	102,974.95	73,260.72	29,714.23
Abnormal spoilage	490.00	7,260.10	5,165.14	2,094.96
WIP ending			12,649.33	3,847.89
		135,780.00	97,370.00	38,410.00

6. Cost of goods completed from the above:

WIP beginning completed	250.00	3,713.77	2,500.00	1,213.77
Normal spoilage		5,333.95	3,794.80	1,539.15
Started and completed this period	6,950.00	102,974.95	73,260.72	29,714.23
Total cost of goods completed	7,200.00	112,022.68	79,555.52	32,467.15
Cost per unit of goods completed		15.56	11.05	4.51

Cost Management: A Strategic Emphasis, 3e by Blocher/Chen/Cokins/Lin
© 2005 by The McGraw-Hill Companies, Inc.

b) Journal entries for production and spoilage costs:

Finished goods inventory   112,022.68
       Work in process inventory   112,022.68

To account for completion of 7,200 units during the period accounted for under FIFO method.

Loss – abnormal spoilage   7,260.10
       Work in process inventory   7,260.10

To account for the cost of 490 units which were spoiled.

Note that normal spoilage is added to the cost of completed production and unit cost is increased by the effect of those units on total production costs.

CHAPTER 12
COST ALLOCATION:
SERVICE DEPARTMENTS AND JOINT PRODUCT COSTS

Highlights:

The two main cost allocation methods are departmental cost allocation and joint product costing. There are three steps in departmental cost allocation; i.e., 1) the tracing of direct costs and initial allocation of indirect costs, 2) the allocation of service department costs to production departments, and 3) the allocation of production department costs to products. There are three methods for allocating service department costs to production departments: the direct method, the step method, and the reciprocal method. The three methods differ in how they deal with service flows among service departments. The direct method ignores these flows to other service departments, while the step method includes some of them, and the reciprocal method includes all. A variation in allocation methods, called dual allocation, makes a distinction between fixed and variable costs in cost allocation. The preferred approach in this regard is to allocate fixed cost based on budgeted percentages and amounts and the variable costs based on predetermined rates and actual usage. This approach leads to better accountability and fairness in charging the users of services. Cost allocation is applicable to manufacturing as well as service organizations.

Joint product costing is a type of costing which arises when two or more products are made simultaneously in a given manufacturing process. The three main methods for costing joint products are: the physical measures method, the sales value at split off method, and the net realizable value method. The physical measures method ignores sales value. The sales value and the net realizable value methods tend to result in similar gross margins among the joint products. The sales value at split off method is used when sales value at split off is known, and otherwise, the net realizable value is used. The four approaches to by-product costing are discussed in the appendix. Basically, by-products that have small values may be reduced from manufacturing costs based on their sales value and kept in inventory until sold, or realized only when the item is sold without accounting for it before it is sold. Also by-products can be considered as "other income" in either of the two cases instead of showing it as a reduction to manufacturing costs.

Questions:

1. What does cost allocation determine?

Learning Objective 1. Identify the strategic role of cost allocation.

---

2. What are the objectives of cost allocation?

3. What are the bases for cost allocation?

4. What is the ethical role of cost allocation?

5. What are the two types of overhead cost allocation?

6. What are the three phases in departmental cost allocation?

7. Explain the three methods of service department cost allocation.

8. How are service department costs allocated?

Cost Management: A Strategic Emphasis, 3e by Blocher/Chen/Cokins/Lin

9. What is the dual allocation method?

10. Discuss some of the problems with cost allocation.

Learning Objective 5. Explain the use of cost allocation in service firms.

Cost allocation is equally applicable to service organizations such as, a bank, a hospital, or a university. The service providing department such as an academic department receives services from college administration, computer center, financial services, the provost's office, the dean's office, the library, maintenance and operations, etc. and in order to determine the cost of the service, an equitable cost allocation method should be used.

Learning Objective 6. Use the three joint product costing methods.

11. What are joint products?

12. What are by-products?

13. What is the split-off point?

14. What are separable costs?

15. What are the most frequently used methods in allocating joint costs?

Learning Objective 7. Use the four by-product costing methods.

---

16. What are the four methods of by-product costing?

Suggested responses to the above questions:

1. What does cost allocation determine?

Cost allocation determines how costs of a shared facility, program, production process, or service should be allocated among its users – cost objectives.

2. What are the objectives of cost allocation?

The objectives of cost allocation are as follows:
- *motivate managers to exert a high level of effort to achieve the goals of top management,*
- *provide the right incentive for managers to make decisions that are consistent with the goals of top management, and*
- *fairly determine the rewards earned by the managers for their effort and skill, and for the effectiveness of their decision making.*

3. What are the bases for cost allocation?

*The most objective basis for cost allocation exists when a **cause and effect relationship** can be determined. **Ability-to-bear** is another basis for cost allocation when cause and effect relationship cannot be established. Another basis is **fairness or benefit received**.*

Cost Management: A Strategic Emphasis, 3e by Blocher/Chen/Cokins/Lin

4. What is the strategic (ethical) role of cost allocation?

Cost allocation should be objective and fair as perceived by those who are affected such as, governmental agencies or internal departments. Cost allocation draws management's attention to the question of shared resources, its economics, and the equity factor in its allocation.

5. What are the two types of overhead cost allocation?

Overhead may be allocated directly to products (job order costing) or first to production departments and then to products (process costing).

6. What are the three phases in departmental cost allocation?

The three phases are a) tracing all direct costs and allocating overhead costs to both the service departments and the production departments, and b) allocating the service department costs to the production departments, and finally c) allocating the production department costs to products.

7. Explain the three methods of service department cost allocation.

- *The direct method is done by taking the service flows to production departments only and determining each production department's share of that service.*
- *The step method uses a sequence of steps in the allocation of service departments to production departments.*
- *The reciprocal method takes into account all the reciprocal flows between service departments through simultaneous equations.*

8. How are service department costs allocated?

Service department costs are allocated upon determining their most appropriate cost drivers. This is a list of suggested allocation bases for certain types of costs:
- *Personnel-related costs -- number of employees*
- *Payroll-related costs -- labor cost*
- *Material-related costs -- material cost or quantity used*
- *Space-related costs -- square feet or cubic feet*
- *Energy-related costs -- motor capacity*
- *Research and development -- estimated time, sales, or assets employed*
- *Public relations -- sales*
- *Executive pay -- sales, assets employed*
- *Property taxes -- square feet, real estate or insurance valuation, market value of assets.*

9. What is the dual allocation method?

Dual allocation method which separates costs into fixed and variable and then finds the most appropriate method for allocation is a better way to allocate costs. Variable costs are allocated based on some measure of actual consumption of goods and services whereas, fixed costs which are often capacity related are allocated based on some predetermined or budgeted basis.

10. Discuss some of the problems with cost allocation.

- *Cause and effect relationship may not be readily established.*
- *Budgeted figures may not be available.*
- *Allocated costs may exceed external purchase value of such services.*
- *Separating costs into fixed and variable may not be readily feasible.*

Cost allocation in service organizations:

Cost allocation is equally applicable to service organizations such as, a bank or a university. The service providing department such as an academic department receives services from college administration, computer center, financial services, the provost's office, the dean's office, the library, maintenance and operations, etc. and in order to determine the cost of the service, an equitable cost allocation method should be used.

11. What are joint products?

Joint products are products from the same production process that have relatively substantial sales values.

12. What are by-products?

By-products are products whose total sales values are minor in comparison with the sales value of the joint products.

13. What is the split-off point?

The split-off point is the first point in a joint production process in which individual products can be identified.

14. What are separable costs?

Separable costs are additional processing costs that occur after the split-off point and can be directly identified with individual products.

15. What are the most frequently used methods in allocated joint costs?

These are a) physical measures, b) sales value, and c) net realizable value methods.

- *The physical measure method uses measures such as gallons, pounds, or yards produced at split-off point to allocate joint costs. This method is easy to use and the basis for allocation can be objectively determined. But it may not be applicable in many situations and can give cost measures that exceed the sales value for the product.*
- *A variation of physical measures called average cost method uses units of output to allocate joint costs to joint products.*
- *The sales value at split-off method allocates joint costs to joint products on the basis of their relative sales values at the split-off point. This method is also easy to calculate, and the cost share is in line with the product's sales value. However, in some industries, sales value change, and in other cases, sales value may not be readily available.*
- *The net realizable value of a product (NRV) is the estimated sales value at the split-off point, determined by subtracting the additional processing and selling costs beyond the split-off point from the ultimate sales value of the product. NRV method is appropriate when the sales value at split-off point is not available.*

16. What are the four methods of by-product costing?

These methods are as follows:
- *Method 1 -- Net realizable value method. This method shows the net realizable value of by-products on the balance sheet as inventory and in the income statement as a deduction from the total manufacturing cost of the joint products. This is done in the period in which the by-product is produced.*
- *Method 2 -- Other income at production point method. This method shows the NRV of by-products in the income statement as other income or other sales revenue. This is also done in the period in which the by-product is produced.*
- *Method 3 -- Other income at selling point method. The net sales revenue from the by-product sold at time of sale is shown in the income statement as other income or other sales revenue.*
- *Method 4 -- Manufacturing cost reduction at selling point method. The net sales revenue from a by-product sold at the time of sale is shown in the income statement as a reduction of the total manufacturing cost.*

Multiple choice questions:

1. The objectives of cost allocation are to
   a) motivate managers to exert efforts to achieve the goals of top management.
   b) provide the right incentive for managers to make decisions that are consistent with the goals of top management.
   c) fairly determine the rewards earned by the managers for their efforts and skills, and for the effectiveness of their decision making.
   d) all of the above.
   e) a and b.

2. The bases used for cost allocation is/are the following:
   a) cause and effect relationship
   b) ability to bear
   c) benefit received
   d) all of the above
   e) a and c

3. In job costing, direct overhead is often
   a) directly traced to jobs.
   b) charged to production departments before being allocated to jobs.
   c) charged to processes before being charged to jobs.
   d) charged to customers before being charged to jobs.
   e) none of the above.

4. The three phases in extended cost allocation include
   a) product costs, production departments, service departments.
   b) production departments, service departments, product costs.
   c) service departments, production departments, product costs.
   d) service departments, product costs, production departments.
   e) none of the above.

5. Direct method of cost allocation is done by
   a) allocating service departments directly to other service departments before allocating any costs to production departments.
   b) allocating service departments directly to production departments before allocating any costs to service departments.
   c) allocating service departments directly to production departments only.
   d) allowing for directly reciprocal allocations before allocating costs to manufacturing departments.
   e) none of the above.

Cost Management: A Strategic Emphasis, 3e by Blocher/Chen/Cokins/Lin

© 2005 by The McGraw-Hill Companies, Inc.

6. Simultaneous equations are used in
   a) direct allocation method.
   b) step allocation method.
   c) reciprocal allocation method.
   d) a and c.
   e) b and c.

7. A reasonable basis for allocating public relations costs is
   a) number of employees
   b) total sales
   c) total assets
   d) total salaries
   e) total square footage

8. A reasonable basis for allocating building property taxes is
   a) number of employees
   b) total sales
   c) total assets
   d) total salaries
   e) total square footage

9. Dual allocation is a method which
   a) separates the costs into fixed and variable costs and allocates them accordingly.
   b) separates the costs into direct and indirect costs and allocates them accordingly.
   c) separates the costs into budgeted and actual costs and allocates them accordingly.
   d) separates the costs into controllable and uncontrollable costs and allocates them accordingly.
   e) none of the above.

10. Joint products are products
   a) from different production processes that have relatively high sales values.
   b) from the same production processes that have relatively high sales values.
   c) from different production processes that have relatively low sales values.
   d) from the same production processes that have relatively low sales values.
   e) none of the above.

11. The split-off point is the first point in a joint production process where
   a) a joint product appears
   b) individual products can be identified.
   c) separable costs disappear.
   d) additional processing costs may not be incurred.
   e) none of the above.

12. The average cost method of cost allocation uses
    a) lbs., gallons, or yards.
    b) units of output.
    c) sales prices.
    d) sales prices less additional processing costs.
    e) b and c.

13. Among the advantages of the physical measure of cost allocation, we can say that
    a) it is easy to use.
    b) sales value is often available.
    c) the criterion for allocation is objectively determined.
    d) a and b.
    e) a and c.

14. The net realizable value of a product is
    a) the sales value of the final product.
    b) same as sales value at split off point.
    c) the estimated sales value of the product at split-off point.
    d) the estimated sales value at split-off point plus any related marketing costs.
    e) none of the above.

15. In the asset recognition method of by-product costing, the by-product may be valued
as
    a) other income at the time of production.
    b) reduction in joint product costs at the time of production.
    c) reduction in joint product costs at the time of sale.
    d) b or c.
    e) a or b.

Exercises:

E1.
Liberty Manufacturing has two service departments, Personnel (P) and Maintenance (M), and two production departments P1 and P2. The statistics regarding these departments are per the following Table.

Item	Personnel	Maintenance	Production 1	Production 2
No. of employees	15	25	30	70
Maintenance hours	100	200	600	1900
Direct overhead	$32,000	$68,000	$495,000	$984,000
Machine hours			2,400	3,600
Direct labor hours			4,200	8,800

P1 overhead is allocated based on machine hours, and P2 overhead is allocated based on labor hours. Product A uses $145 of material, $22 of labor, 1.2 machine hours in P1 and 2.8 labor hours in P2.

Cost Management: A Strategic Emphasis, 3e by Blocher/Chen/Cokins/Lin

Required:
a) Use direct allocation to close service department costs, determine the overhead rates in P1 and P2, and compute the final cost of product A.
b) Use step allocation to close service departments with M to be allocated first, determine the overhead rates in P1 and P2, and compute the final cost of product A. Would it make any difference if P is allocated first? Why and by how much?
c) Use reciprocal allocation to close service departments, determine the overhead rates in P1 and P2, and compute the final cost of Product A.

E2.

Kindercare School has a computer center the costs of which need to be allocated to the two divisions that use its services. The costs of the computer center are as follows:

	Budget	Actual
Supervision	$ 4,800	$ 4,700
Data entry	3,200	3,900
Computer lease	6,200	6,100
Supplies	400	900
Division A share	30%	20%
Division B share	70%	80%

From the above costs, only data entry and supplies costs are variable and the balance are fixed costs.

Required:
What would be the most logical way of allocating the computer department costs to division A and B? Use dual allocation method, show your computations, and explain your logic.

E3.

Abadan Petrochemical Company produces two products resulting from a joint process. 245,000 gallons of product A which sells for $2.60 per gallon and 355,000 gallons of B which sells for $4.95 per gallon after going through an additional process that costs $532,500. B can be sold at split off point for $2.95 per gallon. The cost of the joint process amounts to $1,080,000. 220,000 gallon of A and 315,000 gallons of B are sold during the current period. There was zero inventory at the beginning of the period. The selling and administrative costs of these products amount to $285,500.

Required:
a) Determine cost per gallon of A and B using the physical measures method.
b) Prepare an income statement using the NRV method - (ignore B's selling price at the split-off point).
c) Determine the inventory values using sales value method.
d) Compute and discuss whether it is a good idea to sell B at split off point or process it further and sell it.

E4.

Abadan Petrochemical Company produces two products resulting from a joint process: 245,000 gallons of product A which sells for $2.60 per gallon and 355,000 gallons of B which sells for $4.95 per gallon after going through an additional process that costs $532,500. B can be sold at split off point for $2.95 per gallon. In addition, 125,000 gallons of by-product C which has a sales value of 45 cents a gallon results from the joint process. The cost of the joint process amounts to $1,080,000. 220,000 gallon of A and 315,000 gallons of B and 95,000 gallons of C are sold during the current period. There was zero inventory at the beginning of the period. The selling and administrative costs of these products amount to $285,500.

Required:

a) **Prepare an income statement under the physical measures method assuming that the by-product is recognized as other income at the time of production.**

b) **Prepare an income statement under the sales value method assuming that the NRV method at the time of production is used for the by-product.**

c) **Prepare an income statement under the NRV method assuming that the by-product is considered as other income at the time of sale.**

d) **Prepare an income statement under the NRV method assuming that by-product is considered as a reduction in cost of joint products at the time of sale.**

E5.

Do an internet search for WalMart. See if you can find the amount of their home office costs as well as the number of their stores domestically and globally as well as other particulars with regard to these stores. Then, attempt to allocate the home office costs to all the stores. Consider various options in cost allocation and discuss the pros and cons of each method based on what you learnt in the chapter as well as the analysis provided in the study guide.

Correct answers to multiple choice questions:
1-d; 2-d; 3-a; 4-c; 5-c; 6-c; 7-b; 8-e; 9-a; 10-b; 11-b; 12-b; 13-e; 14-c; 15-e.

Suggested answers to exercises:

E1.

a) Direct allocation method:

Item	Service 1	Service 2	Prod. 1	Prod. 2	Total
Direct overhead costs	32,000	68,000	495,000	984,000	1,579,000
Personnel (sevice1)	(32,000)		9,600	22,400	
Maintenance (serv. 2)		(68,000)	16,320	51,680	
Total	-	-	520,920	1,058,080	1,579,000
Allocation base			2,400	8,800	
Rate per hour			217	120	

Cost of product A:

Material		145.00
Labor		22.00
Overhead:	1.2 * 217.05 = 260.46	
	2.8 * 120.24 = 336.67	597.13
Total cost per unit		764.13

b) Step allocation:

Item	Service 1	Service 2	Production 1	Production 2	Total
Direct overhead costs	68,000	32,000.00	495,000.00	984,000.00	1,579,000
Maintenance (service 1)	(68,000)	2,611.20	15,694.40	49,694.40	
Personnel (service 2)		(34,611.20)	10,383.36	24,227.84	
Total	-	-	521,077.76	1,057,922.24	1,579,000
Allocation base			2,400.00	8,800.00	
Cost per hour			217.12	120.22	

Cost per unit of product A

Material and labor		167.00
Overhead:	(1.2 * 217.12) + (2.8 * 120.22) =	597.16
Total cost per unit		764.16

If we allocate personnel costs first, we will arrive at a different result because of the impact of those costs on other service units. The student is encouraged to do this as an additional reinforcement of the topic.

c) Reciprocal allocation:

$P = 32{,}000 + (100/2600) M$
$M = 68{,}000 + (25/125)P$
$M = 68{,}000 + [(25/125) * (32{,}000 + (100/2600) M)]$
Solving for M results in $74,976.57
Solving for P results in $34,883.71

Direct costs	68,000.00	32,000.00	495,000.00	984,000.00	1,579,000
Allocate Maintenance (S1)	74,976.57	2,883.71	17,302.29	54,790.57	
Allocate Personnel (S2)	6,976.74	34,883.71	8,372.09	19,534.88	
Total	-	-	520,674.38	1,058,325.45	1,579,000
Allocation base			2,400.00	8,800.00	
Cost per hour			216.95	120.26	

Product A cost per unit: $(167) + (1.2 * 216.95) + (2.8 * 120.26) = \$764.07$

Note that in this problem, there is not a substantial difference in cost based on the allocation method used. As such, it is best to stick with the simplest method available.

E2.
The most logical system of allocation is a dual allocation where actual fixed costs would be allocated based on budgeted percentages and actual variable costs would be allocated based on actual percentages. Use of budgeted usage is preferred for fixed cost allocation, because these costs are capacity related and actual fluctuation of service does not change the basic commitments. On the other hand, use of actual usage for allocation of variable costs is recommended because such fluctuations are the result of change in usage of those services as compared to budgeted volumes.

Alternatively, we can also allocate budgeted fixed costs based on budgeted percentages and use budgeted variable cost per unit times actual usage of those services. Use of budgeted fixed costs and budgeted variable cost rates is preferred because it keeps the computer department accountable for changes in costs to which the users have not agreed to and still charges them for higher consumption of services (actual volume of variable services). However, such an approach would result in a residual unallocated cost which may be written off directly on the income statement while identifying the departmental responsibility.

We have used the former approach in solving this problem:
Division A:
Variable costs $4,800 * 20\% = 960$
Fixed costs $10,800 * 30\% = 3,240$
Total Division A $960 + 3,240 = 4,200$

Cost Management: A Strategic Emphasis, 3e by Blocher/Chen/Cokins/Lin

Division B:

Variable costs	4,800 * 80% = 3,840
Fixed costs	10,800 * 70% = 7,560
Total Division B	3,840 + 7,560 = 11,400

The student is encouraged to attempt the problem based on budgeted numbers as suggested above as well.

E3.

a) Cost per gallon using the physical measures method:

Product	Gallons	Percent	Amount	Per unit
A	245,000	0.4083	440,964	1.799853
B	355,000	0.5917	639,036	1.800101
	600,000		1,080,000	

Additional processing cost per unit	532,500 / 355,000 = 1.50
B's final cost per unit	1.80010 + 1.50000 = 3.30010

b) Income statement using NRV method:

Product B's price at split off point   4.95 - 1.50 = 3.45

Product	Gallons	Sell. price	Sales value	Percent	Cost	Per unit
A	245,000	2.60	637,000	0.3422	369,576	1.508473
B	355,000	3.45	1,224,750	0.6578	710,424	2.001194
	600,000		1,861,750		1,080,000	

Cost of B after further processing 2.00119 + 1.50000 = 3.50119

Item	Gallons	Price	Amount A	Gallons	Price	Amount B	Total $
Sales	220,000	2.60000	572,000.00	315,000	4.95000	1,559,250.00	2,131,250
Cost of S	220,000	1.50847	331,863.40	315,000	3.50119	1,102,874.85	1,434,738
Gross Profit			240,136.60			456,375.15	696,512
S&GA Expense							285,500
Profit							411,012

c) Inventory values using the sales value method:

Item	Gallons	Price	Amount	Percent	Cost	Per unit
A	245,000	2.60	637,000	0.3782	408,456	1.667167
B	355,000	2.95	1,047,250	0.6218	671,544	1.891673
			1,684,250		1,080,000	

Cost per unit of B after further processing: $1.891673 + 1.50 = 3.39167$

Product	Production	Sales	Inventory	Cost/unit	Total $
A	245,000	220,000	25,000	1.66717	41,679.25
B	355,000	315,000	40,000	3.39167	135,666.80
Total					177,346.05

d) Sell B or process it further?

Price of B after further processing	4.95
Price of B at split off point	2.95
Incremental revenue of further processing	2.00
Incremental cost of further processing	1.50*
Additional benefit of further processing per unit	.50

Additional profit of further processing: $.50 * 355,000 = 177,500$

$* 532,500 / 355000 = 1.50$

E4.

a) Income statement using physical measures - the by-product is recognized as other income at the time of production.

Item	Gallons	price	Amount A	Gallons	Price	Amount B	Total $
Sales	220,000	2.60000	572,000	315,000	4.9500	1,559,250.00	2,131,250.00
Cost of S.	220,000	1.79985	395,967	315,000	3.3001	1,039,531.50	1,435,498.50
Gross Profit			176,033			519,718.50	695,751.50
S&GA							285,500.00
Profit							410,251.50
Other income (Product C)				125,000	0.4500		56,250.00
Total profit							466,501.50

Cost Management: A Strategic Emphasis, 3e by Blocher/Chen/Cokins/Lin

b) Income statement using sales value method - the by-product is recognized as a reduction of joint product costs at the point of production.

Item	Gallons	price	Amount A	Gallons	Price	Amount	Total $
Sales	220,000	2.60000	572,000.00	315,000	4.95000	1,559,250.00	2,131,250.00
Cost of S.	220,000	1.66717	366,777.40	315,000	3.39167	1,068,376.05	1,435,153.45
By-product C				125,000	0.45000	(56,250.00)	(56,250.00)
Gross Profit			205,222.60			547,124.00	752,346.60
S & GA							285,500.00
Profit							466,846.60

c) Income statement using NRV method - the by-product is considered as other income at the time of sale.

Item	Gallons	price	Amount A	Gallons	Price	Amount B	Total $
Sales	220,000	2.60000	572,000.00	315,000	4.95000	1,559,250.00	2,131,250.00
Cost of S.	220,000	1.50847	331,863.40	315,000	3.50119	1,102,874.85	1,434,738.25
Gross Profit			240,136.60			456,375.15	696,511.75
S & GA							285,500.00
Profit							411,011.75
Other income (Product C)				95,000	0.45000		42,750.00
Total profit							453,761.75

d) Income statement using NRV - the by-product is considered as a reduction of cost of joint products at the time of sale.

Item	Gallons	price	Amount A	Gallons	Price	Amount B	Total $
Sales	220,000	2.60000	572,000.00	315,000	4.95000	1,559,250.00	2,131,250.00
Cost of S.	220,000	1.50847	331,863.40	315,000	3.50119	1,102,874.85	1,434,738.25
By-product sale (C)				95,000	0.45000		42,750.00
Gross Profit			240,136.60			456,375.15	739,261.75
S & GA							285,500.00
Profit							453,761.75

CHAPTER 13
THE FLEXIBLE BUDGET AND STANDARD COSTING: DIRECT MATERIALS AND DIRECT LABOR

Highlights:

A flexible budget can play an important role in assessing operating efficiency. Using the budget and the flexible budget for the period together with actual income, the operating income variance can be computed and separated into the sales volume and flexible budget variances. The sales volume variance is the difference between the master budget and the flexible budget. It measures the effects of changes in sales units on sales, expenses, contribution margins, and operating income. The flexible budget variance is the difference between the actual operating result and the flexible budget. It measures efficiency in using resources.

Establishing a standard requires careful analysis of operations. A standard can be an ideal standard or a currently attainable standard. A manufacturing operation usually has a standard cost sheet that details the standard quantity and standard cost for all the significant manufacturing elements of the operation. A firm can use activity analysis, historical data, benchmarks, market expectation, and strategic decisions to set the standards. Typical standards include standards for direct materials and direct labor. Comparing actual direct materials and direct labor costs to standard costs for direct materials and direct labor, respectively, a firm can identify materials purchase price variance, materials usage variance, labor rate variance, and labor efficiency variance.

Recent advances in manufacturing technology such as JIT, flexible manufacturing, computer integrated manufacturing, total quality management, and theory of constraints have had great impacts on manufacturing and standard costs. Among the impacts are decreased significance of materials purchase price variance, labor variances, and variances of non-bottleneck operations. The focus in using standard costs should be on influencing behavior with positive reinforcements and motivation, not on penalties and punishments. Unreasonable standards, secrecy in standard settings, authoritarian control, poor communication, inflexibility, unfair performance evaluation, uneven rewards, and excessive emphasis on profits among other facts, often make a good standard cost system a failure.

Questions:

Learning Objective 1: Evaluate the effectiveness and efficiency of an operation and calculate and interpret the operating income variance.

1. What is effectiveness?

2. Why are effective operations important?

3. What is an efficient operation?

4. What is the operating income variance?

Learning Objective 2: Develop and use flexible budgets to conduct additional analyses of the operating income variance for control of operations and performance evaluation, as well as calculate and interpret the sales volume and flexible budget variances.

5. What is a flexible budget?

6. What is the flexible budget variance?

7. What are the major distinctions between the master budget and the flexible budget?

8. What is sales volume or activity variance?

9. What is the operating income flexible budget variance?

Learning Objective 3: Set proper standard costs for planning, control, and performance evaluation.

10. What is a standard?

Cost Management: A Strategic Emphasis, 3e by Blocher/Chen/Cokins/Lin

11. What is an ideal standard?

12. What is a currently attainable standard?

13. What kind of standards is a world-class firm likely to use?

14. What are the sources that firms often use in determining appropriate standards?

15. What is activity analysis?

16. What is the advantage of using benchmarks in setting standards?

17. What is a target cost that may also be used in setting standards?

18. What are the three facets of standard costs for direct materials?

19. What is a standard cost sheet?

Learning Objective 4: Identify factors that contribute to operating income flexible budget variance and analyze and explain (1) sales price variance, (2) direct materials price and usage variances, and (3) direct labor rate and efficiency variances.

20. What does flexible budget operating income variance include?

21. What is sales price variance?

22. What is flexible budget variable expense variance?

23. What are the two components of direct material variance, and how are they computed?

24. What is materials usage ratio?

25. What is direct labor variance and what are its components?

Cost Management: A Strategic Emphasis, 3e by Blocher/Chen/Cokins/Lin

Learning Objective 5: Assess the effects of contemporary manufacturing environment on operational control and standard costing.

26. What is the influence of the contemporary manufacturing environment on operational control and standard costing?

Learning Objective 6: Recognize behavioral implications in implementing standard cost systems.

27. What are the behavioral implications in implementing standard costs?

Learning Objective 7: Describe cost flows through general ledger accounts and prepare journal entries for the acquisition and uses of direct materials and direct labor in a standard cost system.

28. Briefly describe the cost flows and ledger entries in a standard costing system.

Suggested responses to the above questions:

1. What is effectiveness?

Effectiveness refers to attainment of the goal set for the operation.

2. Why are effective operations important?

Effective operations are essential for a successful strategy. Ineffective operations can lead to a disaster.

3. What is an efficient operation?

An efficient operation wastes no resources.

4. What is the operating income variance?

Operating income variance of a period is the difference between the actual operating income of the period and master budget operating income projected for the period.

5. What is a flexible budget?

The flexible budget is a budget that adjusts revenues and costs for changes in output achieved.

6. What is the flexible budget variance?

The flexible budget variance is the difference between the actual operating result and the flexible budget at the actual operating level of the period.

7. What are the major distinctions between the master budget and the flexible budget?

The master budget is always prepared before the period in question. It is for a single activity level, and is prepared for all aspects of an operation. On the other hand, the flexible budget may be prepared before, during, or after the period being analyzed. It may be for one or more levels of activity, and it is often prepared for selected aspects of an operation.

8. What is sales volume or activity variance?

The sales volume variance measures the effect of sales, expenses, or operating income of changes in units of sales.

9. What is the operating income flexible budget variance?

The operating income flexible budget variance is the difference between the flexible budget operating income and the actual operating income.

10. What is a standard?

A standard is the cost a firm expects to incur for an operation.

11. What is an ideal standard?

An ideal standard is a standard that demands perfect implementation and maximum efficiency in every aspect of the operation. It is not easily attainable and could discourage employees rather than serving as a motivating factor.

 Cost Management: A Strategic Emphasis, 3e by Blocher/Chen/Cokins/Lin

12. What is a currently attainable standard?

A currently attainable standard sets the performance criterion at a level that workers with proper training and experience can attain most of the time without extraordinary effort.

13. What kind of standards is a world-class firm likely to use?

A world-class firm can ill afford any inefficiency and, most likely, would use ideal standards for its operations, but the achievement of goals are often the function of using state of the art equipment and trained workers who operate those systems.

14. What are the sources that firms often use in determining appropriate standards?

A firm can use one or more of the following sources in determining standards:
- *activity analysis*
- *historical data*
- *benchmarking*
- *market expectation*
- *strategic decisions*

15. What is activity analysis?

Activity analysis is the process of identifying, delineating, and evaluating the activities required to complete a job, project, or operation.

16. What is the advantage of using benchmarks in setting standards?

Benchmarking has the advantage of using the best performance anywhere as the standard. Using such standards can help the firm to maintain a competitive edge in today's global competition.

17. What is a target cost that may also be used in setting standards?

Target costing for a product is the cost that will yield a desired profit margin for the product. It is computed as the difference between the sales price and the desired profit margin for the product.

18. What are the three facets of standard costs for direct materials?

The three facets of standard costs for direct materials are quality, quantity, and price.

19. What is a standard cost sheet?

A standard cost sheet specifies for a product the standard price and quantity of each manufacturing cost element for the production of one unit of the product.

20. What does flexible budget operating income variance include?

The operating income variance includes sales price variance, flexible budget variable expense variance, and fixed expense flexible budget variance.

21. What is the sales price variance?

The sales price variance is the difference between the total actual sales revenue of the period and the total flexible budget sales revenue for the units sold during the period. It is computed by taking the difference between actual selling price and budgeted selling price times actual units sold.

22. What is the flexible budget variable expense variance?

The flexible budget variable expense variance is the difference between the actual variable expenses incurred and the total standard variable expenses for the units sold. This variance includes direct materials variances, direct labor variances, variable overhead variances, and variable selling and administrative expenses variances. At this point and without additional information, they cannot be broken down into their price and efficiency components.

23. What are the two components of direct material variance, and how are they computed?

Direct material variances include material price variance and material usage variance. Price variance can be computed by taking the difference between actual price and flexible budget (standard) price times the actual quantity purchased (purchase price variance) or times the actual quantity used (material used price variance). Usage variance can be computed by taking the actual quantity used minus standard quantity (allowed quantity per unit times number of units produced) times standard prices. The former variance is an indicator of purchasing efficiency while the latter is an indicator of manufacturing efficiency.

24. What is the materials usage ratio?

Materials usage ratio is the ratio of quantity used over quantity purchased. A low ratio may be indicative of high stock levels.

Cost Management: A Strategic Emphasis, 3e by Blocher/Chen/Cokins/Lin

25. What is direct labor variance and what are its components?

Direct labor variance is the difference between actual direct labor cost and the flexible budget amount. It is composed of direct labor rate variance (LRV) and direct labor efficiency variance (LEV). LRV is computed by taking the difference between the actual and standard hourly wage rate multiplied by the actual direct labor hours used in production. LEV is the difference between the actual and standard direct labor hours for the units manufactured multiplied by the standard hourly wage rate.

26. What is the influence of the contemporary manufacturing environment on operational control and standard costing?

Computation of material price variance is less important. Most such companies enter into long-term contracts with reputable suppliers. Computation of labor efficiency variance in high tech firms with flexible manufacturing systems is also less significant. These firms attach little or no importance to labor rate and efficiency variances. These firms emphasize zero-defect and continuous improvement in quality. Considering the theory of constraint, the focus on improving overall efficiency of a firm lies in improving throughput time that relates to efficiency in bottleneck areas.

27. What are the behavioral implications in implementing standard costs?

The focus should be on influencing behavior through positive reinforcement. Unreasonable standards and expectations can make a good standard a failure.

28. Briefly describe the cost flows and ledger entries in a standard costing system.

Items purchased are debited to a raw materials inventory account at standard cost. The material purchased price variance is preferably recognized at the point of purchase. Standard usage (what should have been used for the products produced at standard rates) is charged to work in process. Any difference is charged to material usage variance. Labor is also charged to production at standard rates for what should have been used. Any difference in rate and efficiency is accumulated in LR and LE variance accounts. Units completed are transferred to finished goods inventory at standard cost. Units sold are cleared from finished goods inventory and charged to cost of goods sold - again at standard prices.

Multiple choice questions:

1. An effective organization
   a) wastes no resources
   b) attains the goals set for the operation.
   c) uses standard costs.
   d) has a large market share.
   e) all of the above.

2. Operating income variance for a period is the difference between
   a) the actual operating income and the master budget operating income for the period.
   b) the actual contribution margin and the projected contribution margin.
   c) the actual gross profit and the budgeted gross profit.
   d) the actual sales and the budgeted sales.
   e) none of the above.

3. The flexible budget is a budget that
   a) adjusts revenues and fixed costs for changes in output achieved.
   b) adjusts revenues and variable costs for changes in output achieved.
   c) adjusts revenues and all costs for changes in output achieved.
   d) adjusts fixed and variable costs for changes in output achieved.
   e) adjusts revenues only for changes in output achieved.

4. A flexible budget is prepared
   a) only before the subject period.
   b) for a single activity level.
   c) for selected aspects of operations.
   d) a and b
   e) a and c

5. A master budget is prepared
   a) only before the subject period.
   b) for a single activity level.
   c) selected aspects of operations.
   d) a and b
   e) a and c

6. The sales volume variance
   a) measures the effect on sales of changes in units of sales.
   b) measures the effect on expenses of changes in units of sales.
   c) measures the effect on operating income of changes in units of sales.
   d) all of the above.
   e) none of the above.

Cost Management: A Strategic Emphasis, 3e by Blocher/Chen/Cokins/Lin

7. Flexible budget variance
   a) measures the effect on sales of changes in sales prices.
   b) measures the effect on expenses of changes in cost prices.
   c) measures the effect on operating income as a result of changes in sales prices and/or cost prices.
   d) all of the above.
   e) none of the above.

8. A standard cost
   a) is the cost a firm expects to incur for an operation.
   b) is same as budgeted cost.
   c) is same as flexible budget.
   d) is same as actual cost.
   e) a and c.

9. A currently attainable standard is a standard that
   a) demand perfect implementation and maximum efficiency in every aspect of the operation.
   b) is expected to be achieved within a 3 to 5-year time span.
   c) sets the performance criterion at a level that workers with proper training and experience can attain most of the time without extraordinary effort.
   d) is same as actual cost.
   e) none of the above.

10. A world class firm often uses
    a) currently attainable standards.
    b) achievable standards.
    c) ideal standards.
    d) negotiable standards.
    e) none of the above.

11. It can be said that managers generally
    a) manage costs.
    b) manage activities.
    c) manage expenses.
    d) manage revenues.
    e) manage profits.

12. A firm can use this (these) source(s) in determining standards:
    a) activity analysis.
    b) historical data.
    c) benchmarking.
    d) market expectations or strategic decisions.
    e) all of the above.

13. Target cost for a product is
    a) the difference between the sales price and the desired profit margin of the product.
    b) the difference between the sales price and the desired cost of the product.
    c) the difference between the desired cost and the desired profit for the product.
    d) the difference between the budgeted cost and the standard cost of the product.
    e) the difference between the standard cost and the actual cost of the product.

14. Standard-setting procedure
    a) is always participative.
    b) is always authoritative.
    c) is neither participative or authoritative.
    d) is either participative or authoritative.
    e) none of the above.

15. The facets of standard costs for materials are
    a) quality and price.
    b) quantity and price.
    c) quality and quantity.
    d) quality, quantity, and price.
    e) quality, quantity, vendor reputation, and price.

16. In contemporary manufacturing environment, there is
    a) more emphasis on material purchase price and usage variances.
    b) more emphasis on direct labor rate and efficiency variances.
    c) more emphasis on quality products and customer satisfaction.
    d) more emphasis on throughput efficiency.
    e) c and d.

Exercises:

E1.

Navid Furniture manufacturing uses 9 yards of fabric A in manufacture of its sofas and 5.5 yards of fabric B in manufacture of its love seats. The budgeted prices are $16 per yard for A and $12 per yard for B. For the month of May 2002, 3,200 yards of A and 2,400 yards of B were purchased for $79,200. From this amount $52,800 was for fabric A. A total of 310 sofas and 340 love seats were manufactured in this time period. The actual usage amounted to 3,050 yards of A and 1,900 yards of B.

Required:
a) **Compute material purchase price variance for A and B.**
b) **Compute material usage variance for A and B.**
c) **Recompute material price variance assuming that price variance is determined at the point of usage.**
d) **Prepare journal entries based on a and b above.**

E2.

Nahid Lamp Company uses two grades of labor. Grade one is budgeted at $8 an hour and grade 2 is budgeted at $11 an hour. Each lamp requires 1.5 hours of grade 1 labor and .8 hours of grade 2. A total of 685 lamps were produced in November 2002. Grade 1 labor for the period amounted to 1,100 hours, and 560 hours of grade 2 labor were used. Total payroll for wage employees amounted to $15,400. $13,850 of this amount is for direct labor, and from this total, $8,250 is for grade 1 labor.

Required:

a) **Computer labor efficiency variance for grade 1 and 2 labor.**
b) **Computer labor rate variance for grade 1 and 2 labor.**
c) **Prepare journal entries base on a and b above.**

E3.

Jamshid Ceramics has sold 1200 fancy jars at $29 a piece for the month of October 2002. These items actually cost the firm $21 a piece. The original budget was set at 1000 units at $31 a piece with a forecasted cost of $19.5 per unit. The only other cost was fixed selling expense of $2,900 that was budgeted at $2,650.

Required:

a) **Prepare an income statement with columns for actual, flexible budget and master budget.**
b) **Compute activity variance in terms of sales, costs, and operating income.**
c) **Compute flexible budget variance in terms of sales, costs, and operating income.**
d) **Reconcile the total operating income variance and summarize your work in one Table.**

E4.

Search the internet for any financial or marketing information on Mercedes Benz, Toyota, and Honda vehicles. Discuss why invariably the products of these firms have been used by other car manufacturers as benchmarks for their production and standard costing systems.

Correct answers to multiple choice questions:
1-b; 2-a; 3-b; 4-c; 5-d; 6-d; 7-d; 8-a; 9-c; 10-c; 11-b; 12-e; 13-a; 14-d; 15-d; 16-e.

Suggested answers to exercises:

E1.

a) Material purchase price variance:		
MPPV (A)	52,800 - (3,200 * 16)	1,600 U
MPPV (B): 79200 - 52800 = 26400	26,400 – (2,400 * 12)	2,400 F
TOTAL MPPV		800 F
b) Material usage variance:		
MUV (A)	(3,050 – [310 * 9]) * 16	4,160 U
MUV (B)	(1,900 – [340 * 5.5]) * 12	360U
TOTAL MUV		4,520 U
c) Material price variance:		
MPV (A) : 52800 / 3200 = 16.5	(16.50 - 16) * 3,050	1,525 U
MPV (B) : 26400 / 2400 = 11	(11 - 12) * 1,900	1,900 F
TOTAL MPV		375 F

Note: It is preferable to compute material price variance at the point of purchase rather than at the point of usage. The reason is that in this manner differences between purchase price and estimated price are immediately identified for management's information or action. In addition, inventory would be maintained at standard cost which will be easier to maintain and keep track of.

d) Journal entries:

Raw material inventory	80,000	
MPPV (A)	1,600	
Accounts payable		79,200
MPPV (B)		2,400
Work in process	67,080	
MUV (A)	4,160	
MUV (B)	360	
Raw material inventory		71,600

Cost Management: A Strategic Emphasis, 3e by Blocher/Chen/Cokins/Lin

E2.

a) Labor efficiency variance:		
LEV (1)	(1,100 – [685 * 1.5]) * 8	580 U
LEV(2)	(560 – [685 * .80]) * 11	132 U
TOTAL LEV		712 U
b) Labor rate variance:		
LRV (1)	(8,250 – [1,100 * 8])	550 F
LRV (2): 13850 - 8250 = 5600	(5,600 – [560 * 11])	560 F
TOTAL LRV		1110 F
Total labor variance:		
LV (1)	(8,250 – [685 * 1.5 * 8])	30 U
LV (2)	(5,600 – [685 * .80 * 11])	428 F
Total labor variance		398 F

c) Journal entries:

Payroll summary	15,400	
Wages payable, etc.		15,400
Administration Expense	1,550	
Work in process	14,248	
LEV 1	580	
LEV 2	132	
LRV 1		550
LRV 2		560
Payroll summary		15,400

E3.
a) income statement; b) activity variance, c) flexible budget variance

Item	Actual	Flexible B	Master B.	Activity V	F. B. Var.
Sales in units	1,200	1,200	1,000	200	
Price	29	31	31	31	
Sales revenue	34,800	37,200	31,000	6,200	(2,400)
Cost of sales, 21, 19.5	25,200	23,400	19,500	3,900	1,800
Gross profit	9,600	13,800	11,500	2,300	(4,200)
Selling expense	2,900	2,650	2,650	-	250
Income	6,700	11,150	8,850	2,300	(4,450)

d) Income reconciliation:

Budgeted income	8,850
+ Activity variance	2,300
- Flexible budget variance	- 4,450
= Actual income	6,700

Cost Management: A Strategic Emphasis, 3e by Blocher/Chen/Cokins/Lin

CHAPTER 14
STANDARD COSTING: FACTORY OVERHEAD

Highlights:

Total factory overhead variance is the difference between the total actual variable factory overhead cost and the total standard variable factory overhead for the number of units manufactured. Variable factory overhead variance can be divided into variable overhead efficiency variance (OEV) and variable overhead spending variance (OSV). OEV is the difference between the standard variable factory overhead for the actual quantity of the cost drivers for applying variable factory overhead and the standard variable factory overhead for the output of the period. OSV is the difference between actual variable overhead and standard variable overhead for the actual level of cost drivers. Because of imperfect association between the cost driver or drivers for applying overhead and the variable factory overhead costs, a variable factory overhead spending variance may include both price and usage variances, while OEV may not measure efficiency in the usage of variable factory overhead items, but merely efficiency in the use of cost drivers.

The fixed overhead application rate is determined by dividing the quantity of the cost driver at the denominator activity level into the budgeted total fixed factory overhead. Fixed factory overhead variances include the fixed overhead spending (budget) variance (FOSV) and the fixed overhead production volume variance (FOVV). FOSV is the difference between the actual and the budgeted fixed factory overhead for the period. Neither the actual units produced nor the actual level of the cost driver incurred during the period has any effect on the amount of the fixed factory overhead spending variance. FOVV is the difference between the budgeted fixed overhead and the total fixed overhead applied to the units manufactured during the period. The difference between the actual and the applied fixed factory overhead is referred to as underapplied or overapplied fixed factory overhead.

Fixed and variable factory overhead can also be viewed in a 2-way or 3-way format. The three-way variance creates a factory overhead spending variance by combining VOSV and FOSV into one variance. VOEV and FOVV remain intact. The two-way variance further combines OSV with VOEV. This combined variance is the factory overhead flexible budget variance.

A firm can dispose of variances in the income statement of the period in which the variance is incurred by charging them to the cost of goods sold of the period. Alternatively, the firm can prorate the variance among the cost of goods sold and ending inventories.

Service firms and other types of operations can also benefit from using standard costing systems. Service organizations are different significantly from manufacturing entities because of absence of WIP and finished goods inventory, labor intensive operations, and high level of fixed costs. Accounting for output measures is also more difficult in service organizations.

Firms in new manufacturing environments no longer use a single cost driver to measure and apply overhead. Increasing number of firms are using ideal, rather than, currently attainable standards. To be globally competitive, many firms mandate continual improvement and strive for perfection. Also, not all variances are calculated. The theory of constraints points out that the denominator activity level should be set at the level of the bottleneck activity of the operation.

Whether to conduct further investigation of variances depends on the type of standard the firm uses, the expectations of the firm, the magnitude and impact of the variances, and the causes and controllability of variances. Variance investigation may be done through the use of a payoff table to assess the cost and benefits associated with investigating or not investigating. Where benefits outweigh costs, variances need to be investigated.

Questions:

Learning Objective 1: Establish proper standard costs for variable overhead.

1. What are the steps involved in establishing the standard variable factory overhead?

2. What are the behavioral patterns of variable factory overhead?

3. How do we select cost drivers for applying variable factory overhead?

Learning Objective 2: Calculate and interpret a variable overhead flexible budget variance, spending variance, and efficiency variance.

4. What is the total variable factory overhead variance?

Cost Management: A Strategic Emphasis, 3e by Blocher/Chen/Cokins/Lin

5. What is the variable factory overhead spending variance?

6. What is the factory overhead efficiency variance?

7. What are the differences between variable factory overhead variances and direct materials and direct labor variances?

8. How can we interpret variable overhead spending variance?

9. How can we interpret variable factory overhead efficiency variance?

Learning Objective 3: Compute and interpret fixed factory overhead variances.

10. Is there a cost driver for applying fixed factory overhead?

11. What is fixed factory overhead application rate?

12. What are the steps in determining a fixed factory overhead rate?

Learning Objective 4: Use two-way and three-way variance procedures to analyze and interpret fixed factory overhead variances.

---

13. What is the fixed factory overhead spending variance?

14. What is fixed factory production volume variance?

15. How can we interpret fixed overhead spending variance?

16. How can we interpret fixed overhead volume variance?

17. What is a three-way analysis of factory overhead variances?

18. When would combining of VOSV and FOSV be necessary?

19. What is the two-way analysis of factory overhead variances?

*Cost Management: A Strategic Emphasis, 3*e by Blocher/Chen/Cokins/Lin

Learning Objective 5: Dispose of variances through financial accounting system.

20. How are variances disposed of in the financial statements?

21. When would prorating of variances be appropriate and when would it be inappropriate?

Learning Objective 6: Apply standard costs to service organizations.

22. What are the main characteristics of service organizations?

Learning Objective 7: Analyze and explain variances in an activity-based standard costing system.

23. How would variance analysis be different in an activity-based costing environment?

Learning Objective 8: Describe the effects of new manufacturing technologies and changes in operating environments on standard costing systems.

24. Discuss the effect of the new manufacturing environment on flexible budgeting?

Learning Objective 9: Determine whether to further investigate variances.

25. When should a variance be investigated? When does a variance not need be investigated?

26. What are the causes of variances?

27. What is a prediction error?

28. What is a modeling error?

29. What is a measurement error?

29. What is an implementation error?

30. What is a statistical control chart?

Suggested responses to the above questions:

1. What are the steps involved in establishing the standard variable factory overhead?

- *Determining the behavioral patterns of variable factory overhead costs,*
- *Selecting one or more appropriate cost drivers for applying variable factory overhead to cost objects (such as, products, services, or divisions).*
- *Ascertaining the intended level of operation and estimating the total variable factory overhead and the corresponding total of the cost driver, and*
- *Computing the standard variable factory overhead rate.*

2. What are the behavioral patterns of variable factory overhead?

The standard variable factory overhead for a manufacturing firm is a function of both the number of units to be manufactured and other activities of the manufacturing process. Use of proper cost drivers is very important.

3. How do we select cost drivers for applying variable factory overhead?

Using a single cost driver such as direct labor hours for applying variable factory overhead is satisfactory as long as the total variable factory overhead relates to the selected cost driver. An activity-based cost driver applies factory overhead to products or services according to the activity level of manufacturing operations. Activities that change the amount of factory overhead may be unit-based, batch-based, product-based, and facility-based. Unit-based cost drivers include machine hours, direct labor hours, and units of materials. Batch-based cost drivers include the number of times materials and parts are moved during manufacturing, number of set-ups, number of times materials and parts are received and inspected. Product-based cost drivers include number of products, number of processes, and number of schedule changes. Facility-based cost drivers relate mostly with the size of operations, not with production activities.

4. What is the total variable factory overhead variance?

Total variable factory overhead variance is the difference between total actual variable factory overhead incurred and total standard variable factory overhead for the output of the period. This is also referred to as flexible budget variance.

5. What is the variable factory overhead spending variance?

VOSV is the difference between variable factory overhead incurred and total standard variable factory overhead based on the actual quantity of the cost driver to apply the overhead.

6. What is the factory overhead efficiency variance?

VOEV is the difference between the total standard variable factory overhead for the actual quantity of the substitute cost driver for applying variable factory overhead and the total standard variable factory overhead cost for the units manufactured during the period.

7. What are the differences between variable factory overhead variances and direct materials and direct labor variances?

In addition to varying with volume, the total variable factory overhead cost also varies with activities that change categorically or at intervals such as the number of production runs, number of batches, and type of product. Second, firms use a single cost driver such as pounds of materials or hours of direct labor to assign direct materials or direct labor costs to cost objects. In contrast, a firm may use two or more cost drivers to assign factory overhead costs because of the many different overhead activities involved.

8. How can we interpret variable overhead spending variance?

VOSV reflects the effects of deviations in prices and, in many instances, quantity differences as well.

9. How can we interpret variable factory overhead efficiency variance?

VOEV reflects the effect of deviation in quantities only if the cost driver for applying the overhead is a perfect surrogate for the unknown actual cost drivers for the overhead.

10. Is there a cost driver for applying fixed factory overhead?

Because the total fixed factory overhead does not vary with changes in the activity level, there is in effect no activity measure for fixed factory overhead during the period. Although an application rate is used for allocation of fixed overhead charges.

11. What is fixed factory overhead application rate?

A fixed factory overhead application rate is the rate at which the firm applies fixed overhead costs to cost objects.

12. What are the steps in determining a fixed factory overhead rate?

- *Determine the total budgeted fixed factory overhead for the period.*
- *Select a cost driver for applying fixed factory overhead.*
- *Calculate the denominator quantity for the selected cost driver.*
- *Compute the fixed factory overhead application rate by dividing the calculated quantity into the total budgeted fixed factory overhead for the period.*

13. What is the fixed factory overhead spending variance?

FOSV is the difference between the actual amount incurred and the budgeted allowance for the fixed factory overhead.

14. What is fixed factory production volume variance?

FOVV of a period is the difference between the budget allowance for fixed factory overhead for the period and the amount of the fixed factory overhead applied to the operations of the period. FOVV may also be viewed as a measure of facility or capacity utilization.

15. How can we interpret fixed overhead spending variance?

Factors contributing to FOSV include:
- *ineffective budget procedures*
- *inadequate control of costs*
- *misclassification of cost items*

16. How can we interpret fixed overhead volume variance?

Factors contributing to FOVV include:
- *management decisions*
- *an unexpected change in market demand*
- *unforeseen problems in manufacturing operations.*

17. What is a three-way analysis of factory overhead variances?

The 3-way analysis separates the differences between the total factory overhead incurred and standard factory overhead costs applied to the operations of the period for both variable and fixed factory overheads into three variances: OSV, VOEV, FOVV. Notice that variable and fixed spending variances are combined?

18. When would combining of VOSV and FOSV be necessary?

Combining of these variances is necessary when variable and fixed overhead accounts are not separated in the chart of accounts and their separation is not economically feasible.

19. What is the two-way analysis of factory overhead variances?

A two-way analysis of factory overhead variances analyzes the difference between the total factory overhead incurred and the total factory overhead applied into two variances: factory overhead flexible budget variance, and factory overhead production volume variance.

20. How are variances disposed of in the financial statements?

There are two ways of disposing of variances - either directly to the period's cost of sales or its proration between cost of sales and inventory balances. Proration of the variance can be in proportion to the balances in raw materials inventory, finished goods inventory, and cost of goods sold account or preferably among the overhead portion of these accounts.

21. When would proration of variances be appropriate and when would it be inappropriate?

Proration of variances would be appropriate if the variances are caused due to inappropriate standards or bookkeeping errors. Proration of variances would be inappropriate if the variances are caused due to operational inefficiencies. In the latter case, direct write off to cost of sales would be more appropriate.

22. What are the main characteristics of service organizations?

Among distinguishing characteristics of service organizations are absence of output inventory, labor-intensive products, the predominance of fixed costs, and lack of uniform measures of output. Service outputs cannot be stored for use in a future period, and service outputs cannot be generated before they are needed. A service organization often uses alternative measures other than units of their outputs as gauges for the amount of their outputs.

23. How would variance analysis be different in an activity-based costing environment?

When using activity-based costing, multiple measures with varying cost drivers are used to determine product or service costs. Recent advances in activity-based costing have led many firms to measure and monitor different overheads based on activities that drive overheads. These firms also use several activity measures in preparing flexible budgets. The budgeted total factory overhead no longer varies with changes of a single activity; instead it uses different activities for different factory overheads. Accordingly, we could have variances for unit-level, batch-level, product-level, and facility-level costs.

24. Discuss the effect of the new manufacturing environment on flexible budgeting?

- *Many firms in the new manufacturing environments no longer use a single cost driver. Recent advances in activity-based costing lead many firms to measure and monitor overheads based on activities that drive overhead costs.*
- *In this environment, many firms choose not to calculate and report variances such as, direct material price, direct material usage, direct labor efficiency, and overhead spending variances.*
- *Overhead flexible budget variances are calculated in more detail with the use of activity-based costing.*

The capacity of the equipment or division that is the "bottleneck" of the manufacturing process is used as the denominator activity level in computation of volume variance. Otherwise, there would be inducement for excess production of non-bottleneck areas which would pile up as long as there are bottlenecks in the system. Note that the production volume variance should never be calculated for performance evaluation purposes because volume variance has nothing to do with efficiency or price variations.

25. When should a variance be investigated? When does a variance not need be investigated?

If the standard set is at the currently attainable level, significant variations should be investigated. Investigation of variances also depends on the level of management's expectations from its employees. Experience is also a factor. A firm in its early stages of using standards may not be alarmed by small deviations.

If the standard set is an ideal standard, significant variances do not need investigation as long as the firm shows consistent progress. The degree to which an organization can control a variance determines whether corrective actions are needed or not.

25. What are the causes of variances?

Causes of variances can be classified into random and systematic variances. Systematic variances can be further classified into four subcategories: prediction, modeling, measurement, and implementation. Random variances are beyond the control of management. Systematic variances are persistent and most likely recur unless corrected.

26. What is a prediction error?

A prediction error is a deviation from standard because of an inaccurate estimation of the amounts of variables used in the standard-setting process.

27. What is a modeling error?

A modeling error is a deviation from standard because of failure to include one or more important relevant variables or inclusion of wrong or irrelevant variables in the standard-setting process.

28. What is a measurement error?

Measurement errors are incorrect numbers caused by improper or inaccurate accounting systems or procedures.

29. What is an implementation error?

An implementation error is a deviation from the standard that occurs during operations as a result of operators' errors.

30. What is a statistical control chart?

A statistical control chart helps managers identify out-of-control variances over time. Variances within the limits are deemed random variances and no further action is needed unless a pattern emerges.

Multiple choice questions:
1. Establishing standard cost for variable factory overhead involves all the following steps **except,**
   a) determining the behavioral patterns of variable factory overhead costs,
   b) selecting one or more appropriate cost drivers for applying variable factory overhead to cost objects,
   c) ascertaining the appropriate level of operation and estimating the total variable factory overhead and the corresponding total of the cost driver,
   d) determining the periodic level of depreciation and supervision costs,
   e) computing the standard variable factory overhead rate.

2. Cooper identifies activities that change the amount of factory overhead to be the following **except,**
   a) unit-based,
   b) batch-based,
   c) product-based,
   d) management-based,
   e) facility-based.

Cost Management: A Strategic Emphasis, 3e by Blocher/Chen/Cokins/Lin

3. Total variable factory overhead variance is the difference between
   a) total actual variable overhead incurred and total budgeted variable factory overhead.
   b) total actual variable overhead and total standard variable factory overhead.
   c) total budgeted variable factory overhead and total variable factory overhead applied.
   d) total actual variable factory overhead and total standard variable overhead for actual units of activity utilized.
   e) total standard variable overhead for units of activity utilized and standard variable factory overhead.

4. Total variable factory overhead spending variance is the difference between,
   a) total actual variable overhead incurred and total budgeted variable factory overhead.
   b) total actual variable overhead and total standard variable factory overhead.
   c) total budgeted variable factory overhead and total variable factory overhead applied.
   d) total actual variable factory overhead and total standard variable overhead for actual units of input.
   e) total standard variable overhead for units of activity utilized and total standard variable factory overhead.

5. Total variable factory overhead efficiency variance is the difference between,
   a) total actual variable overhead incurred and total budgeted variable factory overhead.
   b) total actual variable overhead and total standard variable factory overhead.
   c) total budgeted variable factory overhead and total variable factory overhead applied.
   d) total actual variable factory overhead and total standard variable overhead for actual units of activity utilized.
   e) total standard variable overhead for units of activity utilized and total standard variable factory overhead allowed for units of output.

6. A variable factory overhead spending variance reflects the effect of deviations in
   a) price only.
   b) quantity only
   c) price and, in many instances, quantity differences as well.
   d) quantity and, in many instances, price differences as well.
   e) none of the above.

7. A variable factory overhead efficiency variance, when the cost driver for applying the overhead is a good surrogate for the actual cost drivers for overhead, reflects the effects of deviations in
   a) price only.
   b) quantity only.
   c) price and, in many instances, quantity differences as well.
   d) quantity and, in many instances, price differences as well.
   e) none of the above.

8. Many firms establish a standard cost for fixed factory overhead because of
   a) the GAAP requirements
   b) the mandate to include fixed factory overhead in pricing for federal government contracts.
   c) the belief that using a standard cost system for fixed factory overhead allows them to determine whether their operations incur fixed factory overhead as expected.
   d) all of the above
   e) a and b

9. The steps in determining a fixed factory overhead rate includes the following **except**,
   a) determining the behavioral patterns of fixed factory overhead.
   b) determining the total budgeted fixed factory overhead for the period.
   c) selecting a cost driver for applying fixed factory overhead.
   d) calculating the denominator quantity for the selected cost driver.
   e) computing the fixed factory overhead application rate.

10. The fixed overhead spending variance is the difference between
    a) the actual amount incurred and the budgeted allowance for fixed factory overhead.
    b) the actual amount incurred and the total standard fixed factory overhead.
    c) the budgeted allowance for fixed factory overhead and the total standard fixed factory overhead.
    d) the total standard overhead and the total standard fixed overhead.
    e) none of the above.

11. The fixed overhead volume variance is the difference between,
    a) the actual amount incurred and the budgeted allowance for fixed factory overhead.
    b) the actual amount incurred and the total standard fixed factory overhead.
    c) the budgeted allowance for fixed factory overhead and the total standard fixed factory overhead for the quantity produced.
    d) the total standard overhead and the total standard fixed overhead.
    e) none of the above.

Cost Management: A Strategic Emphasis, 3e by Blocher/Chen/Cokins/Lin

12. The fixed overhead total variance is the difference between,
   a) the actual amount incurred and the budgeted allowance for fixed factory overhead.
   b) the actual amount of fixed overhead and the total standard fixed factory overhead.
   c) the budgeted allowance for fixed factory overhead and the total standard fixed factory overhead.
   d) the total standard overhead and the total standard fixed overhead.
   e) none of the above.

13. Reasons for fixed factory overhead production volume variance are the following **except**,
   a) unanticipated fluctuations in fixed costs such as salaries or property taxes.
   b) management decisions.
   c) unexpected change in market demand.
   d) machine breakdown resulting to less output.
   e) shortage of labor or material leading to less production.

14. The three-way analysis of factory overhead variances combines,
   a) the variable overhead spending variance and fixed overhead spending variance.
   b) the variable overhead spending variance and the variable overhead efficiency variance.
   c) the variable overhead spending variance and the fixed overhead volume variance.
   d) the fixed overhead spending variance and the fixed overhead volume variance.
   e) none of the above.

15. The two-way analysis of factory overhead combines,
   a) the variable overhead spending variance and fixed overhead spending and volume variances.
   b) the variable and fixed overhead spending and variable overhead efficiency variances.
   c) the variable spending and fixed overhead efficiency and volume variances.
   d) the variable and fixed spending variance and fixed overhead efficiency variance.
   e) none of the above.

16. The overhead variances that are often not computed in the new manufacturing environment are
   a) direct material price and efficiency and direct labor price and efficiency variances.
   b) direct material price and efficiency, direct labor efficiency, and overhead spending variances.
   c) direct material, direct labor, and overhead spending variances.
   d) direct material, direct labor, and overhead efficiency variances.
   e) fixed overhead spending, variable overhead spending and efficiency variances.

17. Whether to investigate or not to investigate depends on
    a) the type of standard used.
    b) the expectation of the firm.
    c) the magnitude and impact of a variance.
    d) causes of variance and its controllability.
    e) all of the above.

18. A prediction error is
    a) a deviation from the standard that occurs during operations as a result of operator's errors.
    b) an incorrect number(s) caused by improper or inaccurate accounting systems or procedures.
    c) a deviation from standard because of failure to include one or more important relevant variables or inclusion of wrong or irrelevant variables in the standard-setting process.
    d) a deviation from standard because of an inaccurate estimation of the amounts of variables used in the standard-setting process.
    e) none of the above.

19. A modeling error is
    a) a deviation from the standard that occurs during operations as a result of operator's errors.
    b) an incorrect number(s) caused by improper or inaccurate accounting systems or procedures.
    c) deviation from standard because of failure to include one or more important relevant variables or inclusion of wrong or irrelevant variables in the standard-setting process.
    d) deviation from standard because of an inaccurate estimation of the amounts of variables used in the standard-setting process.
    e) none of the above.

20. A measurement error is
    a) a deviation from the standard that occurs during operations as a result of operator's errors.
    b) an incorrect number(s) caused by improper or inaccurate accounting systems or procedures.
    c) deviation from standard because of failure to include one or more important relevant variables or inclusion of wrong or irrelevant variables in the standard-setting process.
    d) deviation from standard because of an inaccurate estimation of the amounts of variables used in the standard-setting process.
    e) none of the above.

*Cost Management: A Strategic Emphasis, 3*e by Blocher/Chen/Cokins/Lin

21. An implementation error is
   a) a deviation from the standard that occurs during operations as a result of operator's errors.
   b) an incorrect number(s) caused by improper or inaccurate accounting systems or procedures.
   c) deviation from standard because of failure to include one or more important relevant variables or inclusion of wrong or irrelevant variables in the standard-setting process.
   d) deviation from standard because of an inaccurate estimation of the amounts of variables used in the standard-setting process.
   e) none of the above.

Exercises:

E1.

Arman Orthopedics Company manufactures two models of wheel chairs. Product A requires material per unit of $115 and direct labor per unit of $44. Product B requires material of $197 and labor of $86 per unit. Each unit of A requires 3 machine hours while B requires 4 machine hours. The forecasted output for the year is 1200 units of A and 1800 units of B. Labor related variable overhead amounts to $83,040 while machine related overhead amounts to $248,400. Fixed overhead amounts to $140,040. Fixed overhead rate is computed as a percentage of total prime cost.

Required:
a) Determine variable and fixed overhead rates.
b) Prepare the forecasted manufacturing budget for the period.
c) Compute standard cost per unit of A and B.

E2.

Arman Cabinet Shop had total budgeted variable overhead of $220,000. Actual variable overhead for the period also amounted to $220,000. The overhead is based on direct labor hours. Other data on the two types of cabinets, M and N, follows:

	M	N
Budgeted hours per unit	12	16
Budgeted production	100	200 units
Actual hours per unit	13	18
Actual number of units	140	160

Required:
a) Determined the budgeted overhead rate.
b) Compute the amount of overhead applied.
c) Compute standard overhead per unit of M and N.
d) Compute VOSV, VOEV, and TVOV.

E3.

Jennifer Pen Company produces regular and deluxe pens. Budgeted fixed overhead amounts to $41,440. Actual fixed overhead amounts to $52,500. Other data follows:

Item	Regular	Deluxe
Budgeted machine hours per unit	.20	.30
Budgeted number of units	3,800	2,400
Actual number of units produced	3,900	2,900

Required:

a) Compute the amount of fixed overhead applied.

b) Compute FOSV, FOVV, FOTV.

E4.

Trish Umbrella Factory makes umbrellas. Other data follows:

	Actual	Budget
Variable overhead	$49,000	$
Fixed overhead	115,500	121,600
Output	41,000	38,000
Labor cost per unit	.70	.80
Overhead % of DL		160%

Required:

a) Prepare a 3-way analysis of overhead.

b) Prepare a 2-way analysis of overhead.

E5.

Factory overhead variances and other account balances for Saba Electronics as of 12/31/1998 were as follows:

VOSV	22,000F
VOEV	32,000U
FOSV	41,000U
FOVV	39,000U

WIP Inventory	199,500	Note: this balance includes $29,000 of overhead.
FG Inventory	248,700	Note: this balance includes $34,800 of overhead.
Cost of goods sold	1,494,900	Note: this balance includes $251,000 of overhead.

Required:

a) Prepare journal entries to close the above variances if variances are closed to cost of goods sold.

Cost Management: A Strategic Emphasis, 3e by Blocher/Chen/Cokins/Lin

b) Prepare journal entries to close the above variances if variances are prorated between cost of sales and inventory accounts.

c) Prepare journal entries to close the above variances if variances are prorated between in proportion to the overhead portion of cost of sales and inventory accounts.

E6.
Search the internet for cost information on Dell or IBM microcomputers, see if you can determine cost figures for these companies major product lines and determine if they use standard costing.

Correct answers to multiple choice questions:
1-d; 2-d; 3-b; 4-d; 5-e; 6-c; 7-b; 8-d; 9-a; 10-a; 11-c; 12-b; 13-a; 14-a; 15-b; 16-b; 17-e; 18-d; 19-c; 20-b; 21-a

Suggested answers to exercises:
E1.
a) Labor related variable overhead rate:

Direct labor cost:	$(44 \times 1{,}200) + (86 \times 1{,}800) = 207{,}600$
Labor related variable overhead rate:	$83{,}040 / 207{,}600 = 40\%$

Machine related variable overhead rate:	
Machine hours	$1200 \times 3 + 1800 \times 4 = 10{,}800$
Machine related variable overhead rate:	$248{,}400 / 10{,}800 = \$23$

Fixed overhead rate:	
Prime costs:	$[(115 + 44) * 1200] + [(197 + 86) * 1800] = 700{,}200$
Fixed overhead rate:	$140{,}040 / 700{,}200 = 20\%$

b) Budget:

Item	Product A	Product B	Total $	
Direct Materials	138,000	354,600	492,600	
Direct Labor	52,800	154,800	207,600	
Variable overhead (labor based)	21,120	61,920	83,040	40% of DL
Variable overhead (machine based)	82,800	165,600	248,400	$23 per hr
Fixed overhead	38,160	101,880	140,040	
Total	332,880	838,800	1,171,680	

c) Standard cost per unit

Item	Product A	Product B
Material	115	197
Labor	44	86
Labor related variable overhead	17.60	34.40
Machine related variable overhead	69.00	92.00
Fixed overhead	31.80	56.60
Total standard cost per unit	277.40	466.00

E2.

a) Variable overhead rate:

Direct labor hours: $(12 \times 100) + (16 \times 200) = 4,400$

Variable overhead rate: $220,000 / 4,400 = \$50$ an hour of DL

b) Variable overhead applied:

Standard hours in output $(12 \times 140) + (16 \times 160) = 4,240$

Variable overhead applied $4,240 \times 50 = \$212,000$

c) Overhead per unit:

Overhead per unit of M: $12 \times 50 = \$600$

Overhead per unit of N: $16 \times 50 = 800$

d) Overhead variances:

VOSV: $220,000 - [(140 \times 13 \times 50) + (160 \times 18 \times 50)] = 15,000F$

VOEV: $235,000 - [(140 \times 12 \times 50) + (160 \times 16 \times 50)] = 23,000U$

Total VOV: $220,000 - 212,000 = 8,000\ U$

E3.

a) Fixed overhead applied:

Budgeted fixed overhead per hour: $41,440 / [(3,800 \times .2) + (2,400 \times .3)] = \$28$ per hour

Fixed overhead applied: $[(3,900 \times .2) + (2,900 \times .3)] * 28 = \$46,200$

b) Variances:

FOSV $52,500 - 41,440 = 11,060\ U$

FOVV $41,440 - 46,200 = 4,760\ F$

Total FOV $52,500 - 46,200 = 6,300\ U$

<u>E4.</u>
a) 3-way variance analysis:

Overhead spending variance:

	Actual	**Standard**
Variable overhead	49,000	45,920 : (41,000 x .70 x 1.60)
Fixed overhead	<u>111,500</u>	<u>121,600</u> (Note: use budgeted fixed costs here)
Total	160,500	167,520

Overhead spending variance: 160,500 - 167,520 = 7,020 F

Overhead efficiency variance:
$$(41,000 \times .7 \times 1.60) - (41,000 \times .8 \times 1.60) = 45,920 - 52,480 = 6,560 \text{ F}$$

Overhead volume variance: 121,600 - (41,000 x 3.2) = 9600 F
Note: FOH per unit - 121,600 / 38,000 = 3.2

b) 2-way variance analysis:
Flexible budget overhead variance: 160,500 - (52,480 + 121,600) = 13,580 F

Overhead volume variance: 121,600 - 131,200 = 9,600 F

5. a) Write off of variances to cost of goods sold:

Cost of goods sold	90,000	
VOSV	22,000	
VOEV		32,000
FOSV		41,000
FOVV		39,000

b) Write off of variances prorated to inventory and cost of goods sold based on their balances:

Item	Amount	Percent	Prorate
WIP	199,500	10.27	9240.39
FG INV.	248,700	12.80	11519.22186
CGS	1,494,900	76.93	69240.38907
TOTAL	1,943,100	100.00	90000.00

Results rounded:

WIP	9,240		
FG INV.	11,519		
CGS	69,241		
VOSV	22,000		
VOEV		32,000	
FOSV		41,000	
FOVV		39,000	

c) Write off of variances to WIP, FG, and CGS prorated based on the overhead component of these accounts.

The preferred way of proration of overhead to the above accounts is to base the allocation on the overhead portion of these accounts. The student is encouraged to redo this section based on the suggested proration figures. Answers are not provided for this question.

CHAPTER 15
PRODUCTIVITY, MARKETING EFFECTIVENESS, AND STRATEGIC PROFITABILITY ANALYSIS

Highlights:

To manage markets effectively, management needs to be fully informed of the effects of changes in selling prices, sales volume, sales mix, market size, and market share on operations and the strategy of the firm. The effects of these changes on operating results need to be monitored so that management can take appropriate action at the earliest time.

Sales variance can be broken down into sales price variance (SPV) and sales volume variance. SPV is the difference between budgeted and actual selling prices times actual quantity of the item sold. The sales volume variance (SVV) accounts for the difference in contribution margins or operating incomes between the flexible budget amount and the master (static) budget. SVV of firms with multiple products need to be further analyzed into sales mix (SMV) and sales quantity variances (SQV). SMV is due to 1) the difference between the actual sales mix and the budgeted sales mix at budgeted contribution margin, with sales mix defined as the ratio of units of the product to the total units of all products, 2) the total units of all products sold during the period, and 3) the standard contribution margin of the product. The SQV is due to 1) the difference between the actual and the budgeted total units of the firm, 2) the budgeted sales mix of the product, and 3) the standard contribution margin of the product.

A SQV can be separated further into the market size (MSV) and the market share (MShV) variances. The MSV assesses the effect of changes in the total market sizes of the industry on the firm's operating income and is determined by the product of three factors: 1) the difference between the actual and the budgeted total units of the market, 2) the budgeted market share of the firm, and 3) the weighted average budgeted contribution margin per unit. The MShV is the product of three elements: 1) the actual total units of the market, 2) the difference between the actual and the budgeted market shares of the firm, and 3) the average budgeted standard contribution margin per unit.

Productivity is the ratio of output to input. Improvements in productivity enable a firm to do more with fewer resources. A productivity measure often is examined relative to performance of prior periods, other firms, or a benchmark.

A partial productivity is the ratio of the output level attained to the amount of an input resource. The higher the ratio is, the better. An operational partial productivity is the required physical quantity of an input resource for the production of one unit of the output. A financial partial productivity is the number of units of output manufactured for each dollar of the input resource the firm spent. A financial partial productivity measure can be separated into changes due to productivity change, input price change, and output change. Productivity change is the difference between the actual and the budgeted quantity of input resources for the manufacturing of the output. The input price change accounts for the effects of differences in prices for the input resource between the actual price paid and the budgeted (or a benchmark) price, while the output change variance accounts for the change in cost due to changes in units of output. Total or financial productivity measures the relationship between output attained and the total input costs.

The same concepts for measuring productivity in manufacturing firms are also applicable to service industries and not-for-profit organizations. Some of the limitations of measuring productivity in service industries and not-for-profit organizations are imprecise output measures, lack of definite relationships between output and input resources, and the absence of revenue for not-for-profit organizations.

Questions:

> **Learning Objective 1: Describe productivity and identify effects of productivity change on operating results.**
>
> **Learning Objective 2: Compute and interpret operational and financial partial productivity.**
>
> **Learning Objective 3: Separate change in financial productivity into productivity change, input price change, and output change.**
>
> **Learning Objective 4: Calculate and interpret total productivity.**
>
> **Learning Objective 5: Identify issues of productivity in the new manufacturing environment and the advantages and limitations of applying productivity measures to service firms and not-for-profit organizations.**
>
> **Learning Objective 6: Disaggregate sales variance into selling price and sales volume variances.**
>
> **Learning Objective 7: Separate sales volume variance into sales mix and sales quantity variances.**
>
> **Learning Objective 8: Explain how market size and market share variances lead to sales quantity variances.**
>
> **Learning Objective 9: Analyze factors leading to changes in profitability.**

1. What is productivity?

2. What is the benchmark for productivity?

3. What is a measure of productivity?

4. What is operational productivity?

5. What is financial productivity?

6. What is partial productivity?

7. What is total productivity?

8. How do we compute partial productivity?

9. Distinguish between changes due to productivity change, input price change, and output change.

10. What are some of the advantages of total productivity measures?

11. What are some of the limitations of total productivity measures?

12. What are some of the limitations of applying productivity measures to firms in service and not-for-profit organizations?

13. What does marketing effectiveness include?

14. What is selling price variance (SPV)?

15. What is sales volume variance (SVV)?

16. What is sales mix variance (SMV)?

17. What is sales quantity variance (SQV)?

Cost Management: A Strategic Emphasis, 3e by Blocher/Chen/Cokins/Lin

18. How is market size variance (MSV) distinguished from market share variance (MShV)?

19. How is market size variance computed?

20. How is market share variance computed?

21. What are some of the strategic implications of marketing variances?

Suggested answers to the above questions:

1. What is productivity?

Productivity is the relationship between what is produced and what is required to produce it. It is the ratio of output to input.

2. What is the benchmark for productivity?

The benchmark for productivity can be the performance of:
- *the previous year*
- *another division of the firm*
- *a competitor, or*
- *a target measure set by management.*

3. What is a measure of productivity?

A measure of productivity can be either operational or financial productivity.

4. What is operational productivity?

Operational productivity uses the number of units of an input factor in the computation of the productivity measure.

5. What is financial productivity?

Financial productivity uses the dollar amount of the input in the computation of the productivity measure.

6. What is partial productivity?

Partial productivity is a productivity measure that focuses on only the relationship between one of the inputs such as, units of materials, persons employed, machine hours, and the output attained. In contrast, total productivity includes all the input resources.

7. What is total productivity?

Total productivity measures the relationship between the output attained and the total input costs of all the required input resources.

8. How do we compute partial productivity?

Partial productivity is computed by taking the units of output manufactured divided by units or cost of a single input resource used. An operational partial productivity is in terms of the units of the input factor. A financial partial productivity is in terms of the dollar amount of the input factor.

9. Distinguish between changes due to productivity change, input price change, and output change.

If each unit of output uses 3 rather than 4 lbs of raw materials and five rather than six hours of labor, the associated difference is due to a productivity change computed at current prices. Next, if the input items used were purchased at a lower or higher price in the prior period, the subject difference is due to input price change. Finally if output for the prior period was different from the current level of output, the difference between actual output at prior period's input levels and prices and prior period's output at prior period's costs is due to output change.

Assume that 100 units are produced, each unit requiring 2 lbs of material at $5 a lb. Last period 90 units were produced that required 1.9 lbs of material at $6 a lb. This difference is explained below:

Cost Management: A Strategic Emphasis, 3e by Blocher/Chen/Cokins/Lin

© 2005 by The McGraw-Hill Companies, Inc.

Productivity change: (100 x 2 x 5) - (100 x 1.9 x 5) = $50 Unfavorable
Input price change: (100 x 1.9 x 5) - (100 x 1.9 x 6) = 190 Favorable
Output level change(100 x 1.9 x 6) - (90 x 1.9 x 6) = 114 Unfavorable
Total difference: (100 x 2 x 5) - (90 x 1.9 x 6)   = 26 Favorable

10. What are some of the advantages of total productivity measures?

Using a total productivity measure decreases the possibility of manipulating one or two manufacturing factors to improve the measure.

11. What are some of the limitations of total productivity measures?

Total productivity is a financial measure. Deterioration in total productivity can be the result of increased costs of resources, which may be beyond the control of manufacturing people. Also, the basis for assessing changes in productivity may change over time. Productivity measures may also ignore the effects on productivity due to changes in demand, changes in selling prices of the goods or services, and special purchasing or selling arrangements. Special arrangements either in sales of the output or in purchases of input resources may also disrupt the underlying constant relation between input and output in computing productivity.

12. What are some of the limitations of applying productivity measures to firms in service and not-for-profit organizations?

Many of the outputs and required tasks of service firms and not-for-profit organizations cannot be measured precisely. Indefinite relationships between output and input resources required in a service firm often lead the service firm to measure only financial productivity. Here both the numerator and denominator of the ratio are measured in dollars. However, dollar amounts can hardly represent a major objective of not-for-profit organizations, and revenues of service firms are more likely determined by the quality of the service rendered, not the cost of input resources.

13. What does marketing effectiveness include?

Marketing effectiveness includes,
- achieving budgeted operating income,
- attaining budgeted market share, and
- adapting to changes in the market.

14. What is selling price variance (SPV)?

SPV is the difference between the actual dollar amount received from all the units sold and the dollar amount the firm would have received had the firm sold these units at the master budgeted selling price per unit.

15. What is sales volume variance (SVV)?

SVV is the difference between the budgeted contribution margin for the actual total units sold and the budgeted contribution margin for the budgeted units.

16. What is sales mix variance (SMV)?

SMV measures the effect on operating income of the difference between the actual sales mix and the budgeted sales mix. It is computed as the percentage of actual sales mix for the product minus budgeted sales mix percentage for the product times actual total units of all products sold times budgeted unit contribution margin of the product.

17. What is sales quantity variance (SQV)?

SQV of a product is the effect of the difference between the budgeted and the actual total sales quantity at the budgeted sales mix and the budgeted contribution margin per unit of the product.

18. How is market size variance (MSV) distinguished from marker share variance (MShV)?

MSV measures the effect on operating income of changes in the total market sizes of the firm's product. MShV assesses the effect on operating income of changes of a firm's proportions of the total market.

19. How is market size variance computed?

MSV = (actual market size - budgeted market size) x budgeted market share x weighted average budgeted contribution margin.

20. How is market share variance computed?

MShV = (Actual market share - budgeted market share) x actual total market in units x weighted average contribution margin per unit.

21. What are some of the strategic implications of marketing variances?

- Price decreases are among the tools firms often use as a competitive weapon to expand market shares, or to implement the strategy of converting the firm into a low-cost provider.
- A firm with an unfavorable selling price variance may be following an appropriate strategy if the firm intends to build its market share because of the great potentials of the products.

Cost Management: A Strategic Emphasis, 3e by Blocher/Chen/Cokins/Lin

- Expansions during periods of declining market sizes can lead to overcapacities, decline in prices, or financial distress. Decreases in market shares of a firm erode the firm's competitive position.

Multiple choice questions:

1. Productivity is the ratio of
   a) input to output
   b) output to input
   c) output to sales
   d) input to sales
   e) none of the above

2. The benchmark for productivity can be the performance of
   a) a previous year.
   b) another division of the firm.
   c) a competitor.
   d) a target measure set by management.
   e) all of the above.

3. A financial productivity measure uses
   a) only dollar amounts for output.
   b) dollar amounts for input.
   c) only quantity for output.
   d) only quantity for input.
   e) none of the above.

4. Units of output manufactured divided by cost of material resources used. This is a measure of
   a) financial productivity.
   b) operational productivity.
   c) partial financial productivity.
   d) partial operational productivity.
   e) none of the above.

5. Marketing effectiveness includes
   a) achieving budgeted operating income.
   b) attaining budgeted market share.
   c) adapting to changes in the market.
   d) all of the above.
   e) a and b.

6. Market size variance + market share variance =
   a) sales price variance.
   b) sales volume variance.
   c) sales quantity variance.
   d) sales mix variance.
   e) sales variance.

7. Sales quantity variance + sales mix variance =
   a) selling price variance.
   b) sales volume variance.
   c) sales contribution variance.
   d) sales variance.
   e) none of the above.

8. Selling price variance + sales volume variance =
   a) sales contribution variance
   b) sales variance
   c) sales quantity variance.
   d) sales mix variance.
   e) none of the above.

9. (number of units sold - budgeted number of units) x budgeted contribution margin equals to,
   a) sales volume variance.
   b) sales quantity variance.
   c) sales mix variance.
   d) sales price variance.
   e) sales variance.

10. (Actual units of market - Budgeted units of market) x Budgeted market share x Weighted average contribution margin per unit equals to
   a) market size variance.
   b) market share variance.
   c) sales quantity variance.
   d) sales mix variance.
   e) none of the above.

Exercises:

E1.

Baher Ceramics produces high quality ceramic tiles. Sales and budget data follows:

Item	Current year	Forecast
Sales of product A	7,500 @ $20	8,000 @ $18
Sales of product B	2,500 @ $30	4,000 @ $28
Market size in units	80,000	120,000
Variable cost of A	$12	$9
Variable cost of B	$21	$16.80

Required:
a) Compute selling price variance.
b) Compute net sales price variance.
c) Compute sales volume variance.
d) Compute sales quantity variance.
e) Compute sales mix variance.
f) Compute market size variance.
g) Compute market share variance.
h) Compute total sales variance and reconcile the above variances.

Note: we use contribution margin rather than selling price for computation of net sales price variance.

E2.

Nader Fabrics has provided us with the following data for the period:

	This Period	Prior Period
Production (yards)	18,000	16,000
DM (lbs)	24,000	22,400
DM	$ 36,000	31,360
DL (hours)	3,000	3,200
DL	$ 18,000	17,920

Required:
a) Determine direct materials' partial operational productivity.
b) Determine direct labor's partial operational productivity.
c) Determine direct materials' partial financial productivity.
d) Determine direct labor's partial financial productivity.
e) Determine direct materials and direct labor's partial financial productivity.
f) Decompose (e) into productivity change, input price change, and output change variances.
g) Discuss the significance of what you found in (f) above.

E2.

Search the internet for any financial and non-financial information for Intel corporation. Determine how some of the financial and non-financial productivity measures may apply to Intel. Use some numbers to prove the point and discuss the results with your team.

Correct answers to multiple choice questions:
1-b; 2-e; 3-b; 4-c; 5-d; 6-c; 7-b; 8-b; 9-a; 10-a

Suggested answers to exercises:

E1.

a) SPV: $\{(20 - 18) * 7,500\} + \{(30 - 28) * 2,500\} = 20,000$ F

b) SPV (net): $\{(7,500 * 1) + (2,500 * 2.2)\} = 13,000$ U

c) SVV: $\{(7,500 - 8,000) * (18 - 9)\} + \{(2,500 - 4,000) * (28 - 16.8)\} = 21,300$ U

d) SQV: $\{(10,000 - 12,000) * 66.67\% * 9\} + \{(10,000 - 12,000) * 33.33\% * 11.2\} = 19,467$ U

e) SMV: $\{(75\% - 66.67\%) * 10,000 * 9\} + \{25\% - 33.33\%) * 10,000 * 11.20\} = 1,833$ U

f) MSV: $\{(80,000 - 120,000) * 10\% * 9.7333\} = 38,933$ U

Computation of budgeted weighted average contribution margin:
$\{(8000 \times 9) + (4000 \times 11.20)\} / 12000 = 9.7333$

g) MShV: $\{(12.50\% - 10\%) * 80,000 * 9.7333 = 19,466$ F

h) Total variance: $\{(7500 \times 8) + (2500 \times 9)\} - \{(8000 \times 9) + (4000 \times 11.20)\} = 34,400$U

TSV = SPV + SVV = 13,000 + 21,300 = 34,400 U

SVV = SQV + SMV = 19,467 + 1,833 = 21,300 U

SQV = MSV + MShV = 38,933 U + 19,466 F = 19,467 U

E2.

	This Period	Prior Period
a) Material partial operational productivity	18,000 / 24,000 = .750	16,000 / 22,400 = .714
b) Labor partial operational productivity	18,000 / 3,000 = 6	16,000 / 3,200 = 5
c) Material partial financial productivity	18,000 / 36,000 = .50	16,000 / 31,360 = .510
d) Labor partial financial productivity	18,000 / 18,000 = 1	16,000 / 17,920 = .893
e) Labor and material partial financial productivity	18,000 / (36,000+18,000) = .333	16,000 / (31,360 + 17,920) = .325

f)
I - Current period production at current levels of productivity at current prices:

DM   24,000 x 1.50 = 36,000
DL   3,000 x 6 =   18,000
Total   54,000

II - Current period production at prior period's levels of productivity at current prices:

DM   18,000 x 1.40 x 1.50 = 37,800
DL   18,000 x .20 x 6   = 21,600
Total   59,400

III - Current period production at prior period's levels of productivity at prior period's prices:

DM   18,000 x 1.40 x 1.40 = 35,280
DL   18,000 x .20 x 5.60 = 20,160
Total   55,440

*IV - Prior period production at prior period's levels of productivity at prior period's prices:

DM   16,000 x 1.40 x 1.40 = 31,360
DL   16,000 x .20 x 5.60 = 17,920
Total   49,280

Productivity change: (I - II) : 54,000 - 59,400 = 5,400 F

Input price change: (II - III) : 59,400 - 55,440 = 3,960 U

Output level change: (III - IV): 55,400 - 49,280 = 6,160 U

g) The analysis in part f reveals that this year's productivity in terms of the level of input for material and labor has improved compared to prior period; input prices have increased compared to prior period; and higher costs can be partially explained because of a higher level of output.

Cost Management: A Strategic Emphasis, 3e by Blocher/Chen/Cokins/Lin

CHAPTER 16
TOTAL QUALITY MANAGEMENT

Highlights:

Quality is the best strategy for firms to maintain long-term profitability. A quality product or service meets or exceeds customer expectations at the price the customer is willing to pay. To achieve quality products or services, many firms adopt total quality management (TQM). TQM requires continuous effort by everyone in an organization to understand, meet and exceed the expectations of both internal and external customers.

Approaches to conform to quality specifications include goalpost or zero-defect conformance, which meets the quality standard within the specified range of the target, and absolute or robust quality conformance, which meets the specification exactly at the target value.

Four common categories for quality costs are prevention, appraisal, internal failure and external failure. Prevention and appraisal costs are costs of conformance. Internal and external failure costs are costs of nonconformance. The first step in generating a quality cost report is to define quality cost categories and to identify all quality costs within each category.

Tools identifying quality problems and finding solutions to the problems include control charts, Pareto diagrams, brainstorming, and cause-and-effect (fishbone or Ishikawa) diagrams. A control chart is a graph that depicts successive observations of an operation taken at constant intervals and is often used in identifying or discovering quality problems. Both histograms and Pareto diagrams depict graphically the frequency of quality problems or observations. A Pareto diagram orders quality problems from the largest to the smallest. Brainstorming is a useful way to elicit ideas in identifying quality problems, finding causes of a quality problem, or developing solutions to a quality problem. The cause-and-effect (fishbone or Ishikawa) diagram represents, graphically, a chain of causes and effects that lead to a quality problem and is a useful way to sort out root causes and to identify relationships between causes or factors and the quality problems.

Questions:

1. What is the Malcolm Baldridge National Quality Award?

2. What is ISO 9000?

3. What is a quality product or service?

4. What is total quality management (TQM)?

5. What is the purpose of a quality audit?

6. What is a gap analysis?

7. What are some of the external initiatives to be launched with suppliers?

8. What is goalpost performance?

9. What is absolute quality conformance?

10. Which of the above two methods is more effective?

11. What is the Taguchi Quality Loss Function?

12. What are some of the costs of nonconformance to quality?

13. What are some of the hidden costs of nonconformance to quality?

Learning Objective 3: Identify four major objectives of quality costs.

14. What are the major costs of quality?

15. What are the four categories of costs of quality?

---

16. What are costs of conformance and costs of non-conformance?

Learning Objective 4: Prepare and interpret cost of quality reports.

17. What is a cost of quality report?

Learning Objective 5: Describe methods commonly used to identify significant quality problems and their causes.

18. What is a control chart?

19. What is a histogram?

20. What is a Pareto diagram?

21. What is brainstorming?

22. What is a cause-and-effect diagram?

Learning Objective 6: Identify distinct characteristics of total quality management in service organizations.

---

23. What is the key difference between quality problems for a manufacturing versus a service entity?

Learning Objective 7: Explain the relationships between total quality management and productivity.

---

24. Why do quality improvements also increase productivity?

Learning Objective 8: Describe the role of management accountants in total quality management and the challenges they face.

---

25. What is the role of management accountants in TQM?

Suggested responses to the above questions:

1. What is the Malcolm Baldridge National Quality Award?

   This award was created in 1987 by the U.S. government to recognize U.S. companies in manufacturing, small business, service, education, and healthcare that excel in quality achievement and quality management.

2. What is ISO 9000?

   ISO 9000 is a set of guidelines for quality management and quality standards developed by the International Organization for Standardization in Geneva, Switzerland.

3. What is a quality product or service?

   It is a product or service that meets or exceeds customer expectations at the price he or she is willing to pay.

4. What is total quality management (TQM)?

TQM is the unyielding and continually improving effort by everyone in an organization to understand, meet, and exceed the expectations of customers. It also requires the unwavering and continuous support of top management.

5. What is the purpose of a quality audit?

A quality audit assesses the firm's quality practices and analyzes the quality performance of the best practices, including those of other companies.

6. What is a gap analysis?

A gap analysis is a type of benchmarking that determines "the gap" in practices between the "best-in-class" and the firm.

7. What are some of the external initiatives to be launched with suppliers?

They include:
- *Reducing the supplier base*
- *Selecting suppliers based on price and their capability and willingness to improve quality, cost, delivery, flexibility, and their dedication to continuous improvement*
- *Forming long-term relationship with suppliers as working partners specifying precise supplier expectations and ensuring suppliers' consistent delivery.*

8. What is goalpost performance?

Goalpost performance is conformance to a quality specification expressed as a specified range around the target. The target is the ideal value for which the process is designed to attain. It is a zero-defect conformance.

9. What is absolute quality conformance?

Absolute quality conformance (robust quality approach) requires all products or services to meet exactly the target value with no variations allowed.

10. Which of the two methods in #8 and #9 above is more effective?

Experience has shown that for a firm that has long-term profitability and customer satisfaction as its goals, absolute conformance is the better approach.

11. What is the Taguchi Quality Loss Function?

It is a function that depicts the relationship between the total loss to the firm due to quality defects and the extent of quality defects. Taguchi believes that a quadratic function provides a good approximation of losses; i.e., when deviations double, losses quadruple.

12. What are some of the costs of nonconformance to quality?

They include items such as rework, warranty repair or replacement, additional production costs, and loss on disposal.

13. What are some of the hidden costs of nonconformance to quality?

They include items such as customer dissatisfaction, loss of future business, loss of market share, additional engineering costs, additional management costs, and additional inventory.

14. What are the major costs of quality?

Costs of quality are costs associated with prevention, identification, repair, and rectification of poor quality, and opportunity costs from lost production time and sales as a result of poor quality.

15. What are the four categories of costs of quality?

They include prevention, appraisal, internal failure, and external failure.
- *Prevention costs are costs incurred to keep quality defects from occurring. As these costs of quality increase, others would decrease. Examples: training, preventive maintenance.*
- *Appraisal costs are costs incurred in measurement and analysis of data to ascertain conformity of products and services to the specifications. Examples: material inspection, equipment maintenance.*
- *Internal failure costs are costs incurred as a result of poor quality found through appraisal prior to delivery to customers. Examples: scrap, rework, reinspection.*
- *External failure costs are costs incurred to rectify quality defects after unacceptable products or services reach the customer, and lost profit opportunity because of the unacceptable products or services delivered. Examples: sales returns and allowances, warranty costs, contribution lost due to lost sales.*

16. What are costs of conformance and costs of non-conformance?

Prevention costs and appraisal costs are costs of conformance so that quality problems would be avoided later on. Internal failure costs and external failure costs, on the other hand, are costs of non-conformance. Spending money for conformance will save the company the substantial non-conformance costs.

17. What is a cost of quality report?

It is a report, preferably incorporated into the firm's information system, that classifies prevention, appraisal, internal failure, and external failure costs by department for management's attention and corrective action where necessary. Year-to-year comparison of such data can provide useful information for management's action.

18. What is a control chart?

A control chart is a graph that depicts successive observations of an operation taken at constant intervals.

19. What is a histogram?

A histogram is a graphical representation of the variation in a given set of data. Such variation is shown by category and frequency of problems identified in a histogram.

20. What is a Pareto diagram?

A Pareto diagram is a graphic representation of frequency of occurrence of the factors contributing to the quality problem, ordered from the most to the least frequent.

21. What is brainstorming?

Brainstorming is a useful way to elicit ideas from a group of people in a short time. It is useful in identifying problems, finding causes of a problem, and developing a solution to a quality problem. It is effective if people are encouraged and respected for their suggestions and recommendations.

22. What is a cause-and-effect diagram?

A cause-and-effect, or Ishikawa, or fishbone diagram is a graphical method that organizes a chain of causes and effects to sort out root causes and identify relationships between causes or variables.

23. What is the key difference between quality problems for a manufacturing versus a service entity?

A manufacturing firm is able to recall the defective merchandise and correct the problem. A service organization can only offer an apology for poor service. Such apology may be too little and too late in many situations.

24. Why do quality improvements also increase productivity?

Firms that spend a lot of effort and money in correcting problems because of defective items contribute to a reduction of productivity, because such efforts do not result in increased productivity. Improvements in quality lead to increases in productivity and sales.

25. What is the role of management accountants in TQM?

Management accountants must be trained and involved in analyzing, measuring, and reporting quality concerns. S/he must not only provide fast and timely feedback to users and managers but must also foster improvement rather than just monitoring.

Multiple choice questions:

1. The Malcolm Baldridge National Quality Award
    a) is the quality award for recognition of US companies in manufacturing.
    b) is the quality award for recognition of US companies in small business.
    c) is the quality award for recognition of US companies in service and education.
    d) is the quality award for recognition of US companies in healthcare.
    e) all of the above.

2. ISO 9000 is a set of guidelines for quality management and quality standards developed by the
    a) American Institute of Management Accountants.
    b) Malcolm Baldridge National Quality Award Committee.
    c) The Securities and Exchange Commission.
    d) The International Organization for Standardization.
    e) None of the above.

3. Improved quality is often related to
    a) decreased productivity.
    b) increased profitability.
    c) higher return on investment.
    d) a and c.
    e) b and c.

4. A quality product or service
    a) meets customer's expectations in price but not quality.
    b) meets customer's expectations in quality but not price.
    c) exceeds customer's expectations in price but not quality.
    d) exceeds customer's expectations in quality but not price.
    e) meets or exceeds customer's expectations in price and quality.

5. Total quality management is the unyielding and continually improving effort by
    a) management in an organization to understand, meet or exceed customers' expectations.
    b) workers in an organization to understand, meet or exceed customers' expectations.
    c) shareholders in an organization to understand, meet or exceed customers' expectations.
    d) everyone in an organization to understand, meet or exceed customers' expectations.
    e) none of the above.

6. The primary features of TQM are,
    a) continuous improvement, focus on the supplier, and involvement of all employees.
    b) continuous improvement, focus on the customer, and involvement of management.
    c) continuous improvement, focus on the customer, and involvement of all employees.
    d) continuous improvement, focus on the supplier, and focus on the customer.
    e) focus on the supplier, focus on the customer, and involvement of all employees.

7. Successful implementation of TQM requires
    a) active leadership from the supervisors but not necessarily senior managers.
    b) active leadership from the senior managers but not necessarily the CEO.
    c) active leadership from the workers but not necessarily the senior managers.
    d) active leadership from the CEO and the senior managers.
    e) none of the above.

8. A gap analysis
    a) is a type of benchmarking.
    b) identifies target areas for quality improvements.
    c) provides a common objective data base for the firm.
    d) all of the above.
    e) a and b.

*Cost Management: A Strategic Emphasis, 3*e by Blocher/Chen/Cokins/Lin

9. Absolute quality conformance
   a) is same as Robust Quality Approach.
   b) requires all products or services to meet exactly the target value with no variation allowed.
   c) is conformance to a quality specification expressed as a specified range around a target.
   d) a and c
   e) a and b.

10. The four components of quality costs are
    a) training, rework, inspection, and warranty costs.
    b) prevention, appraisal, internal failure, and external failure.
    c) scrap, rework, inspection, and equipment testing.
    d) training, scrap, rework, and sales returns.
    e) prevention, rework, equipment testing, and warranty costs.

11. Examples of appraisal costs include
    a) training and promotion costs.
    b) scrap and rework costs.
    c) inspection and testing costs
    d) sales allowances and warranty costs.
    e) none of the above.

12. Examples of prevention costs include
    a) training and promotion costs.
    b) scrap and rework costs.
    c) inspection and testing costs
    d) sales allowances and warranty costs.
    e) none of the above.

13. Examples of external failure costs include
    a) training and promotion costs.
    b) scrap and rework costs.
    c) inspection and testing costs
    d) sales allowances and warranty costs.
    e) none of the above.

14. Examples of internal failure costs include
    a) training and promotion costs.
    b) scrap and rework costs.
    c) inspection and testing costs
    d) sales allowances and warranty costs.
    e) none of the above.

15. An Ishikawa diagram is a
   a) graphic representation of the variations in a given set of data.
   b) graphic representation of frequency of occurrence of the factors contributing to the quality problem, ordered from the most to the least frequent.
   c) relaxed yet structured group session for exchanging ideas for a common solution to a problem.
   d) is a graphical method that organizes a chain of causes and effects to sort out root causes and identify relationships between causes or variables.
   e) none of the above.

16. A histogram is a
   a) graphic representation of the variations in a given set of data.
   b) graphic representation of frequency of occurrence of the factors contributing to the quality problem, ordered from the most to the least frequent.
   c) relaxed yet structured group session for exchanging ideas for a common solution to a problem.
   d) is a graphical method that organizes a chain of causes and effects to sort out root causes and identify relationships between causes or variables.
   e) none of the above.

17. Brainstorming is
   a) graphic representation of the variations in a given set of data.
   b) graphic representation of frequency of occurrence of the factors contributing to the quality problem, ordered from the most to the least frequent.
   c) relaxed yet structured group session for exchanging ideas for a common solution to a problem.
   d) is a graphical method that organizes a chain of causes and effects to sort out root causes and identify relationships between causes or variables.
   e) none of the above.

18. A Pareto diagram is
   a) graphic representation of the variations in a given set of data.
   b) graphic representation of frequency of occurrence of the factors contributing to the quality problem, ordered from the most to the least frequent.
   c) relaxed yet structured group session for exchanging ideas for a common solution to a problem.
   d) is a graphical method that organizes a chain of causes and effects to sort out root causes and identify relationships between causes or variables.
   e) none of the above.

19. Quality problems in service organizations are often
   a) less serious than those in a manufacturing firm.
   b) more serious than those in a manufacturing firm.
   c) as serious as those in a manufacturing firm.
   d) more serious than those at a university.
   e) more serious than those at a health clinic.

20. Quality improvements often result in
   a) decreased productivity because of additional training and inspection needs.
   b) increased productivity in spite of additional training and inspection needs.
   c) same level of productivity because of offsetting training and inspection needs.
   d) same level of productivity because of offsetting scrap and rework costs.
   e) decreased productivity in spite of warranty and sales allowance costs.

Exercises:

E1.
KTT Plastics Company has determined that no customer will accept plastic sheets deviating more than .06" from the target value in thickness. The target value for thickness is .60", and the cost to the firm for each rejected job is $18,000.
Required: Determine loss per unit if the actual thickness of a unit is .57.

E2.
Irana Tiles Company has determined that no customer will accept its tiles deviating more than .03 from the target value in thickness. The target value for thickness is .40", and the cost to the firm for each rejected job is $2,250.
Required: Determine loss per unit if the actual thickness is .42.

E3.
Use the data in Exercise 2 and also assume that 20% of output has a thickness of .37, 20% has a thickness of .39, 30% has a thickness of .40, 15% has a thickness of .42, and the balance has a thickness of .43.
Required: Determine the expected loss given the above scenario.

E4.
Printing Impression company spends $5,000 per period on employee training and quality planning, $12,000 on testing and inspection; cost of rework and rejections amounts to $18,000, and warranties and customer losses are estimated to be around $32,000. It is estimated that an increased expenditure of 60% on prevention costs plus an additional increase in appraisal costs by 50% will result in reduction of internal failures by 30% and external failures by 60%. Sales is anticipated to remain at the current level of $700,000 with the current profit amounting to 9% of sales.
Required: Determine if such changes will increase profitability, and if so by how much. What is this change in profit as a percentage of current profit.

<u>E5.</u>
Printing Impression Company has determined that its quality problems for the prior periods have been caused by the following items: 35 problems due to inferior quality of paper, 25 problems due to worker's inefficiency, 62 problems due to problems with machines; 12 problems due to mistakes by the graphic artist, and 17 problems due to customer's errors in specifications. The company had a total of 2,000 jobs for the period. **Required: Prepare a histogram, a Pareto diagram, and a fishbone diagram depicting the above-mentioned problems.**

<u>E6.</u>
The following companies have been among the winners of Malcolm Baldrige National Quality Award since 1987 when the Congress established the award: 3M, Cadillac, Federal Express, GTE, Milliken, Motorola, Texas Instruments, Ritz-Carlton, Westinghouse, and Xerox. Do an internet search for at least two of these companies to find more about these companies and for what reason they received this prestigious award.

<u>Correct answers to multiple choice questions:</u>
1-e; 2-d; 3-e; 4-e; 5-d; 6-c; 7-d; 8-d; 9-e; 10-b; 11-c; 12-a; 13-d; 14-b; 15-d; 16-a; 17-c; 18-b; 19-b; 20-b.

<u>Suggested answers to exercises:</u>
<u>E1.</u>
   $k = \$18,000/ (.06)^2 = \$5,000,000$
   $L (.57) = 5,000,000 * (.57-.60)^2 = 5,000,000 * .0009 = \$4,500$

<u>E2.</u>
   $k = \$2,250/(.03)^2 = \$2,500,000$
   $L (.42) = 2,500,000 * (.42 - .40)^2 = \$1,000$

<u>E3.</u>
Using the formula used in Exercises 1 and 2 results in the following:

L (.37) =	$2,250;	2,250 * 20% = 450
L (.39) =	250;	250 * 20% = 50
L (.40) =	0;	0 * 30% = 0
L (.42) =	1,000;	1,000 * 15% = 150
L (.43) =	2,250;	2,250 * 15% = 337.5

Adding the above totals results in an expected loss of $987.50.

E4.

Quality Cost Summary

	Now	After change
Prevention costs	$ 5,000	$8,000
Appraisal costs	12,000	18,000
Internal failures	18,000	12,600
External failures	32,000	12,800
Total quality costs	67,000	51,400

Increased profit after the change = $15,600

Current profit: 700,000 * 9% = $63,000
Increase in profit as a percentage of current profit: 24.76%

E5.

List of identified problems

- Inferior quality of paper   35
- Workers' inefficiency   25
- Machine problems   62
- Mistakes in graphics   12
- Customer errors   17
- Total number of errors   151

Please refer to the textbook for drawing the required diagrams. Note that histogram is often prepared in the order that data is provided, and Pareto diagram is prepared in the order from the most frequent to the least frequent. In the fishbone diagram, the relationship between the number of problems and the resulting percentage of defects is established.

A. Histogram:

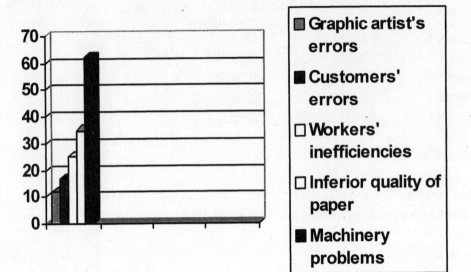

B. Pareto diagram:

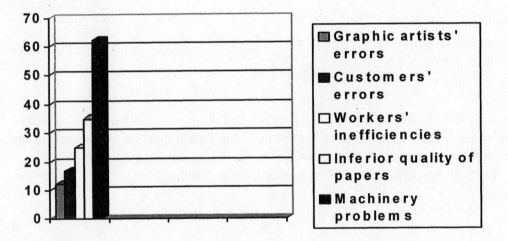

C. Fishbone diagram:

Inferior quality of paper (35); Workers' inefficiency (25)

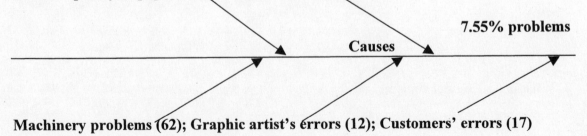

Machinery problems (62); Graphic artist's errors (12); Customers' errors (17)

CHAPTER 17
MANAGEMENT CONTROL AND
STRATEGIC PERFORMANCE MEASUREMENT

Highlights:

The goal of top management in using strategic performance measurement is to motivate managers to provide a high level of effort, to guide them to make decisions that are congruent with the goals of top management, and to provide a basis for fair compensation for the managers. Strategic performance measurement systems are implemented in any of four different forms, depending upon the nature of the manager's responsibilities -- the revenue strategic business units (SBUs), cost SBU, profit SBU, and investment SBU. Such SBUs are employed in manufacturing as well as service and not-for-profit firms.

The contribution margin income statement is sometimes called variable costing income statement. It has the benefit of not being affected by changes in finished goods inventory. In contrast, the conventional income statement based on absorption costing is biased by inventory changes. A useful guide is that the amount of the bias in the absorption income statement is the amount of fixed cost in the change in inventory.

A key issue in the effective use of strategic performance measurement systems is the integration of strategic considerations into the evaluation. This requires an identification of the critical success factors of the firm, and appropriate measurement and reporting of these factors, commonly in the form of a balanced scorecard. In many cases, a substantial portion of these factors will be non-financial, including operating and economic data from sources external to the firm. A balanced scorecard provides a comprehensive measure of a firm's performance.

Questions:

1. What is performance evaluation?

Learning Objective 1: Identify the objectives of management control.

---

2. What is management control?

3. What is operational control?

Study Guide   263
© 2005 by The McGraw-Hill Companies, Inc.

4. What is a strategic business unit?

5. What are the objectives of management control?

6. How can goal congruence between the firm and its management be achieved?

7. What are the elements of uncertainty and lack of observability in conjunction with the principal-agent model of a contract?

8. What are the three principles of effective contracting?

Learning Objective 2: Identify the types of management control systems.

9. Who is interested in evaluating the performance of the organization?

10. Consider the various aspects of control; i.e., what is being evaluated and when should the performance evaluation be done.

11. What are the formal and informal types of management control?

12. What are the three types of formal management control systems?

Learning Objective 3: Define strategic performance measurement and show how centralized, , decentralized, and team-oriented organizations can apply it.

13. What is strategic performance measurement?

14. What are the advantages of centralization?

15. What are the advantages of decentralization?

16. What are the four types of strategic business units?

Learning Objective 4: Explain the objectives and applications of strategic performance measurement in three common types of strategic business units: cost SBUs, revenue SBUs, and profit SBUs.

17. What are the key strategic issues in implementation of cost SBUs?

18. What is meant by cost shifting?

19. What is excessive short-term focus?

20. What is budgetary slack?

21. What are the two methods for implementing cost SBUs for producing and support departments?

22. What is outsourcing?

23. What should be the criteria for cost allocation from service to manufacturing units?

24. What is the dual cost allocation method?

25. Why are revenue drivers often used in the evaluation of the performance of revenue SBUs?

26. What are the two types of costs incurred by the marketing department?

27. What are the three strategic issues that cause firms to choose profit SBUs?

28. What is contribution margin income statement?

29. What are controllable fixed costs?

30. What is a controllable margin?

31. What are non-controllable fixed costs?

32. Contrast variable costing to absorption costing.

33. To what extent would variable costing income be different from absorption costing income?

34. What is the role of the balanced scorecard?

35. In which key areas does the balanced scorecard measure the SBU's performance?

36. What are the major two motivating factors for outsourcing Information Technology (IT)?

Suggested responses to the above questions:

1. What is performance evaluation?

Performance evaluation can be thought of as the process by which managers at all levels in the firm gain information about the performance of tasks within the firm and judge that performance against pre-established criteria as set out in budgets, plans, and goals.

2. What is management control?

Management control refers to the evaluation by upper-level managers of the performance of mid-level managers.

3. What is operational control?

Operational control means the evaluation of operating level employees by mid-level managers.

4. What is a strategic business unit?

A strategic business unit (SBU) consists of a well-defined set of controllable operating activities over which a SBU manager is responsible.

5. What are the objectives of management control?

The objectives of management control are to:
- *motivate managers to exert a high level of effort to achieve the goals of top management,*
- *provide the right incentive for managers to make decisions that are consistent with the goals of top management, and*
- *fairly determine the rewards managers' earn for their effort and skill, and for the effectiveness of their decision making.*

6. How can goal congruence between the firm and its management be achieved?

Goal congruence is achieved when the manager acts independently in such a way as to simultaneously achieve top manager's objectives.

7. What are the elements of uncertainty and lack of observability in conjunction with the principal-agent model of a contract?

Uncertainty involves the factors over which the manager has no control such as unexpected machine breakdowns or external factors. Lack of observability concerns the fact that many of managers' decisions are not observable by top management.

8. What are the three principles of effective contracting?

- *Separate the outcome of the manager's actions from the effort and decision-making skill of the manager.*
- *Exclude known uncontrollable factors.*
- *Compensate for the expected relative risk aversion of the manager.*

9. Who is interested in evaluating the performance of the organization?

- *The owners, directors, or shareholders,*
- *The creditors,*
- *The governmental units affected by the operations of the firm, and*
- *The employees of the firm.*

10. Consider the various aspects of control; i.e., what is being evaluated and when should the performance evaluation be done?

The focus of the evaluation could be the manager or the SBU. The manager's performance could be compared to other business units or to the budget. The manager may negotiate with top management regarding resources needed to achieve certain goals.

11. What are the formal and informal types of management control?

Formal systems are developed from explicit management guidance, while informal systems arise from the unmanaged, and sometimes unintended, behavior of managers and employees. Informal systems reflect the managers' and employees' reactions and feelings that arise from the positive and negative aspects of the work environment.

12. What are the three types of formal management control systems?

They are a) hiring practices, b) promotion policies, and c) strategic performance measurement systems.

13. What is strategic performance measurement?

Strategic performance measurement is an accounting system used by top management for the evaluation of SBU managers.

14. What are the advantages of centralization?

Centralization has the advantage of top management retaining control over the key business functions so that a desired level of performance is assured. Also the expertise of top management can be effectively utilized, and the activities of the different units within the firm can be effectively coordinated. Finally, there will be no need for coordination of the work of lower level managers.

15. What are the advantages of decentralization?

Top management lacks the necessary local knowledge, and decentralization can be more effective. Decentralization also helps in making timely decisions. It can also provide better motivation for managers.

16. What are the four types of strategic business units?

The four types of strategic business units are cost SBUs, revenue SBUs, profit SBUs, and investment SBUs.

17. What are the key strategic issues in implementation of cost SBUs?

The strategic issues of cost SBUs are cost shifting, excessive short-term focus, and the problem of budget slack.

18. What is meant by cost shifting?

A manager of a cost SBU that is evaluated on controllable costs has the incentive to replace variable costs with fixed costs. Cost shifting undermines the motivation and fairness of the performance evaluation systems.

19. What is excessive short-term focus?

Many performance measurement systems focus excessively on annual cost figures. So cost SBUs should also use non-financial strategic considerations.

20. What is budgetary slack?

Budgetary slack is the difference between budgeted performance and expected performance.

21. What are the two methods for implementing cost SBUs for producing and support departments?

The two methods are discretionary-cost method and the engineered-cost method. The former method is input-oriented, since costs are considered largely uncontrollable and discretion is applied at the planning stage. The latter method is the output-oriented approach since costs are variable and therefore "engineered," that is, controllable.

22. What is outsourcing?

Outsourcing is the term used for a firm's decision to have the service or product provided by a support department supplied by an outside firm.

23. What should be the criteria for cost allocation from service to manufacturing units?

The criteria should be to a) motivate the managers to exert a high level of effort, b) provide the incentive for managers to make decisions that are consistent with top management's goals, and c) provide a basis for a fair evaluation of managers' performance.

24. What is the dual cost allocation method?

Dual allocation is a method in which fixed and variable costs are separated. Variable costs are directly traced to user departments, and fixed costs are allocated on some logical basis.

25. Why are revenue drivers often used in the evaluation of the performance of revenue SBUs?

Revenue drivers are the factors which affect sales volume, such as price changes, promotions, discounts, customer service, changes in product features, delivery dates, and other value-added factors.

26. What are the two types of costs incurred by the marketing department?

*The two types of costs incurred by the marketing department are **order-getting** and **order-filling** costs. The former are costs to advertise and promote the product. These costs are often discretionary. The latter include freight, warehousing, packing, shipping, and the cost of collections. These costs are often engineered with a relatively clear relationship to sales volume.*

27. What are the three strategic issues that cause firms to choose profit SBUs?

The three strategic issues which cause firms to choose profit SBUs are: First, profit SBUs provide the incentive for the desired coordination among the marketing, production, and support functions. Second, it helps motivate managers to think of their product as marketable to outside customers. Third, it helps motivate managers to develop new ways of making profit from their products and services. Managers have the incentive to develop creative new products and services, since the profit SBU evaluation rewards the incremental profits.

28. What is contribution margin income statement?

The contribution margin income statement is an income statement based on contribution margin which is developed for each profit SBU and for each relevant group of profit SBUs.

29. What are controllable fixed costs?

Controllable fixed costs are those fixed costs that the profit SBU manager can influence in the period of approximately a year or less such as, advertising and sales promotion.

30. What is controllable margin?

Controllable margin is determined by subtracting controllable fixed costs from the contribution margin, and this is a useful measure of the profit SBU manager's performance in controlling costs.

31. What are non-controllable fixed costs?

Non-controllable fixed costs are those that are not controllable within a year's time, and these usually include facilities-related costs such as depreciation, taxes, and insurance.

32. Contrast variable costing to absorption costing.

The use of the contribution margin income statement is often called variable costing, since it separates variable and fixed costs. In contrast, absorption costing includes fixed manufacturing cost as part of product cost which will go to cost of goods sold. The latter is used for financial accounting and for tax purposes. Variable costing, on the other hand, meets the three objectives of management control systems. In addition, net income using variable costing is not affected by changes in inventory levels.

33. To what extent is variable costing income different from absorption costing income?

Absorption costing net income will exceed variable costing net income by the amount of fixed cost in the inventory change when inventory increases; i.e., production > sales.

34. What is the role of the balanced scorecard?

The balanced scorecard looks at both financial and non-financial factors of performance. It considers no one measure as adequate for monitoring the SBU's progress to strategic success.

35. In which key areas does the balanced scorecard measure the SBU's performance?

The balanced scorecard measures the SBU's performance in four key areas
a) financial performance, b) customer satisfaction, *c) internal business processes, d) learning and growth.*

36. What are the major two motivating factors for outsourcing Information Technology (IT)?

First, it can help to dramatically reduce the overall cost of IT in the firm. Second, and perhaps most importantly, it helps the firm to keep up with advancing technology, by partnering with an application service provider or consulting firm with a high level of expertise.

Multiple choice questions:

1. The two important aspects of the principal-agent model of a contract are:
   a) uncertainty and lack of observability.
   b) uncertainty and controllability.
   c) controllability and lack of observability.
   d) influence and behavior
   e) none of the above.

2. The principles of effective contracting include,
   a) separating the outcome of the manager's actions from the effort and decision-making skill of the manager.
   b) excluding known uncontrollable factors.
   c) compensating for the expected relative risk aversion of the manager.
   d) all of the above.
   e) a and b.

3. The important aspects of a formal management control system include,
   a) hiring practices.
   b) promotion policies.
   c) strategic performance measurement systems.
   d) all of the above.
   e) a and c.

4. Strategic performance measures are used by
   a) lower management for the evaluation of workers.
   b) middle management for the evaluation of supervisors.
   c) top management for the evaluation of SBU managers.
   d) SBU managers for the evaluation of top management.
   e) none of the above.

5. Investment SBU's are
   a) production or support SBUs within the firm that have the goal of providing the best quality product or service at the lowest cost.
   b) marketing SBUs by product line or geographical area.
   c) SBUs that generate both revenue and costs for producing those revenues.
   d) SBUs that include assets employed as well as profits in the performance evaluation.
   e) none of the above.

6. Strategic issues in conjunction with cost SBUs include,
   a) cost shifting.
   b) tendency to an excessive focus on short-term objectives.
   c) tendency for managers and top management to mis-communicate because of the pervasive problem of budget slack.
   d) all of the above.
   e) a and c.

Cost Management: A Strategic Emphasis, 3e by Blocher/Chen/Cokins/Lin

7. The methods for implementing cost SBUs include,
   a) the discretionary-cost method.
   b) the engineered-cost method.
   c) the accountability-approach method.
   d) all of the above.
   e) a and b.

8. The discretionary cost method considers costs to be primarily,
   a) controllable.
   b) uncontrollable.
   c) variable.
   d) mixed.
   e) step.

9. The objective(s) for management control is (are)
   a) to motivate the managers to exert a high level of effort.
   b) to provide the incentive for managers to make decisions that are consistent with top management's goals,
   c) provide a basis for a fair evaluation of managers' performance,
   d) all of the above.
   e) a and b.

10. The criteria for choosing the cost allocation method are (is)
   a) to motivate the managers to exert a high level of effort.
   b) to provide the incentive for managers to make decisions that are consistent with top management's goals,
   c) provide a basis for a fair evaluation of managers' performance,
   d) all of the above.
   e) b and c.

11. The absorption cost net income will exceed variable cost net income by the amount of fixed cost in the inventory change when,
   a) production > sales.
   b) production < sales.
   c) production = sales.
   d) production > or = sales.
   e) production < or = sales.

12. The balanced scorecard measures the SBU's performance in
   a) customer satisfaction.
   b) financial performance.
   c) internal business processes.
   d) learning and growth.
   e) all of the above.

Exercises:

<u>E1.</u>

Taher Publishing Company has three divisions, A, B, and C. The revenues of these divisions are $29,000, 48,000, and 63,000 respectively. Variable costs of these divisions amounts to 57%, 59%, and 64% of the given revenues. The divisions' controllable fixed costs are $4,200, 5,200, and 6,200 respectively. The divisions' uncontrollable fixed costs amount to $3,800, 4,900, and 5,700 in the order given. The Company's other uncontrollable costs amount to $7,150.

Required: Prepare a contribution margin income statement in good form.

<u>E2.</u>

Heshmat Blankets Factory produced 4,000 blankets in January and 2,000 blankets in February. However, it sold 2,000 blankets in January and sold the remaining 4,000 in February. There was no beginning inventory. Variable cost per unit amounts to $19 while fixed factory costs amount to $40,000 per month. Fixed administration expenses amount to $12,000 per month. Variable selling expense amounts to $5 per blanket. Blankets are sold at the price of $49 per unit.

Required:

a) **Prepare an income statement for January and February and cumulative two-month period under absorption costing.**

b) **Prepare an income statement for January and February and cumulative two-month period under variable costing.**

c) **Compute the inventory value under both methods at the end of January.**

d) **Reconcile the difference between the operating income amount under both methods at the end of each month.**

<u>E3</u>

Ryan Toy Company's total sales amounts to $120,000. Cost of sales amounted to 60% of sales. Selling expenses amounted to $12,000. Sales were 10% more than last year while costs were 5% higher than prior year and selling expenses were 9% of sales in the prior year. There were 400 sales items with 20 returns as compared to 30 returns on the same number of sales items last year. There were five accidents in the plant as compared to 7 in the prior year. The employees spent 450 hours in training sessions this year as compared to 230 hours the year before. The additional time spent this year dealt with business ethics and best practices of competing firms.

Required:

Without showing the detailed calculations, prepare a short balanced scorecard and indicate where the basic information will be shown and provide some comments and explanation with regard to each entry.

Cost Management: A Strategic Emphasis, 3e by Blocher/Chen/Cokins/Lin

E4.

The Outsourcing Insitute (www.outsourcinginstitute.com) indicates that firms go to outsourcing to save on operating costs and to focus the company's operations on core activities. **Go to this site and see what else you can find with regard to outsourcing practices.**

Correct answers to multiple choice questions:
1-a; 2-d; 3-d; 4-c; 5-d; 6-d; 7-e; 8-b; 9-d; 10-d; 11-a; 12-e.

Suggested answers to exercises:

E1.

Departmental income statement for Taher

ITEM	Division A	Division B	Division C	Total
Revenue	29,000	48,000	63,000	140,000
Variable cost of sales	16,530	28,320	40,320	85,170
Contribution margin	12,470	19,680	22,680	54,830
Controllable fixed costs	4,200	5,200	6,200	15,600
Controllable margin	8,270	14,480	16,480	39,230
Uncontrollable fixed costs	3,800	4,900	5,700	14,400
Unontrollable margin	4,470	9,580	10,780	24,830
Common uncontrollable costs				7,150
Operating income				17,680

E2.

a) Absorption costing income statement

ITEM	JANUARY	FEBRUARY	TOTAL
Revenue: 2000, 4000 @ 49	98,000	196,000	294,000
Cost of goods sold @ 29	58,000	58,000	116,000
@39		78,000	78,000
Gross profit	40,000	60,000	100,000
Variable selling expense @$5	10,000	20,000	30,000
Administration expense	12,000	12,000	24,000
Operating income	18,000	28,000	46,000

b) Variable costing income statement

ITEM	JANUARY	FEBRUARY	TOTAL
Revenue: 2000, 4000 @ $49	98,000	196,000	294,000
Variable cost of sales @ 19	38,000	76,000	114,000
Manufacturing margin	60,000	120,000	180,000
Variable selling expense @ $5	10,000	20,000	30,000
Contribution margin	50,000	100,000	150,000
Fixed manufacturing costs	40,000	40,000	80,000
Fixed administration costs	12,000	12,000	24,000
Operating income	(2,000)	48,000	46,000

c) Cost of production and unit cost

ITEM	JANUARY	FEBRUARY
Production (units)	4,000	2,000
Unit variable cost	19	19
Total variable costs	76,000	38,000
Fixed manufacturing costs	40,000	40,000
Total cost of production	116,000	78,000
Cost per unit	29	39

d) Reconciliation of operating income:

January operating income under absorption costing	18,000
January operating income under variable costing	-2,000
Difference	20,000

Change in inventory @ fixed cost per unit: (2,000 * $10) - 20,000

February operating income under absorption costing	28,000
February operating income under variable costing	48,000
Difference	20,000

Change in inventory @ fixed cost per unit: (2,000 * $10) = 20,000

Note that for the two periods combined profit is the same amount under both methods.

Cost Management: A Strategic Emphasis, 3e by Blocher/Chen/Cokins/Lin

<u>E3.</u>

1. Financial: Sales have improved by 10% from last years, but costs have increased by 5% and selling expenses have increased by 1%. These changes need be explained and complimented with more detail provided in the other sections of the balanced scorecard.
2. Customer satisfaction: Our sales returns this year amounted to 5% of our total sales activity as compared to 8% for the prior year. This is in part due to better employee training as explained below.
3. Internal Business Processes: We still need to work more closely with our supervisors and workers. However, the accident rates are lower (5) compared to last year (7).
4. Learning and innovation: We had 220 more training hours this year as compared to last year, almost twice as many hours of the prior year. The additional hours were spent on business ethics and best practices of other firms. While current results reflect in part the benefits of this investment in employees, we expect to get higher dividends from this effort in future years.

CHAPTER 18
STRATEGIC INVESTMENT UNITS
AND TRANSFER PRICING

Highlights:

ROI and **RI** are two of the most common and well-understood financial measures in business today. Both measures have a short-term focus which is inconsistent with a strategy-based approach. In spite of this short-coming, firms continue to use these measures but often together with the balanced scorecard and the economic value added **(EVA)** approaches.

The objectives of transfer pricing are performance evaluation, evaluation of business units, tax minimization, management of foreign currencies and risks, and other strategic objectives. Especially for multinational firms, the determination of transfer prices is likely to have important implications on profits and the achievement of strategic goals. Management considers the availability and quality of outside supply, the capacity utilization of the internal selling unit, and the strategic objectives of the firm in determining the proper transfer price - cost-based, market price, or a negotiated price. Value chain analysis can help by identifying strategically important activities in the value chain, and how competitive the firm is in providing these activities within the industry.

Questions:

1. What is return on investment?

2. When is the use of ROI preferable to profitability alone?

Learning Objective 1: Identify the objectives of strategic investment units.

3. What is the strategic role of investment SBUs?

Learning Objective 2: Explain the use of return on investment (ROI) and identify its advantages and limitations.

4. How is the amount of investment determined?

5. What is return on equity?

6. What is the expanded formula for ROI?

7. What is the significance of return on sales (ROS) and asset turnover (ATO)?

8. What criteria should be used to ascertain the usefulness of ROI?

9. What accounting policies have an impact on ROI?

10. What are the specific accounting policies for measurement of inventory and long-lived assets that affect income and investment?

11. What are other factors that affect income and should be considered when using ROI?

Cost Management: A Strategic Emphasis, 3e by Blocher/Chen/Cokins/Lin

12. Which assets should be included in the investment base?

13. What is a good way of allocating joint costs for ROI evaluation purposes?

14. What are the different ways that the investment base are calculated?

15. Why use balance scorecard in conjunction with ROI?

Learning Objective 3: Explain the use of residual income and identify its advantages and limitations.

16. What is residual income?

17. What is the advantage of using RI rather than ROI?

18. What are some of the unique limitations of RI?

Learning Objective 4: Explain the use of economic value added (EVA) in evaluating strategic investment units.

19. What is EVA?

20. What is cost of capital?

21. What are some of the characteristics of EVA?

Learning Objective 5: Explain the objectives of transfer pricing, the different transfer pricing methods, and when each method should be used.

22. What is transfer pricing?

23. When is transfer pricing important?

24. What are the objectives of transfer pricing?

25. What are some of the other objectives in international transfer pricing?

26. What are the basic methods used in transfer pricing and when should each method be used?

27. What are the three questions to be asked in setting a transfer price?

Learning Objective 6: Discuss the important international tax issues in transfer pricing.

28. What are the important international tax issues in transfer pricing?

29. What are the three most common arms length pricing methods?

30. What is an advance pricing agreement?

Suggested responses to the above questions:

1. What is return on investment?

ROI is profit divided by investment in the business unit.

2. When is the use of ROI preferable to profitability alone?

   Using profitability as a measure of a unit's performance over time can be adequate and effective. However, in comparing a unit's performance to other units, we must also know the investment base to be able to provide a meaningful comparison.

3. What is the strategic role of investment SBUs?

   The strategic role of investment SBUs are to:
   - *motivate managers to exert a high level of effort to achieve the goals of the firm,*
   - *provide the right incentive for managers to make decisions that are consistent with the goals of top management, and*
   - *fairly determine the rewards earned by the managers for their effort and skill.*

4. How is the amount of investment determined?

   For external reporting purposes, investment is defined as either the gross or book value of all assets. For internal reporting purposes, assets may be valued in terms of their replacement cost or market value.

5. What is return on equity?

   Return on equity (ROE) which is sometimes also referred to as return on investment is the return determined when investment is measured as shareholders' equity. ROE is of major interest to shareholders.

6. What is the expanded formula for ROI?

   ROI = Return on sales X Asset turnover
   Return on sales (ROS) = profit / sales
   Asset turnover (ATO) = Sales / assets

7. What is the significance of ROS and ATO?

   ROS measures the manager's ability to control expenses and increase revenues in order to improve profitability.
   AT measures the manager's ability to produce increased sales from a given level of investment.

8. What criteria should be used to ascertain the usefulness of ROI?

   In order for ROI measurement to be useful, it must be determined consistently and fairly.

9. What accounting policies have an impact on ROI?

There are two types of accounting policies that affect ROI: a) revenue and expense recognition policies, and b) asset measurement methods. These policies impact on the amount of income and investment.

10. What are the specific accounting policies for measurement of inventory and long-lived assets that affect income and investment:

The accounting policies that affect income and investment are:
- *depreciation policy*
- *capitalization policy*
- *inventory measurement methods*
- *absorption costing*
- *disposition of variances*

11. What are other factors that affect income and should be considered when using ROI?

Other measures affecting ROI are:
- *Non-recurring items such as promotion costs for introducing a new product.*
- *Income taxes when divisions operate in different countries.*
- *Foreign exchange when units in foreign countries are subject to exchange rate fluctuations that can affect income.*
- *Joint cost sharing would affect income differently depending on the allocation method used.*

12. Which assets should be included in the investment base?

A key criterion for including an asset in ROI is the degree to which it is controllable by the unit. If one unit leases fixed assets and another purchases them, it causes a problem for comparative purposes. In general, leased assets should be included in the investment base. Idle assets if controlled by the division manager should be included in the investment base. It can motivate the manager to dispose of them if there is no alternative use for such assets.

13. What is a good way of allocating joint costs for ROI evaluation purposes?

It is best to allocate joint costs at peak demand of each individual unit. Because it is for such levels that a certain capability level needs to be maintained.

14. What are the different ways that the investment bases are calculated?

The investment base can be calculated as,
- *historical cost of current assets plus the net book value of the long-lived assets.*

- gross book value (historical costs without the reduction for depreciation) may be used to avoid the effect of declining asset base as equipments get older.
- replacement cost to avoid the misleading nature of historical cost.
- liquidation value if the firm is considering disposal of the unit.

15. Why use a balanced scorecard in conjunction with ROI?

ROI focuses on short-term. It may tempt managers to cut on research and development, advertising, etc. that could enhance long-term profitability but negatively impact short-term profits. The balanced scorecard with its focus on customer satisfaction, internal business processes, and learning and growth provides a balance for evaluation purposes.

16. What is residual income?

Residual income (RI) is a dollar amount equal to the income of the business unit less a charge for the investment in the unit.

17. What is the advantage of using RI rather than ROI?

RI has the same limitations as ROI. RI, however, has the advantage that a unit will pursue an investment opportunity as long as the return from the investment exceeds the minimum rate of return set by the firm. A firm can also adjust the required rates of return (RRR) depending on the riskiness of the project. Different RRRs may also be used for current assets as compared to fixed assets.

18. What are some of the unique limitations of RI?

Some of the limitations of RI are the following:
- *RI is not a percentage and is not useful in comparison of different units.*
- *It is not as intuitive as ROI.*
- *Obtaining a minimum rate of return may be difficult.*

19. What is EVA?

EVA is a business unit's income after taxes and after deducting the cost of capital.

20. What is cost of capital?

Cost of capital is usually obtained by calculating a weighted average of the cost of the firm's two sources of funds - borrowing (net of tax) and selling stock.

21. What are some of the characteristics of EVA?

EVA is used to focus managers' attention on creating value for shareholders, by earning profits greater than the firm's cost of capital. Expenses that contribute to the long-term value of the firm are capitalized.

22. What is transfer pricing?

Transfer pricing is the determination of an exchange price when different business units within a firm exchange products or services.

23. When is transfer pricing important?

Transfer pricing is common among companies that are vertically integrated.

24. What are the objectives of transfer pricing?

The objectives of transfer pricing are a) to motivate managers, b) to provide an incentive for managers to make decisions consistent with the firm's goals, and c) to provide a basis for fairly rewarding the managers. In addition, the method used should satisfy the firm's overall strategic goals such as, minimizing the overall tax.

25. What are some of the other objectives in international transfer pricing?

The other objectives include minimizing custom charges, dealing with currency restrictions of foreign governments, and dealing with the risk of expropriation.

26. What are the basic methods used in transfer pricing and when should each method be used?

*The basic methods used in transfer pricing are **variable cost, full cost, market price, and negotiated price.** Variable cost method is suitable when the selling unit has excess capacity. The full cost method is well understood but it can cause improper short-term decisions. The market price method is most preferred. It is objective, but market price may not always be available. The negotiated price is desirable when the two units have a conflict, but the method can reduce the units' autonomy. A dual pricing scheme may be used when the buyer and seller do not use the same method and the difference is absorbed at the higher level in the organization.*

27. What are the three questions to be asked in setting a transfer price?

The key questions asked are,
- *Is there an outside supplier?*
- *Is the variable cost of the seller less than the market price?*
- *Does the selling unit have excess capacity?*

28. What are the important international tax issues in transfer pricing?

The important international tax issues in transfer pricing are, a) the arms-length standard, and b) the comparative price method. The arms length standard says that transfer prices should be set so they reflect the price that would have been set by unrelated parties acting independently. The comparable price method establishes an arm's length price by using the sales prices of similar products made by unrelated firms.

29. What are the three most common arms length price methods?

The three most common arms length price methods are,
- *the comparable price method which establishes an arm's length price by using the sales prices of similar products made by unrelated firms.*
- *the resale price method which is based on determining an appropriate markup, where the markup is based on gross profits of unrelated firms selling similar products.*
- *the cost plus method which determines the transfer price based on the seller's costs, plus a gross profit percentage determined from comparison of sales of the seller to unrelated parties.*

30. What is an advance pricing agreement?

Advance pricing agreements (APAs) are agreements between the Internal Revenue Service (IRS) and the firm using transfer prices, which sets out the agreed-upon transfer price.

Multiple choice questions:

1. The objectives of strategic investment units are to,
   a) motivate managers to exert a high level of effort to achieve the goals of the firm.
   b) provide the right incentive for managers to make decisions that are consistent with the goals of top management.
   c) fairly determine the rewards earned by the managers for their effort and skill.
   d) all of the above.
   e) a and b.

2. The expanded formula for ROI is
   a) Return on sales x Asset turnover.
   b) Return on sales x Inventory turnover.
   c) Gross profit x Asset turnover.
   d) Contribution margin x Asset turnover.
   e) Operating income x Inventory turnover.

Cost Management: A Strategic Emphasis, 3e by Blocher/Chen/Cokins/Lin

3. Asset turnover is
   a) profit over sales.
   b) sales over profits.
   c) sales over assets.
   d) assets over sales.
   e) profit over assets.

4. For ROI to be useful,
   a) income must be determined consistently and fairly.
   b) investment must be determined consistently and fairly.
   c) assets should be at net book value.
   d) all of the above.
   e) a and b.

5. The asset base used in ROI computations can be
   a) net book value or gross book value.
   b) replacement cost or liquidation value.
   c) gross book value plus accumulated depreciation.
   d) all of the above.
   e) a and b.

6. To get a better picture of the unit's performance,
   a) the balanced scorecard must be used.
   b) the ROI method must be used.
   c) the balanced scorecard + ROI must be used.
   d) the balanced scorecard focusing on financial performance and ROI focusing on operational performance must be used.
   e) none of the above.

7. The balanced scorecard focuses on,
   a) profit and investment.
   b) customer satisfaction and internal business processes.
   c) learning and growth.
   d) b and c.
   e) a and b.

8. Residual income is
   a) income over investment.
   b) income plus a charge for the investment in the unit.
   c) remaining income over investment.
   d) income less a charge for cost of capital.
   e) none of the above.

9. Residual income's limitations include,
    a) favors large units when the minimum rate of return is low.
    b) not as intuitive as ROI
    c) the difficulty to obtain a minimum rate of return.
    d) all of the above.
    e) b and c.

10. The cost of capital is
    a) a weighted average cost of all the funds borrowed.
    b) a weighted average cost of equity.
    c) a weighted average cost of debt and equity.
    d) a weighted average number representing company's expected return.
    e) none of the above.

11. Economic value added (EVA) is
    a) a business unit's contribution margin less fixed costs.
    b) a business unit's income after taxes.
    c) a business unit's net income less a charge for cost of capital.
    d) a business unit's operating income less the cost of capital.
    e) none of the above.

11. Transfer pricing when goods are imported from a home country to a host country should be,
    a) set high if the objective is to minimize custom charges in the host country.
    b) set low if the objective is to minimize custom charges in the host country.
    c) set regardless of consideration for custom charges.
    d) set low if there is currency restrictions.
    e) set low if there is a chance of expropriation.

12. The transfer prices used may be,
    a) variable cost or full cost.
    b) market price or negotiated price.
    c) dual price.
    d) all of the above.
    e) a and b.

13. Variable costing method of transfer pricing is
    a) easy to implement.
    b) intuitive and easily understood.
    c) preferred by tax authorities over full cost method.
    d) causes the seller to act as desired.
    e) all except c.

*Cost Management: A Strategic Emphasis, 3*e by Blocher/Chen/Cokins/Lin

14. Market price approach in transfer pricing,
    a) helps to preserve unit autonomy.
    b) provides incentive for the selling unit to be competitive with outside suppliers.
    c) has arm's-length standard desired by taxing authorities.
    d) may be the most practical approach when there is significant conflict.
    e) all of the above.

15. If there is no outside market, the transfer price can be,
    a) cost.
    b) negotiated price.
    c) dual price.
    d) any of the above.
    e) a and b.

16. If there is an outside market and the seller works at full capacity, then the transfer price should be,
    a) cost.
    b) market price.
    c) dual price.
    d) variable cost.
    e) negotiated price.

17. The resale price method in transfer pricing is,
    a) an arm's length price used in sales of similar products.
    b) based on cost plus a markup based on gross profit of the firm.
    c) based on cost plus a markup based on gross profit of unrelated firm's selling of similar products.
    d) is based on cost plus a markup based on gross profit of unrelated firm's selling of dissimilar products.
    e) none of the above.

18. Advance pricing agreements are agreements between the firm and,
    a) OECD which sets out the agreed-upon transfer price.
    b) IRS which sets out the agreed-upon transfer price.
    c) the host country which sets out the agreed-upon transfer price.
    d) SEC which sets out the agreed-upon transfer price.
    e) none of the above.

Exercises:

E1.

Arman Athletics has three divisions; Athletic shoes, Athletic clothing, Athletic equipment. Income, sales, and investment information for the years 1998 and 1999 follow:

Division	Income	Income	Investment	Investment	Sales	Sales
	1998	1999	1998	1999	1998	1999
Shoes	12,000	15,000	120,000	180,000	240,000	275,000
Clothing	7,000	8,000	100,000	100,000	154,000	168,000
Equipment	18,000	24,000	270,000	384,000	180,000	216,000

Required:
a) **Prepare comparative and extended ROI for the three divisions and for both years.**
b) **Comment on the comparative nature of this information between 1998 and 1999 and among the three divisions.**
c) **Compute the divisions' RI with a required rate of return of 5%.**
d) **Compute the divisions' EVA assuming that the given income is the operating income; the tax rates are at 30%, 20%, and 10% and the costs of capital are at 4%, 6%, and 8% respectively.**

E2.

Consider the same facts in exercise 1 but also assume that the gross book value of assets, replacement cost of assets, and liquidation value of assets are as follows:

Division	Gross BV	Gross BV	Repl Cost	Repl Cost	Liq Value	Liq Value
	1998	1999	1998	1999	1998	1999
Shoes	180,000	270,000	200,000	300,000	100,000	150,000
Clothing	150,000	150,000	180,000	180,000	90,000	90,000
Equipment	340,000	400,000	380,000	500,000	200,000	320,000
Total	670,000	820,000	760,000	980,000	390,000	560,000

Required:
a) **Compute ROI for both years and for the three divisions.**
b) **Comment on the results obtained.**

E3.

Ariana Toys has three divisions located in the US, France, and Germany. The US division sells its product A and B to the other two divisions at $29 and $49 a unit respectively. During 1999, 5000 units of A were sold to France Division, and 6000 units of B were sold to German Division. The US division also sold 9000 each of the two products to other customers at the same prices. France Division converts this product at the cost of $15 a unit and German division converts this product at the cost of $27 per unit and sell it to outsiders at $54 and $84 respectively. A has a variable cost of $12 and

Cost Management: A Strategic Emphasis, 3e by Blocher/Chen/Cokins/Lin

B has a variable cost of $23. Fixed costs for the year amounted to $98,600 for the US division, $40,000 for the France Division, and $54,000 for the German division. Applicable tax rates are 30%, 40%, and 50% for US, France, and Germany respectively.

Required:
a) **Prepare a consolidated income statement for the three divisions assuming that there is no inventory beginning or ending.**
b) **Recompute the income statement assuming that transfers are at variable product costs.**
c) **Recompute the income statement assuming that transfers are at full product costs.**
d) **Recompute the income statement assuming that transfers are at full cost plus a 20% margin.**
e) **Assuming some possible flexibility, at what prices should transfer prices take place to minimize the company's overall tax bill.**

E4.

Do a computer search for Coke Company that produces and sells the highly profitable proprietary concentrate to the bottlers and the bottling company, Coca-Cola Enterprises. Get their income before interest and taxes figures and total operating asset amounts and **compute their ROI for the last couple of years. Redo the exercise computing the ROI's in the expanded version.**

Correct answers to multiple choice questions:
1-d; 2-a; 3-c; 4-e; 5-e; 6-c; 7-d; 8-d; 9-d; 10-c; 11-b; 12-d; 13-e; 14-e; 15-d; 16-b; 17-b; 18-b.

Suggested answers to exercises:

E1.
a) ROS = Return on Sales; ATO = Asset turnover; ROI = Return on investment

DIVISION	ROS	ROS	ATO	ATO	ROI	ROI
	1998	1999	1998	1999	1998	1999
SHOES	0.05	0.054545	2	1.527778	0.1	0.083333
CLOTHES	0.045455	0.047619	1.54	1.68	0.07	0.08
EQUIPMENT	0.1	0.111111	0.666667	0.5625	0.066667	0.0625
TOTAL	0.06446	0.07132	1.171429	0.99247	0.07551	0.070783

b) The above analysis shows that although ROS has improved in Shoes division, but ROI has decreased because of lower ATO. Clothing ROI has increased because of improvement in both ROS and ATO. Equipment ROI has decreased because of lower ATO even though ROS has improved. Total ROI has slightly decreased because of lower ATO in spite of improved ROS. Comparing the three divisions, it appears that the divisions' performance can be ranked as first, Shoes, second, Clothes, and third,

Equipment for both years. However, this may be misleading because the risk factor in the three divisions may not be the same.

c) RI

DIVISION	RESIDUAL INCOME 1998	RESIDUAL INCOME 1999
SHOES	12,000 - (120,000 X 5%) = 6,000	15,000 - (180,000 X 5%) = 6,000
CLOTHES	7,000 - (100,000 X 5%) = 2,000	8,000 - (100,000 X 5%) = 3,000
EQUIPMENT	18,000 - (270,000 X 5%) = 4,500	24,000 - (384,000 X 5%) = 4,800
TOTAL	37,000 – (490,000 X 5%) = 12,500	47,000 - (664,000 X 5%) = 13,800

Note that with RI, Equipment division shows a better ranking compared to the Clothes division because of higher investment amount. Looking at both ROI and RI is preferable.

d) EVA

DIVISION	EVA 1998	EVA 1999
SHOES	12,000 * .70 - (120,000 * 4%) = 3,600	15,000 * .70 - (180,000 * 4%) = 3,300
CLOTHES	7,000 * .80 - (100,000 * 6%) = -400	8,000 * .80 - (100,000 * 6%) = 400
EQUIPMT.	18,000 * .90 - (270,000 * 8%) = -5400	24,000 * .90 - (384,000 * 8%) = - 9,120
TOTAL	N/A	N/A

Note that the divisions do not have the same cost of capital and the same applicable tax rates. Considering the taxes and cost of capital, the equipment division shows negative returns in both years and Clothes division shows negative returns in 1998.

E2.
a) ROI

DIVISION	GBV	GBV	REPL. C	REPL. C	LIQ VALU	LIQ VALU
	1998	1999	1998	1999	1998	1999
SHOES	0.066667	0.055556	0.06	0.05	0.12	0.1
CLOTHES	0.046667	0.053333	0.038889	0.044444	0.077778	0.088889
EQUIPMT	0.052941	0.06	0.047368	0.048	0.09	0.075
TOTAL	0.055224	0.057317	0.048684	0.048958	0.094872	0.714286

b) Comments:
The important point to note here is that ROI based on gross book value and replacement costs are considerably lower for all divisions for both years as compared to ROI based on

Cost Management: A Strategic Emphasis, 3e by Blocher/Chen/Cokins/Lin

net book value of assets. Gross book value provides more consistency from year to year, and using replacement costs may be more relevant. However, replacement costs may be somewhat subjective.

E3.

a) Consolidated income statement: transfer price = market price

Item	Qty.	USA	France	Germany	Total
Sales – A	14,000	406,000	270,000		531,000
Sales – B	15,000	735,000		504,000	945,000
Total Sales		1,141,000	270,000	504,000	1,476,000
VCS – A	14,000	168,000	145,000		168,000
VCS – B	15,000	345,000		294,000	345,000
Fixed Costs		98,600	40,000	54,000	192,600
Total Costs		611,600	185,000	348,000	705,600
Operating Income		529,400	85,000	156,000	70,400
Inc. Tax .30, .40, .50		158,820	34,000	78,000	270,820
Net Income		370,580	51,000	78,000	499,580

b) Income statement - transfer price at variable cost

Item	Qty.	USA	France	Germany	Total
Sales – A	9,000	261,000	270,000		531,000
Sales – B	9,000	441,000		504,000	945,000
Sales to Fr.	5,000	60,000			
Sales to Ge.	6,000	138,000			
Total Sales		900,000	270,000	504,000	1,476,000
VCS – A	14,000	168,000	60,000		168,000
VCS – B	15,000	345,000		138,000	345,000
Fixed Costs		98,600	40,000	54,000	192,600
Total Costs		611,600	100,000	192,000	705,600
Operating Income		288,400	170,000	312,000	770,400
Inc. Tax .30, .40, .50		86,520	68,000	156,000	310,520
Net Income		201,880	102,000	156,000	459,880

c) Income statement - transfer price at full cost

Item	Qty.	USA	France	Germany	Total
Sales – A	9,000	261,000	270,000		531,000
Sales – B	9,000	441,000		504,000	945,000
Sales to Fr.	5,000	77,000			
Sales to Ge.	6,000	158,400			
Total Sales		937,400	270,000	504,000	1,476,000
VCS – A	14,000	168,000	77,000		168,000
VCS – B	15,000	345,000		158,000	345,000
Fixed Costs		98,600	40,000	54,000	192,600
Total Costs		611,600	117,000	212,400	705,600
Operating Income		325,800	153,000	291,600	770,400
Inc. Tax .30, .40, .50		97,740	61,200	145,800	304,740
Net Income		228,060	91,800	145,800	465,660

d) Income statement - transfer price at full cost + 20% margin

Item	Qty.	USA	France	Germany	Total
Sales – A	9,000	261,000	270,000		531,000
Sales – B	9,000	441,000		504,000	945,000
Sales to Fr.	5,000	92,400			
Sales to Ge.	6,000	190,080			
Total Sales		984,480	270,000	504,000	1,476,000
VCS – A	14,000	168,000	92,400		168,000
VCS – B	15,000	345,000		190,080	345,000
Fixed Costs		98,600	40,000	54,000	192,600
Total Costs		611,600	132,400	244,080	705,600
Operating Income		372,880	137,600	259,920	770,400
Inc. Tax .30, .40, .50		111,864	55,040	129,960	296,864
Net Income		261,016	82,560	129,960	473,536

Cost Management: A Strategic Emphasis, 3e by Blocher/Chen/Cokins/Lin

e) Income statement using a transfer price to minimize taxes

Item	Qty.	USA	France	Germany	Total
Sales – A	9,000	261,000	270,000		531,000
Sales – B	9,000	441,000		504,000	945,000
Sales to Fr.	5,000	230,000			
Sales to Ge.	6,000	450,000			
Total Sales		1,382,000	270,000	504,000	1,476,000
VCS – A	14,000	168,000	230,000		168,000
VCS – B	15,000	345,000		450,000	345,000
Fixed Costs		98,600	40,000	54,000	192,600
Total Costs		611,600	270,000	504,000	705,600
Operating Income		770,400	0	0	770,400
Inc. Tax .30, .40, .50		231,120	0	0	321,120
Net Income		539,280	0	02	539,280

In this final exercise, we increased the transfer price from the US Division to France and German subdivision to the extent that those divisions' total costs would equal their total revenues and produce no taxable income. All income is thus shifted to the US division where the tax rate is the lowest. The end result is that the overall company's net income will be at the highest level as compared to the other alternatives. While transfer pricing may still be a good tool for overall tax minimization, the firm should be careful in making sure that they are acting lawfully and within the tax guidelines. Where clear market prices exist, there may not be room for playing with internally beneficial schemes for profit maximization.

CHAPTER 19
MANAGEMENT COMPENSATION
AND BUSINESS VALUATION

Highlights:

There are three principal objectives for management compensation, which follow directly from the objectives for management control -- the motivation of the manager, the incentive for proper decision making, and fairness to the manager. There are three main types of compensation -- salary, bonus, and benefits. The bonus is the fastest growing part of total compensation and often also the largest part. There are three important factors in the development of a bonus plan -- the base for computing the bonus (strategic performance measures, stock price, and critical success factors), the source of funding for the bonus (the business unit or the entire firm), and the payment options (current and deferred bonus, stock options, and performance shares).

Recent and unprecedented level of top management abuse in companies such as Enron, Worldcom, Tyco International, Global Crossing, and Arthur Andersen could have serious impact on the future viability of U.S. economy. Management compensation and management's ethical conduct must be reviewed so that they become more accountable to their employees, their shareholders, and the general public.

Tax planning and financial reporting concerns are important in compensation planning because of management's desire to reduce taxes and to report financial results favorably. Thus, taxes and financial reporting issues are also considered in the development of a compensation plan for managers.

The second part of the chapter deals with evaluation of the firm which is not the same as evaluation of the manager. The valuation of the firm is important to investors, and as one part of an overall assessment of the performance of top management. There are two approaches -- a financial analysis approach which focuses on critical success factors and accounting measures, and a valuation approach which focuses on market valuation. There are four methods for assessing the market value of the firm -- market value of shares, asset valuation, the discounted cash flow method, and the earning multiplier.

Questions:

Learning Objective 1: Identify and explain the types of management compensation.

1. What are the three components of most management compensation plans?

2. How can compensation plans be tailored for different strategic conditions?

3. How can managers' risk aversion be handled?

4. What is the link between compensation plans and ethics?

5. What are the objectives of management compensation?

6. What are the three key aspects of bonus pay plans?

7. What are the three ways to determine the bonus?

8. What are the advantages/disadvantages of various bases for bonus plans?

9. Identify and discuss unit-based and firm-wide-based compensation pools.

10. What are some of the advantages/disadvantages of unit-based compensation pools?

11. Discuss current bonus, deferred bonus, stock options, and performance shares.

12. Discuss some of the advantages/disadvantages of various bonus payment options.

Learning Objective 4: Describe the role of tax planning and financial reporting in management compensation planning.

13. What are the key tax and financial report effects of compensation?

Learning Objective 5: Explain how management compensation plans are used in service firms and not-for-profit organizations.

14. How are management compensation plans used in service firms and not-for-profit organizations?

Learning Objective 6: Apply the different methods for business evaluation and business valuation.

15. How is financial analysis used for firm valuation purposes?

16. How is valuation approach used?

17. How is market value of the firm determined?

18. What does the term liquidity refer to?

19. What are the key measures of liquidity?

20. What are the key profitability ratios?

21. What is a firm's economic valued added (EVA)?

22. What are the methods used for directly measuring the value of a firm?

23. What are the options in asset valuation?

24. What is the discounted cash flow method used for company valuation?

25. What is the earnings-based valuation?

Suggested responses to the above questions:
1. What are the three components of most management compensation plans?

     The three components of most management compensation plans are salary, bonus, and benefits. Salary is a fixed payment, while a bonus is based upon the achievement of performance goals for the period. Perks include special services and benefits for the employee, such as travel, membership in a fitness club, life insurance, medical benefits, tickets to entertainment events, and other "extras" paid for by the firm.

2. How can compensation plans be tailored for different strategic conditions?

Compensation plans can be tailored for different strategic conditions. During the introductory phase of the product life cycle, high salary, low bonus and benefits may be appropriate, because of substantial uncertainties. During the growth phase, salaries may be set low with high bonus and competitive benefits to induce managers to work harder in achieving the organization's goals. During the maturity phase of the product life cycle where the major task is maintaining of the firm's position in the industry, salary, bonus, and benefits can be set at competitive levels. During the decline phase where in spite of managers' efforts, the decline would still continue, setting high salaries with low bonus and competitive benefits may be appropriate.

3. How can managers' risk aversion be handled?

Managers are often risk averse with a tendency to prefer decisions with assured outcomes over those with uncertain outcomes. Compensation plans can manage risk-aversion effectively by carefully choosing the mix of salary and bonus included in total compensation. The larger the proportion of bonus in total compensation, the more the incentive to the manager to avoid risky outcomes.

4. What is the link between compensation plans and ethics?

The author cites several examples where managers resorted to manipulation of financial statements or engaged in fraudulent billing practices to reach an established goal and receive a bonus. Through promotion of ethical behavior, internal controls, strong audit teams, and reasonably achievable and participatory goals, managerial ethical lapses can be minimized.

5. What are the objectives of management compensation?

The essential objectives of a management compensation plan are,
- *to motivate managers to exert a high level of effort to achieve the firm's goals. Example - a bonus plan.*
- *to provide the right incentive for managers, acting autonomously, to make decisions that are consistent with the firm's goals. Example - critical success factors.*
- *to fairly determine the rewards earned by the manager for their effort and skill, and for the effectiveness of their decision making. Note: make the plan simple, clear, and consistent.*

Cost Management: A Strategic Emphasis, 3e by Blocher/Chen/Cokins/Lin

6. What are the three key aspects of bonus pay plans?

The three key aspects of bonus pay plans are,
- *the base of the compensation, that is, how the bonus pay is determined. The three most common bases are (1) stock price, (2) cost, revenue, profit, or investment SBU-based performance, and (3) the balanced scorecard.*
- *compensation pools, that is, the source from which the bonus pay is funded. The two most common compensation pools are (1) earnings in the manager's own SBU, and (2) a firm-wide pool, based on total earnings for the firm.*
- *payment options, that is, how the bonus is to be awarded. The two common options are cash and stock (typically common shares). The cash or stock can either be awarded currently or deferred to future years. Also, the stock can either be awarded directly or granted in the form of stock options.*

7. What are the three ways to determine the bonus?

The bonus can be determined based on a comparison in prior year(s), budget or predetermined target, or other managers.

8. What are the advantages/disadvantages of various bases for bonus plans?

- *Using stock price is consistent with shareholder's interests. However, there is lack of controllability on stock prices.*
- *Using strategic performance measures (cost, revenue, profit, investment SBUs) are generally good measures of economic performance. They are also intuitive, clear, and easily understood. But such measures usually have a short-term focus, may contribute to inaccurate reporting, and are subject to differences in accounting conventions and methodology.*
- *Using the balanced scorecard can be strongly motivating if non-controllable factors are excluded. It is consistent with management's strategy, and if carefully defined and measured, CSFs are likely to be perceived as fair. But this measure may also be subject to inaccurate reporting, and there is the potential for measurement problems.*

9. Identify and discuss unit-based and firm-wide based compensation pools.

A unit based pool is a method for determining a bonus based upon the performance of the unit. A firm-wide pool is a method of determining bonus available to all managers through an amount that is set aside for this purpose.

10. What are some of the advantages/disadvantages of unit-based compensation pools?

- *Unit-based compensation pools provide strong motivation for an effective manager. But it is an incentive for not cooperating with other units and does not separate the performance of the unit from the performance of the manager.*
- *Firm-wide compensation pools help to attract and retain good managers throughout the firm, even in economically weaker units. It promotes doing good for the benefit of the firm as a whole. It separates the performance of the manager from that of the unit. It also appears to be fairer to shareholders and others concerned about the level of the executive pay.*

11. Discuss current bonus, deferred bonus, stock options, and performance shares.

- *Current bonus which is based on current performance is the most common form of bonus.*
- *Deferred bonus, earned currently but not paid for two or more years, are used to avoid or delay taxes, or affect the future total income stream of the manager in some way, and enhance the possibility of retaining the manager.*
- *Stock options are used to motivate the manager to increase stock price for the benefit of the shareholders.*
- *Performance shares are stock granted for achieving certain performance goals over a two or more year period.*

12. Discuss some of the advantages/disadvantages of various bonus payment options.

- *Current bonus provides strong motivation for current performance, but it has a short-term focus, and risk averse managers avoid risky projects.*
- *Deferred bonus also provides a strong motivation for current performance (but not as strong as the former approach). It has somewhat of a short -term focus, and risk averse managers avoid risky projects.*
- *Stock options are highly motivating but delayed rewards may reduce motivation. It focuses on long term and provides better risk incentives. However, managers may be induced to manipulate income and cheat the market in order to cash in on their stock options. This should not happen in an ethical world and in an ideal setting, but unfortunately, it does.*
- *Performance shares have similar advantages as stock options. It also considers long-term performance, and provides rewards consistent with shareholder interests and firm's strategy.*

Cost Management: A Strategic Emphasis, 3e by Blocher/Chen/Cokins/Lin

13. What are the key tax and financial report effects of compensation?

- *Salary is considered as current business expense and is taxed currently on the manager.*
- *Current bonus is considered as current expense and is also taxed currently on the manager.*
- *Deferred bonus is a deferred expense and its tax will also be deferred.*
- *Stock options (nonqualified plans) - accounting rules encourage but do not require recognition as expense. It is a deductible expense for tax when exercised, and will be taxed as ordinary income on the manager when exercised.*
- *Stock options (qualified plans) - similar accounting rules apply here too, but no deduction is allowed for tax purposes and is taxed as capital gains when stock is sold (if held for at least 18 months).*
- *Certain retirement plans are considered as current expense with current deduction for taxes but deferred deduction on the manager.*
- *Other perks such as company car, club membership, etc. may be considered as current expense but never taxed on the manager.*

14. How are management compensation plans used in service firms and not-for-profit organizations?

An example provided in the text book explains the use of balanced scorecard approach with focus on financial results, client satisfaction, and improvement in the process of developing and providing the services. Financial results are evaluated in terms of profitability, efficiency with regards to staff utilization, and collection of accounts.

15. How is financial analysis used for firm valuation purposes?

The financial analysis approach uses the balanced scorecard, financial ratio analysis, and economic value added as benchmarks in the evaluation. While this approach evaluates the firm's overall performance, it does not develop a dollar value for the firm.

16. How is valuation approach used?

The valuation approach evaluates the firm by estimating its total market value, which can then be compared to the market value for prior periods or for comparable firms.

17. How is market value of the firm determined?

Market value of the firm is a complex mix of asset values, profitability, quality factors, human resource values, etc.

18. What does the term liquidity refer to?

Liquidity refers to the firm's ability to pay its current operating expenses (usually a year or less) and maturing debt.

19. What are the key measures of liquidity?

The key measures of liquidity are:
- *accounts receivable turnover*
- *inventory turnover*
- *current ratio*
- *quick ratio*
- *cash flow ratio*

20. What are the key profitability ratios?

The key profitability ratios are:
- *gross margin percentage*
- *return on assets*
- *return on equity*
- *earnings per share*

21. What is a firm's economic valued added (EVA)?

A firm's EVA is the business unit's income after taxes and after deducting the cost of capital.

22. What are the methods used for directly measuring the value of a firm?

The four methods used for measuring the value of a firm are:
- *market value*
- *asset valuation*
- *the discounted cash flow method*
- *earnings-based valuation*

23. What are the options in asset valuation?

There are four options when using the asset valuation method,
- *net book value*
- *gross book value*
- *replacement cost*
- *liquidation value*

Cost Management: A Strategic Emphasis, 3e by Blocher/Chen/Cokins/Lin

The net book value and gross book value method are affected by the firm's accounting policies. Replacement cost and liquidation values are more relevant for valuation, although there is problem with lack of objectivity.

24. What is the discounted cash flow method used for company valuation?

The discounted cash flow (DCF) method develops the value of the firm as the discounted present value of the firm's net free cash flows. To get the net valuation of the firm, we add the discounted value of six-year-plus cash flows to the value of current non-operating investments such as marketable securities, and we subtract the market value of long term debt.

25. What is the earnings-based valuation?

The earnings-based method computes value as the product of expected annual accounting earnings times a multiplier.

Multiple choice questions:

1. A proper strategic compensation plan must include,
   a) high salary and low bonus and benefits during product introduction phase.
   b) low salary and high bonus during the growth phase of the business.
   c) competitive salary, bonus, and benefits during the maturity phase.
   d) high salary and low bonus during the decline phase.
   e) all of the above.

2. The objectives of management compensation plan include,
   a) motivation of managers to exert a high level of effort to achieve the firm's goals.
   b) providing the right incentive for managers, acting autonomously, to make decisions that are consistent with the firm's goals.
   c) determining the rewards earned by the manager for their effort and skill, and for the effectiveness of their decision making.
   d) all of the above.
   e) a and b.

3. Using the stock option as part of management compensation has the advantage of
   a) controllability.
   b) consistency with shareholder's interests.
   c) fairness.
   d) all of the above.
   e) b and c.

4. Using cost, revenue, profit, or investment as a base for management compensation has the advantage of being,
   a) strongly motivating if non-controllable factors are excluded.
   b) having long-term focus.
   c) intuitive, clear, and easily understood.
   d) all of the above.
   e) a and c.

5. Using cost, revenue, profit, or investment as a base for management compensation has the disadvantage of,
   a) not being a good measure of economic performance.
   b) typically having a short-term focus.
   c) differing accounting and financing conventions.
   d) all of the above.
   e) b and c.

6. A firm-wide performance measure has the advantage of
   a) helping to attract and retain good managers.
   b) rewarding for the overall good of the firm.
   c) separating the performance of the manager from that of the unit.
   d) all of the above.
   e) none of the above.

7. The impact of nonqualified stock option plans as management bonus is that
   a) it can be recognized as expense of the current period.
   b) it is tax deductible to the firm when exercised.
   c) it is taxed as ordinary income to the manager when exercised.
   d) all of the above.
   e) a and c.

8. The impact of qualified stock option plans as management bonus is that
   a) it can be recognized as expense of the current period.
   b) it is tax deductible to the firm when exercised.
   c) it is taxed as ordinary income to the manager when exercised.
   d) all of the above.
   e) a and c.

9. As part of a firm's valuation,
   a) net book value or gross book value of assets may be used.
   b) replacement cost or liquidation value of assets may be used.
   c) net income or cash flow may be used.
   d) all of the above.
   e) b and c.

10. Liquidity ratios include,
    a) accounts receivable and inventory turnovers.
    b) quick and current ratios.
    c) cash flow ratios.
    d) all of the above.
    e) b and c.

11. Profitability ratios include,
    a) accounts receivable and inventory turnovers.
    b) gross margin percentage and return on assets.
    c) return or equity and earnings per share.
    d) all of the above.
    e) b and c.

12. The methods for directly measuring the value of a firm include,
    a) market value or asset valuation.
    b) multiplier of earnings-based valuation
    c) the discounted cash flow method.
    d) all of the above.
    e) a and c.

Comprehensive exercise:

Mona Pharmaceutical Company is considering to sell one of its divisions. Total assets at the beginning of the year for this division amounted to $360,000 from this amount $100,000 was accounts receivable and $80,000 was inventory. There were no preferred stocks and the number of shares have remained at 5000 during the past two years. Cost of debt before tax is at 10% and cost of equity has averaged to 12%. Company shares are traded at $62 a share in the market. It is estimated that liquidation value of assets is about 70% of fixed assets. Replacement cost of fixed assets is approximately 1.6 times their net book values. The company uses a discount rate of 12% and Financial information for the current year and the coming five years are summarized below:

ITEM	Yr 2002	Yr 2003	Yr 2004	Yr 2005	Yr 2006	Yr 2007
Cash	20,000	25,000	35,000	40,000	45,000	50,000
Receivable	120,000	130,000	135,000	140,000	145,000	150,000
Inventory	40,000	45,000	50,000	55,000	60,000	65,000
Fixed assets - net	220,000	230,000	240,000	250,000	260,000	270,000
Total assets	400,000	430,000	460,000	485,000	510,000	535,000
Current liabilities	20,000	25,000	35,000	40,000	45,000	50,000
Long-term debt	200,000	210,000	220,000	230,000	240,000	250,000
Equity	180,000	195,000	205,000	215,000	225,000	235,000
Total L + E	400,000	430,000	460,000	485,000	510,000	535,000
Revenue	800,000	820,000	840,000	860,000	880,000	900,000
Cost of goods sold	480,000	492,000	504,000	516,000	528,000	540,000
Expenses (cash)	70,000	80,000	85,000	90,000	95,000	100,000
Expenses (noncash)	70,000	75,000	80,000	85,000	90,000	100,000
Operating income	180,000	173,000	171,000	169,000	167,000	160,000
Income tax 32%	57,600	55,360	54,720	54,080	53,440	51,200
Net income	122,400	117,640	116,280	114,920	113,560	108,800

Required:
a) Compute accounts receivable turnover
b) Compute inventory turnover
c) Current ratio
d) Quick ratio
e) Cash flow ratio
f) Gross margin percent
g) Return on assets
h) Return on equity
i) Earnings per share
j) Cost of capital
k) Economic value added - you can round the cost of capital computed above.
l) Company value using the market value approach.
m) Company value using asset valuation approach.
n) Company value using the discounted cash flow method.
o) Company value using earning-based valuation.
p) Company value using a weighted average value: .15 (k), .20 (l), .30(m), .35 (o).
    The letters in parenthesis refer to the above requirements of k through o.
q) What do we primarily learn and infer from this exercise?

E2.
Search the internet and find at least three articles dealing with the scandals concerning Kenneth Lay, CEO of Enron, Andrew Fastow, CFO of Enron, Scott Sullivan, CFO of Worldcom, Dennis Kozlowski, CEO of Tyco International, and Gary Winnick, CEO of Global Crossing.

Suggested answer to the comprehensive exercise:

ITEM	Yr 2002	Yr 2003	Yr 2004	Yr 2005	Yr 2006	Yr 2007
Cash	20,000	25,000	35,000	40,000	45,000	50,000
Receivable	120,000	130,000	135,000	140,000	145,000	150,000
Inventory	40,000	45,000	50,000	55,000	60,000	65,000
Fixed assets - net	220,000	230,000	240,000	250,000	260,000	270,000
Total assets	400,000	430,000	460,000	485,000	510,000	535,000
Current liabilities	20,000	25,000	35,000	40,000	45,000	50,000
Long-term debt	200,000	210,000	220,000	230,000	240,000	250,000
Equity	180,000	195,000	205,000	215,000	225,000	235,000
Total L + E	400,000	430,000	460,000	485,000	510,000	535,000
Revenue	800,000	820,000	840,000	860,000	880,000	900,000
Cost of goods sold	480,000	492,000	504,000	516,000	528,000	540,000
Expenses (cash)	70,000	80,000	85,000	90,000	95,000	100,000
Expenses (noncash)	70,000	75,000	80,000	85,000	90,000	100,000
Operating income	180,000	173,000	171,000	169,000	167,000	160,000
Income tax 32%	57,600	55,360	54,720	54,080	53,440	51,200
Net income	122,400	117,640	116,280	114,920	113,560	108,800
a) A/R turnover	7	7	6	6	6	6
b) Inventory turnover	8	12	11	10	9	9
c) Current ratio	9	8	6	6	6	5
d) Quick ratio	7	6	5	5	4	4
e) Cash flow ratio	10	8	6	5	5	4
f) Gross margin ratio	0	0	0	0	0	0
g) Return on assets	0	0	0	0	0	0
h) Return on equity	1	1	1	1	1	0
i) Earning per share	24	24	23	23	23	22
j) Cost of capital	0	0	0	0	0	0
k) EVA	85,347	77,634	73,462	69,755	66,048	58,940
l) Market value	310,000	310,000	310,000	310,000	310,000	310,000
m1) Liquidation value	154,000	161,000	168,000	175,000	182,000	189,000
m2) Replacement cost	352,000	368,000	384,000	400,000	416,000	432,000
n) Discounted CF	413,464					
o) Earning based val	571,200					
p) Weighted average	476,059					

q) This exercise shows clearly that there are various ways to value an entity. None of these methods are exact, but they provide valuable insight with regard to various aspects of value. Ultimately, management judgment and negotiation skills are necessary to finalize a deal.

CHAPTER 20
CAPITAL BUDGETING

Highlights:

Capital budgeting processes include project identification, project evaluation and selection, and monitoring and review. The primary focus in analyzing capital investments often is on cash flow. An investment is not a good investment if the investor receives less cash from the investment than the amount the investor puts in.

Cash flows in investments occur at three stages. These stages are initial acquisition, operations, and final disinvestment. Cash flows at initial acquisition include cash disbursement for the purchase of equipment and facilities, commitment of working capital needed during operation of the investment, and cash proceeds from disposal of the asset the investment replaced or cash disbursement for disposing of the replaced assets and facilities.

An investment generates net cash inflows during its operation either through increases in revenues or through decreases in expenses. The final disinvestment may generate additional cash proceeds through sales of the investment. Final disinvestment leads to cash expenditures for disposal, restoration of facilities, relocations, retraining of personnel, etc.

Many investments are available for analyzing capital investments. Among the techniques often used are payback period and book rate of return and discounted cash flow methods such as net present value and internal rate of return. For computations using the latter techniques which consider time-value of money, one needs to understand the concept of cost of capital; i.e., the cost of money that an entity needs to consider in capital budgeting decisions. Cost of capital is computed by taking the weighted average of after-tax cost of debt plus cost of equity. Cost of equity is composed of dividend and growth as a percentage of market value of the company's stock.

A capital investment analysis needs to take into consideration the firm's competitive advantage, effects of the investment on both upstream and downstream activities in the firm's value chain, and impact of strategic structural and executional cost drivers.

Questions:

1. What is a capital investment?

2. What is capital budgeting?

3. What are the three successive steps in capital budgeting? Briefly discuss these steps.

4. How does data for use in capital budgeting differ from data used in financial reporting?

5. What is the tax effect of cash flow in capital budgeting?

6. What are the effects of asset acquisition on cash flow?

7. What is the working capital effect in capital budgeting?

8. What is the paypack period method?

9. What are some of the advantages and disadvantages of the payback period method?

10. What is the book rate of return method?

11. What are some of the advantages and disadvantages of book rate of return?

12. What is the desired rate of return?

13. What is cost of capital?

14. What is the net present value (NPV) method?

15. What are some of the advantages and disadvantages of the net present value method?

16. What is the present value of discounted payback period or breakeven time (BET)?

17. What is internal rate of return (IRR) method?

18. What are some of the advantages and disadvantages of the IRR method?

Learning Objective 4: Identify underlying assumptions of the two discounted cash flow methods.

19. In what situations may the results from NPR and IRR be different?

Learning Objective 5: Explain the relationships between strategic cost management and capital budgeting.

20. What is the relationship between strategic cost management and capital budgeting?

21. What is the significance of value chain and capital budgeting?

22. What is the significance of cost driver analysis in capital budgeting?

Cost Management: A Strategic Emphasis, 3e by Blocher/Chen/Cokins/Lin

23. What are some of the important behavioral factors in capital budgeting to consider?

Suggested responses to the above questions:

1. What is a capital investment?

A capital investment is an investment that requires commitment of a large sum of funds and has expected expenditures and benefits that stretch well into the future.

2. What is capital budgeting?

Capital budgeting is the process of making capital investment decisions.

3. What are the three successive steps in capital budgeting? Briefly discuss these steps.

They are project identification, evaluation, and periodic post-audit and review.
At the outset, it is important and critical to identify the potential projects and their importance to the firm. Evaluation of capital investments requires projection of revenues or benefits, costs, and cash flows for the entire life of the project. There are also important non-financial reasons for committing major capital expenditures such as, the safety of employees or the public, pollution control, legal requirements, etc. Continuous monitoring and review of a project are important. The situation may change, and there may be a need for altering the course of action or modifying the current plan.

4. How does data for use in capital budgeting differ from data used in financial reporting?

Data used for capital budgeting is for the life period of the project. Financial reporting data is usually annual. In capital budgeting, we are interested in cash flow; i.e., the actual cash revenue and expenditure. In financial accounting, we primarily use accrual accounting. Finally, in capital budgeting the time horizon is always future events and transactions. In financial accounting, the time horizon is the historical events and transactions. The cash flow in a capital budget occurs at its inception (for purchase of the new system), during its lifetime for its operation, and at the end of the project for disposal of the system.

5. What is the tax effect of cash flow in capital budgeting?

*In a tax bracket of say, 40%, a $10,000 cash revenue is reduced by $4,000 for taxes, and a cash expenditure of $6,000 is reduced by $2,400 for its tax advantage. Alternatively, a cash income of $4,000 is reduced by $1,600; [(10,000 -6,000) * .40] for its tax effects. A non-cash expenditure (depreciation) is irrelevant in capital budgeting except for its tax effect (often referred to as depreciation tax shield); i.e., because of depreciation, we pay less taxes. Thus, in the above example, if our only expenditure was depreciation for the amount of $6,000, we would still pay a tax of $1,600, however, our cash flow will not be $2,400; ($4,000 * .60), rather, it would be $2,400 + 6,000 = $8,400. The $6,000 expenditure did not require any cash resource, and it is added back*

6. What are the effects of asset acquisition on cash flow?

*The primary components are a) cost of equipment and associated costs until it becomes ready for operation (outflow), and b) the depreciation of the asset during its life provides a cash inflow because of its tax effect (depreciation * tax rate). The disposal of the asset at the end of project's life provides a final additional cash inflow. It often has some tax effect due to gain or loss on disposal of an asset that must be considered.*

7. What is the working capital effect in capital budgeting?

Purchase of a fixed asset often has an impact on working capital (the increase in cash, receivables, and inventory needs less payables). It is important to add this item to initial cash requirements and then consider it as an inflow at the end of the project's life.

8. What is the paypack period method?

The payback period method finds the length of time required to recoup the investment in the project. For equal cash inflows, we divide the initial investment by the annual cash inflow to determine the payback period. For unequal cash-flows, add the cumulative cash-flows until such time that total inflows equal total outflows. If inflows continue beyond payback, the project may be worth considering.

9. What are some of the advantages and disadvantages of the payback method?

The payback method a) is simple to use and understand, b) measures liquidity, and c) allows for risk tolerance. However, it a) ignores timing and time value of money, b) ignores cash flows beyond payback period.

Cost Management: A Strategic Emphasis, 3e by Blocher/Chen/Cokins/Lin

10. What is the book rate of return method?

This method is the net income or the return from an investment as a percentage of its book value. The numerator is the average annual expected net income from the investment over its useful life. The denominator is either total initial investment or the average investment (book value) over the useful life of the project.

11. What are some of the advantages and disadvantages of book rate of return?

The advantages are a) readily available data, b) consistency between data for capital budgeting and data for performance evaluation, and c) easily identifiable impact on financial measures. Disadvantages include, a) no adjustment for time value of money, b) arbitrary measurements, c) periodic net income not equal to cash flow.

12. What is the desired rate of return?

Desired rate of return is the minimum rate of return that the investing firm requires for the investment. It is used as an alternative to the true opportunity cost which is usually not readily available.

13. What is cost of capital?

Cost of capital is a composite of the cost of various sources of funds comprising a firm's capital structure. It may be used as a substitute for the desired rate of return. The weighted average after-tax cost of capital is the after-tax cost to the firm in securing funds with a given capital structure. Debt is computed after tax, and equity is computed before tax.

14. What is the net present value (NPV) method?

This method considers the excess of the present value of future cash flow returns over the initial investment considering the time value of money. The present value factor is based on the cost of capital. PV of even cash flows can be computed by taking the annual flow times PV of annuity. Annuity is the number of time periods involved. For uneven cash flows, we must compute the PV for each year separately. A NPV amount over zero indicates that the project is favorable.

15. What are some of the advantages and disadvantages of the net present value method?

NPV a) considers time value of money, b) uses realistic discount rate for reinvestment, and c) shows the additive effect on combined investments. However, it is not meaningful for comparing projects requiring different amounts of investment.

16. What is the present value of discounted payback period or breakeven time (BET)?

BET of an investment is the span of time for the cumulative present value of cash inflows to be equal to the initial investment of the project. So we start discounting the annual cash flows until such amounts equal the initial investment.

17. What is internal rate of return (IRR) method?

IRR method is a discounted cash flow method that estimates the discount rate which makes the present value of subsequent cash flow returns equal the initial investment. The IRR method compares the project's rate of return to the desired rate of return. If the cash flows are even, the IRR rate is computed by taking the initial cash outlay divided by annual returns from the investment. The factor so arrived at is found across the Table of PV rates for the number of periods involved. If cash flow is uneven, we must use trial and error realizing that if initial cash flows are higher, then, the rate of return is probably higher than the average rate of return that is computed through the earlier method.

18. What are some of the advantages and disadvantages of the IRR method?

IRR a) considers time value of money, and b) is easy for comparing projects requiring different amounts of investment. Disadvantages include a) the assumption on reinvestment rate of return may be unrealistic, and b) it is complex to compute if done manually.

19. In what situations would the results from NPR and IRR be different?

Results may be different if projects differ in a) required initial investment, b) cash flow pattern, c) length of useful life, d) varying cost of capital, and e) multiple investments. Also note that the NPV method assumes that all cash inflows an investment generates earn a return equal to the cost of capital of the firm. The IRR method assumes that all cash inflows earn the same rate of return as the internal rate of return of the investment. The result is that the IRR is often more optimistic compared to the NPV. Both methods favor projects with longer lives. The NPV method can accommodate multiple discount rates easily while it is rather difficult for the IRR method to handle multiple costs of capital or desired rates of return. NPV's of multiple investment projects are additive while internal rates of return of these projects are not.

Cost Management: A Strategic Emphasis, 3e by Blocher/Chen/Cokins/Lin

20. What is the relationship between strategic cost management and capital budgeting?

A proper analysis of a capital investment needs to include the firm's competitive advantage, assessments of effects of the firm's value chain, and inclusion of strategic cost drivers.

During early phases of a product life cycle (build), capital expenditure decisions need to be less formal with more emphasis on non-financial data and expectation for longer payback periods. The expected rates of return may be relatively low, and investment analysis may be more subjective and qualitative. Project approval limits at business unit levels may be relatively high with frequent post-audit review.

During later phases (harvest), capital expenditure decisions are generally more formalized. There is more emphasis on financial data with shorter payback expected. Discount rates used are usually high. Capital investment analysis is more quantitative. Project approval limits at business levels is relatively low, and there is less frequent post-audits.

21. What is the significance of value chain and capital budgeting?

A value-chain analysis that includes impacts to both upstream and downstream operations provides a better picture of the benefits of a proposed investment project.

22. What is the significance of cost driver analysis in capital budgeting?

Structural and executional cost drivers are more critical factors than volume. They must be seriously considered in capital budget analysis. Structural cost drivers are factors that relate to the firm's strategic choices regarding economic structure. These strategic choices include technology, scale, product-line complexity, scope of vertical integration, or experience.

Executional cost drivers are major determinants of a firm's cost position that hinge on its ability to work successfully within the economic structure it chooses. They include items such as, workforce involvement and commitment to continuous improvement, adherence to total quality management concepts, utilization of effective capacity, efficiency of production flow layout, effectiveness of product design or formulation, exploiting linkages with suppliers and customers all along the value chain.

23. What are some of the important behavioral factors in capital budgeting to consider?

Firms need to be more careful not to allow aggressive managers to overestimate projections in attempts to earn approval of capital investment for their divisions. Sunk costs should have no effect on decisions. Research has found that sunk costs play an important role influencing the framing of decisions. Intolerance of uncertainty often leads managers to require short payback periods for capital investments. Once a project pays for itself, the amount of risk is reduced. Many projects, however, require a lengthy time for installation, testing, adjusting, personnel training, and market acceptance.

Multiple choice questions:

1. A capital investment is an investment that
   a) requires commitment of a large sum of funds and has expected expenditures and benefits during the current time period.
   b) requires commitment of a small sum of funds and has expected expenditures and benefits well into the future.
   c) requires commitment of a large sum of funds and has expected expenditures and benefits well into the future.
   d) requires commitment of a large sum of funds and has expected expenditures during the current period and benefits well into the future.
   e) none of the above.

2. Capital investment decisions are important to
   a) manufacturing industries
   b) agricultural industries
   c) service industries
   d) information technologies
   e) all of the above

3. With regard to capital budgeting (CB) versus financial reporting (FR),
   a) CB time horizon is future events and transactions whereas FR's is historical events and transactions.
   b) CB's measurement object is accrual revenues and expenses and FR's is cash flows.
   c) CB's data period is life of the project whereas FR's is annual.
   d) a and c.
   e) a and b.

4. With regard to cash flow (CF) and net income (NI) concepts,
   a) cash flow may vary with choices of discretionary accounting policy and procedure whereas, net income is objective and precise.
   b) cash flow and net income are often the same amount.
   c) net income may vary with choices of discretionary accounting policy and procedures whereas, cash flow is objective and precise.
   d) none of the above.
   e) a and b.

5. With regard to capital investments, cash flows occur
   a) at project initiation.
   b) during project operation.
   c) at final disposal.
   d) all of the above.
   e) a and b.

6. In capital budgeting, depreciation tax shield represents the amount of
   a) additional cash flow because of using depreciation as a period expense.
   b) additional tax because of using depreciation as a period expense.
   c) additional expense because of using depreciation as a period expense.
   d) additional revenue because of using depreciation as a period expense.
   e) none of the above.

7. Among payback period method advantages are that it
   a) considers time value of money and is easy for comparing projects.
   b) considers time value of money, uses realistic discount rates, and is additive for combined projects.
   c) is consistent with other financial measures and, data is readily available.
   d) is simple to use and understand, measures liquidity, and allows for risk tolerance.
   e) none of the above.

8. Among book return method advantages are that it
   a) considers time value of money and is easy for comparing projects.
   b) considers time value of money, uses realistic discount rates, and is additive for combined projects.
   c) is consistent with other financial measures, and data is readily available.
   d) is simple to use and understand, measures liquidity, and allows for risk tolerance.
   e) none of the above.

9. Among net present value method advantages are that it
   a) considers time value of money and is easy for comparing projects.
   b) considers time value of money, uses realistic discount rates, and is additive for combined projects.
   c) is consistent with other financial measures and, data is readily available.
   d) is simple to use and understand, measures liquidity, and allows for risk tolerance.
   e) none of the above.

10. Among internal rate of return method advantages are that it
    a) considers time value of money and is easy for comparing projects.
    b) considers time value of money, uses realistic discount rates, and is additive for combined projects.
    c) is consistent with other financial measures and, data is readily available.
    d) is simple to use and understand, measures liquidity, and allows for risk tolerance.
    e) none of the above.

11. Among the discounted payback method advantages are that it
    a) considers time value of money and is easy for comparing projects.
    b) considers time value of money, uses realistic discount rates, and is additive for combined projects.
    c) is consistent with other financial measures and, data is readily available.
    d) is simple to use and understand, measures liquidity, and allows for risk tolerance.
    e) none of the above.

12. Payback period method weaknesses include the fact that it
    a) ignores timing and time value of money and uses accounting numbers rather than cash flows.
    b) ignores timing and time value of money and ignores cash flows beyond recovery of the investment.
    c) assumes a reinvestment rate of return which may be unrealistic, and is difficult to compute manually.
    d) is not meaningful for comparing projects requiring different amounts of investment.
    e) none of the above.

13. Book rate of return method weaknesses include the fact that it
    a) ignores timing and time value of money and uses accounting numbers rather than cash flows.
    b) ignores timing and time value of money and ignores cash flows beyond recovery of the investment.
    c) assumes a reinvestment rate of return which may be unrealistic, and is difficult to compute manually.
    d) is not meaningful for comparing projects requiring different amounts of investment.
    e) none of the above.

14. Net present value method weaknesses include the fact that it
    a) ignores timing and time value of money and uses accounting numbers rather than cash flows.
    b) ignores timing and time value of money and ignores cash flows beyond recovery of the investment.
    c) assumes a reinvestment rate of return which may be unrealistic, and is difficult to compute manually.
    d) is not meaningful for comparing projects requiring different amounts of investment.
    e) none of the above.

15. Internal rate of return weaknesses include the fact that it
    a) ignores timing and time value of money and uses accounting numbers rather than cash flows.
    b) ignores timing and time value of money and ignores cash flows beyond recovery of the investment.
    c) assumes a reinvestment rate of return which may be unrealistic, and is difficult to compute manually.
    d) is not meaningful for comparing projects requiring different amounts of investment.
    e) none of the above.

Cost Management: A Strategic Emphasis, 3e by Blocher/Chen/Cokins/Lin

16. With regard to the net present value (NPV) and the internal rate of return (IRR) methods,
    a) IRR favors projects with large investments, and the amount of investment has no effect on the calculated IRR.
    b) the NPV method favors projects with large investments, and the amount of investment has no effect on the calculated NPV.
    c) the NPV method favors projects with large investments, and the amount of investment has no effect on the calculated IRR.
    d) the IRR method favors projects with large investments, and the amount of investment has no effect on the calculated NPV.
    e) none of the above.

17. With regard to NPV and IRR methods,
    a) both methods assume that cash inflows earn a return equal to the cost of capital.
    b) both methods assume that all cash inflows earn the same project's rate of return.
    c) NPV assumes that cash inflows earn a return equal to the cost of capital and IRR assumes a rate of return equal to that of the project.
    d) NPV assumes a rate of return equal to that of the project and IRR assumes that all cash inflows earn a return equal to the cost of capital.
    e) none of the above.

18. In the initial phases of a product's life cycle (build), capital expenditure decisions and evaluation criteria are often,
    a) less formal and with more emphasis on financial data.
    b) less formal and with more emphasis on non-financial data.
    c) more formal and with more emphasis on financial data.
    d) more formal and with more emphasis on nonfinancial data.
    e) none of the above.

19. In the final phase of a product's life cycle (harvest), capital investment analysis is often
    a) more quantitative and financial.
    b) more quantitative and non-financial.
    c) more subjective and financial.
    d) more subjective and qualitative.
    e) none of the above.

20. Cost of capital includes,
    a) a simple average of before tax cost of debt and after tax cost of equity
    b) a simple average of after tax cost of debt and before tax cost of equity
    c) a weighted average of before tax cost of debt and after tax cost of equity
    d) a weighted average of after tax cost of debt and before tax cost of equity
    e) none of the above

Comprehensive exercise:

ABC company is considering replacing of its current computer system. The current system has a book value of $40,000 and a current salvage value of $10,000 with a remaining life of 4 years. Salvage value will be zero after two years. The operating cost of the old system is $45,000 a year. The new system will have a life of 4 years and costs $105,000 with additional working capital requirement of $20,000, and a salvage value of $5,000. The operating cost of the new system is $15,000 a year. The desired rate of return is 8% and the tax rate is at 30%. Use straight-line depreciation. The company has a total assets of 2 million dollars with 75% debt and the balance in equity. Interest on debt is at 5% per year.

Required:
a) Compute the project's payback period.
b) Compute the project's book rate of return.
c) Compute the project's net present value.
d) Compute the project's internal rate of return.
e) Compute the company's rate of return on its equity.
f) When would a company use a desired rate of return higher than its average cost of capital?
g) When would a company accept a project even if it cannot fully justify it on financial grounds.

E2.

Search the internet for the financial statements of the three major U.S. vehicle manufacturers – General Motors, Ford, and Chrysler/Dodge. Review their amounts of fixed assets as a percentage of total assets and as a percentage of sales and profit. How do they compare?

Correct answers to multiple choice questions:

1-c; 2-e; 3-d; 4-c; 5-d; 6-a; 7-d; 8-c; 9-b; 10-a; 11-e; 12-b; 13-a; 14-d; 15-c; 16-c; 17-c; 18-b; 19-a; 20-d.

Suggested answer to comprehensive exercise:

a) Payback period:

Cost of the computer	$105,000
Working capital needs	20,000
Salvage value of the old system	(10,000)
Tax savings on loss of the old system	(9,000)*
Net initial cash outlay	106,000

·   Computation of tax gain on loss of the old system: (40,000 - 10,000) * .30

Annual cash inflow (savings):
Difference between the new and old operating costs: 45,000 - 15,000 = 30,000

Cost Management: A Strategic Emphasis, 3e by Blocher/Chen/Cokins/Lin

Savings net of tax: 30,000 * .70 = 21,000
Depreciation tax shield: (105,000 - 5,000) * 25% * .30 = 7,500
Total annual savings: 21,000 + 7,500 = 28,500

Payback period: 106,000 / 28,500 = 3.7 years
As the project has a life of 4 years, this initial calculation shows that it may be considered if no better alternative is found.

b) Book rate of return:
Net income / average investment
Net income: (30,000 - 25,000) * (1 - .30) = $3,500

Average investment:

Year	Beginning of the year	End of the year	Average
1	$105,000	$ 80,000	$ 92,500
2	80,000	55,000	67,500
3	55,000	30,000	42,500
4	30,000	5,000	17,500
Total			220,000
Average investment: 220,000 / 4 =			55,000

Book rate of return: 3,500 / 55,000 = 6.36%

c) Net present value:

Present value of annual savings net of tax:	30,000 * .70 * 3.312 =	69,552
Present value of depreciation tax shield:	25,000 * .30 * 3.312 =	24,840
Present value of salvage on the new computer:	5,000 * .735 =	3,675
Present value of working capital recovery:	20,000 * .735 =	14,700
Total present value of cash inflows		112,767
Present value of cash outflows		(106,000)
Net present value		6,767

This project appears acceptable due to its positive NPV after consideration of any other option which may be available.

d) Internal rate of return:
As NPV is positive, the IRR (the return that produces an NPV of zero) should be more than 8%. Repeat this exercise with a discount rate of 10% and you will still get a positive NPV of $1,420. This means that IRR is even higher. Now repeat the exercise with a discount rate of 12%, and you will get a negative NPV of 3,545. So the project's IRR should be between 10% and 12%. We can interpolate by dividing the amount of $1,420 by the difference of the NPV at 10% and 12% which amounts to $4,965 and multiply it by 2; the difference between 10% and 12%. The result is .6 meaning that the project's IRR is approximately 10.6%.

e) Company's return on equity:

Cost of capital = 8%

Cost of capital = cost of debt (net of tax) + return on equity

Cost of debt (net of tax) in percentage = 5% * .70 * 75% = 2.625%

Return on equity = 8% - 2.625% = 5.375%

Rate of return on equity: 5.375/.25 = 21.5%

Proof:

Cost of debt in dollars:	2,000,000 * 75% * 5% * .7 =	$52,500
Return on equity in dollars:	2,000,000 * 25% * 21.5% =	107,500
Cost of capital:	2,000,000 * 8% =	160,000
Or	52,500 + 107,500 =	160,000

f) The company may require a rate of return higher than its cost of capital if the project is considered to be riskier than the average projects.

g) The company may accept a project even if it cannot be totally justified financially because of legal requirements or because of the necessity to remain competitive. Other intangible factors such as strategic positioning, employee morale, training possibilities, better customer service, etc. may also play an important role in the final decision in terms of accepting or rejecting a project.

Cost Management: A Strategic Emphasis, 3e by Blocher/Chen/Cokins/Lin